Common OpenStack Deployments

Common OpenStack Deployments

Real-World Examples for Systems Administrators and Engineers

Elizabeth K. Joseph
with Matthew Fischer

PRENTICE
HALL

Boston • Columbus • Indianapolis • New York • San Francisco • Amsterdam • Cape Town
Dubai • London • Madrid • Milan • Munich • Paris • Montreal • Toronto • Delhi • Mexico City
São Paulo • Sydney • Hong Kong • Seoul • Singapore • Taipei • Tokyo

For information about buying this title in bulk quantities, or for special sales opportunities (which may include electronic versions; custom cover designs; and content particular to your business, training goals, marketing focus, or branding interests), please contact our corporate sales department at corpsales@pearsoned.com or (800) 382-3419.

For government sales inquiries, please contact governmentsales@pearsoned.com.

For questions about sales outside the U.S., please contact intlcs@pearson.com.

Visit us on the Web: informit.com/ph

Library of Congress Control Number: 2016944433

ISBN-13: 978-0-13-408623-1
ISBN-10: 0-13-408623-6
Text printed in the United States on recycled paper at RR Donnelley in Crawfordsville, Indiana.

1 16

This book is dedicated to the OpenStack community. Of the community, I'd also like to specifically call out the help and support received from the Puppet OpenStack Team, whose work directly laid the foundation for the deployment scenarios in this book.

❖

Contents

x   Contents

Preface

*And suddenly you know: It's time to start something new
and trust the magic of beginnings.*
Meister Eckhart

Companies today are heavily relying upon virtualized and cloud-based solutions in their infrastructures. Whether they are off-loading their work to third-party cloud providers, using a virtualized solution in-house or building clouds in their own data centers, OpenStack has a lot to offer. This book provides an introduction to using and deploying OpenStack, open source software for creating private and public clouds, in your own organization.

OpenStack as an open source project has only existed since 2010 but quickly gained support of companies around the world and the broader open source community. At open source conferences OpenStack talks quickly sprang up by the time the project was just three years old to the extent that some In the community joked that the "OS" in open source conference names no longer stood for "Open Source" but for "OpenStack." Demand for talent in the field has risen along with interest, with OpenStack experts demanding a premium as companies expand their private cloud deployments.

Audience

The audience for this book is Linux and Unix systems administrators and network engineers seeking to learn the basics of OpenStack and to run sample deployment scenarios that can be transitioned into real-world deployments. It also provides insight into the most popular ways OpenStack is being used and how your organization can get there.

Though detailed commands are given, literacy with Linux systems administration is expected so you can focus on learning about OpenStack and simplify the task of troubleshooting. If you are doing these deployments in a series of virtual machines rather than bare metal servers, familiarity with a virtual machine technology is expected. This book does provide a reference deployment using virtualization with KVM and QEMU on Ubuntu if you wish to have step-by-step instructions. However, the intent is to leave virtualization preference up to the reader and make it easier to transition to a physical setup.

Basic networking experience is recommended since networking is such an important part of OpenStack, but diagrams in Chapter 3, "Networking," will help guide you through the OpenStack network architecture we're demonstrating.

Goals and Vision

I was inspired to write this book after attending several open source conferences where OpenStack was becoming an increasingly popular topic. In spite of all these talks, I'd still get practical usage questions from friends and colleagues about how they could use Open-Stack in their organizations. To that end, each chapter with a deployment scenario begins with a series of real-world examples of how it is being used by organizations in production. From serving up fleets of web servers to log storage, backups and data processing, these usage examples help you to find a place for OpenStack to accomplish a variety of tasks that span organizations across various industries, universities and governments.

Whether you're seeking to do an OpenStack deployment yourself or work with a vendor, this book also provides a guide through these sample deployments. You learn the basics of how to configure various OpenStack components and then walk through interactions with them via a web dashboard and the OpenStack command-line client. The mechanics of how the components interact with each other are also explained, so you have an understanding of how you're interacting with the systems.

System Prerequisites

In order to run most of the deployment scenarios in this book you need, at minimum, two computers with combined resources of 6G of RAM and 50G of hard drive space. A laptop with 8G of RAM is sufficient if you're using virtualization, including use of our tested reference deployment described in Appendix A, "Reference Deployment." If you choose to use real hardware, you will need two computers and two switches. One of the switches must be connected to a network with access to the Internet so you can install system packages and pull in configuration management tooling on your systems.

Diagrams of both virtualized and physical environment options, including a breakdown of specifications for each, are included in Chapter 3.

Ubuntu

You need to download the latest Ubuntu 14.04 ISO image to complete the deployment scenarios. Ubuntu is a Linux distribution based on Debian, which had its first release in 2004. Initially aimed at making Linux easier for regular people, growth of Ubuntu on servers has exploded over the past five years. It's now the number one choice for cloud deployments, both in OpenStack and on other cloud platforms such as Amazon Elastic Compute Cloud (EC2).

OpenStack's beginnings are also intertwined with the Ubuntu community. A number of the early project contributors come from the Ubuntu project. The decision to use Ubuntu comes from the expertise of the authors and a desire to focus on understanding the types of deployments and basics surrounding OpenStack itself rather than the underlying operating system.

Although the OpenStack ecosystem is much broader than Ubuntu, with professional services built around Red Hat Enterprise Linux (RHEL) and even a move to other operating systems beyond Linux, this book uses Ubuntu 14.04 LTS (Long Term Support) as the base installation for OpenStack.

This will impact configuration to some extent, since the Ubuntu Cloud Archive (see Chapter 1, "What Is OpenStack?") referenced in this book will be different from that of RHEL, CentOS openSUSE, Fedora and others. However, the core OpenStack knowledge and the deployment examples will be exportable to other systems once you start making plans to move into production with your system of choice.

Puppet

With an initial release in 2005, today Puppet is one of the most popular configuration management systems in the world. The Puppet OpenStack modules were one of the first configuration management system projects to reach maturity in the OpenStack community. Puppet modules for each release are made available within weeks of the OpenStack release itself.

Like the selection of Ubuntu, the selection of Puppet for configuration management was made so we can focus less on fundamental deployment and management, and more on learning about OpenStack. While you will be using Puppet commands for these deployments, the basic concepts are explained and prior knowledge of Puppet is not required. Additionally, the creators of the Puppet modules for OpenStack are a diverse group of developers and operators from around the world and are formally supported by multiple organizations. They are known to be flexible enough for a variety of environments.

We will be using the default installed Puppet version on Ubuntu 14.04. If you're seeking to run Puppet in production, the OpenStack Puppet team recommends using the Puppet version directly from Puppet instead. This is covered in Appendix C, "Long-Lived Puppet." The OpenStack Puppet modules for OpenStack are currently tested on both Ubuntu and CentOS.

Appendix B, "Other Deployment Mechanisms," has been provided to give you an overview of other configuration management and orchestration services you may be interested in using, should your organization prefer Chef, Ansible or something else.

Tour

The following is a short tour of what to expect from each chapter and the appendices.

- **Chapter 1: What Is OpenStack?** This first chapter provides a brief introduction to cloud computing before moving into an introduction to OpenStack itself. It goes on to provide descriptions of each component of OpenStack that are explored in depth in later chapters. The chapter concludes by talking about the OpenStack release cycle and how Ubuntu and Puppet factor into this cycle and their usage in this book.

- **Chapter 2: DevStack**   Built as a non-production development tool, DevStack is also a great introductory tool for a single-server deployment of OpenStack and for getting familiar with it quickly. You learn how to use it, launch your first compute instance and execute basic debugging techniques.

- **Chapter 3: Networking**   Networking is an important and complicated component of OpenStack and will drive decisions you make as you build your own deployments. This chapter is devoted to explaining key concepts for networking in OpenStack and to dive into the networking decisions and requirements used in our deployment scenarios. Diagrams and written descriptions help guide you through these concepts.

- **Chapter 4: Your First OpenStack**   Before getting into chapters using configuration management, this chapter walks you through a manual install of the basic components of OpenStack, Nova compute, Keystone Identity, Glance image storage and Neutron networking. This will give you a firm understanding of how the pieces fit together, from the databases to the service users in Keystone, which are handled in later chapters automatically by configuration management to the queuing system.

- **Chapter 5: Foundations for Deployments**   This chapter serves as a basis for all your subsequent deployment scenarios using Puppet. It explains the core components and sets up your basic controller and compute node and concludes with some basic usage tests to confirm it is working.

- **Chapter 6: Private Compute Cloud**   The first of our Puppet-driven deployment scenarios, this chapter provides usage examples and then walks you through the basics of interacting with a private compute cloud. You learn how to add a compute flavor and your first operating system image, how to launch and interact with a Nova compute instance from both the Horizon dashboard and the command line client and then complete a basic web service demonstration.

- **Chapter 7: Public Compute Cloud**   Your next deployment scenario adds metering to your cloud with Ceilometer. Ceilometer tracks usage of RAM, CPU, networking and more for your deployments, which you can then feed into systems to do monitoring and billing. Usage examples are given, as well as a basic introduction to Ceilometer itself and a walkthrough of how to use it with a strong focus on the command-line client.

- **Chapter 8: Block Storage Cloud**   Moving on from compute-focused deployments, this chapter introduces the concept of block storage and provides example usage. The basics of OpenStack Cinder block storage architecture are explained, and then you are walked through configuration. You then attach a Cinder block storage device to a compute instance, partition it, give it a filesystem and mount it inside your compute instance so you can add files to it.

- **Chapter 9: Object Storage Cloud**   Continuing with storage, this chapter introduces you to the concept of object storage using Swift. You learn about basic Swift concepts and deployment considerations, and then build your own tiny Swift deployment. Using this deployment scenario, you create storage containers, upload files and build upon your earlier web service demonstration by including an image served by object storage on a compute instance.

- **Chapter 10: Bare Metal Provisioning**   Moving on from our deployment scenarios, usage examples and an architecture overview of bare metal provisioning with OpenStack Ironic are provided. Though you aren't doing an actual deployment for this chapter since we couldn't make assumptions about your hardware, guidance is given for how you might.

- **Chapter 11: Controlling Containers**   In this, another non-deployment chapter, you learn why you may wish to use containers in an OpenStack deployment. The chapter continues with a basic introduction to OpenStack Magnum and considerations for your own deployments.

- **Chapter 12: A Whole Cloud**   Coming back to our deployment scenarios, this chapter provides one final scenario where all the components from Chapters 6-9 are brought together in a single scenario. This demonstrates how they can be used together, and you're encouraged to do your own tests with this feature-rich cloud scenario.

- **Chapter 13: Troubleshooting**   OpenStack is a complicated infrastructure project, and every engineer running it needs to get very good at troubleshooting. You are walked through understanding error messages and log files, tooling for troubleshooting network problems, common mistakes in configuration files and basic Puppet debugging. The chapter concludes with tips for how you can mitigate breakage in your deployment and tips for asking for help.

- **Chapter 14: Vendors and Hybrid Clouds**   The final chapter of this book introduces you to the broader OpenStack ecosystem through vendors and hybrid clouds, which blend a local OpenStack deployment with hosted solutions. Evaluation considerations for choices you make from cost to data sovereignty and security are covered.

- **Appendix A: Reference Deployment**   In case you run into trouble with your own environment selections, or simply don't have a preference, this appendix provides a tested, virtualized reference deployment you may use.

- **Appendix B: Other Deployment Mechanisms**   We use Puppet throughout this book, but this appendix introduces you to other ways you can deploy OpenStack, from Chef and Ansible to where to find vendor-specific tooling.

- **Appendix C: Long-Lived Puppet**   The Puppet examples in this book are triggered manually. This appendix gives direction for your options when building a proper, maintainable Puppet system.

- **Appendix D: Contributing Code to OpenStack**   Feel inspired to contribute back to OpenStack? Or need a feature or bug fix? This appendix gives an introduction to how you go about contributing code to the OpenStack open source project, including how community members communicate and how to use the development tooling.

- **Appendix E: OpenStack Client (OSC)**   The OpenStack Client is rapidly replacing individually maintained clients for each project. This appendix provides some background and a quick reference of some common commands.
- **Appendix F: Finding Help with OpenStack**   The final appendix provides a quick tour of the support options in the OpenStack community, both online and in person. It concludes with tips for finding paid support as well.

Conventions

Instead of using the root user, sudo is used throughout this book. As such, all commands are prefixed with a dollar sign to indicate that it's a command you should be typing into a shell. For instance, when you're preparing your Ubuntu systems and want to update the Ubuntu sources before installing anything, we show that as:

```
$ sudo apt-get update
```

When lines are wrapping, we use the bash syntax of \ to indicate that the command wraps to the next line. The creation of a compute instance is a good example of this:

```
$ openstack server create --flavor m1.tiny --image "CirrOS 0.3.4" \
  --security-group default --nic net-id=Network1 \
  --availability-zone nova my_first_instance
```

For most of the OpenStack commands, we have provided sample output of what to expect when you run each command. For the output of standard tooling for things like Ubuntu package installation, git clones and MySQL commands, this output is generally not included.

Supplementary Materials

As discussed, you will need a copy of the Ubuntu 14.04 ISO to install Ubuntu on your initial OpenStack controller and compute nodes. Later, the Ubuntu 14.04 server QCOW2 cloud image will need to be loaded into Glance for our deployment example using Ubuntu as a compute instance. All Puppet modules and other packages are downloaded through scripts you're instructed to use or through Puppet itself.

This book also has an accompanying git project hosted on GitHub at https://github.com/DeploymentsBook.

This project is broken into several repositories:

- **http-files**—Used for our basic web server examples.
- **puppet-data**—The repository you clone to bootstrap your installation of Puppet on your OpenStack nodes. It also includes your core configuration file, hiera/common.yaml, which you will be editing.

- **puppet-deployments**—Pulled in automatically by setup.py in puppet-data, this is the composition module used for all of our deployment scenarios. It includes service profiles and the foundation roles used in each chapter. It also includes a README.md file for the latest known issues and work-arounds that will be updated throughout the life of this book.

- **scripts-and-configs**—Miscellaneous scripts, commands and configuration file examples provided so you have a place from which to view or copy them as needed. The commands provided in this directory for the deployment chapters are particularly valuable for viewing OpenStack client output that doesn't fit well on a printed page.

Finally, a blog and the latest updates to other materials being made available throughout the lifespan of this book can be found on our web site at http://deploymentsbook.com/. You can also follow us on Twitter for updates @DeploymentsBook.

Register your copy of *Common OpenStack Deployments* at informit.com for convenient access to downloads, updates, and corrections as they become available. To start the registration process, go to informit.com/register and log in or create an account. Enter the product ISBN (9780134086231) and click Submit. Once the process is complete, you will find any available bonus content under "Registered Products."

Acknowledgments

When I began working on this book, I knew I had my work cut out for me and that I would need help from various members of the community. OpenStack is a huge infrastructure project. Every aspect of the project is continually being refined and revised, and even the official project documentation struggles to keep up. New projects are always being added, and the existing ones are reaching various states of maturity.

A few months into writing I brought in my contributing author, Matt Fischer. He put in a massive amount of work across three releases of OpenStack to get our Puppet composition module working. This book wouldn't have made it past the theoretical stage without his efforts. Colleen Murphy of the OpenStack Puppet team also spent time working with us on changes and by doing review of chapters and appendices. Clayton O'Neill, Eric Peterson and Adam Vinsh, working with Matt directly, assisted with Puppet configuration questions. We also had the project team lead of the OpenStack Puppet project, Emilien Macchi, pitch in with advice and getting required changes needed upstream.

Thanks to members of various teams who took time as subject matter experts to review individual chapters, including: Mike Perez, Gordon Chung, Donagh McCabe, Matthew Oliver, Hisashi Osanai, Christian Schwede, Kota Tsuyuzaki, Julia Kreger and Charlie Crawford. Pasi Lallinaho helped by turning our basic HTML page examples into something considerably more palatable. We also had help from my friends and fellow systems and network engineers Jonathan DeMasi, Ola Peters, Joe Gordon, Eric Windisch, James Downs and Brent Saner on several of the chapters.

We had several multi-chapter reviewers with varying backgrounds to thank, including José Antonio Rey, Mohammed Arafa, Doug Hellman and Christian Berendt.

Throughout this process, my husband Mike Joseph has been incredibly supportive of my work. Even during the most difficult times when I wasn't sure I could finish it, he was ready with encouragement.

Finally, I'd like to thank my editors at Pearson. Thanks to my editor and primary contact at Pearson, Debra Williams Cauley, for offering advice on how to approach each section and for keeping me on track throughout this process. Also to editor Chris Zahn, who made his way through editing the entire book.

About the Author

Elizabeth K. Joseph is a Systems Administrator working on the OpenStack Infrastructure project. In her role on this team, she supports OpenStack developers as they make contributions to the project and is active on OpenStack development mailing lists, and has worked on test engineering for the OpenStack on OpenStack (TripleO) project. She has given tutorials on the basics of OpenStack for San Francisco Bay Area organizations and regularly attends the bi-annual OpenStack Design Summits. A regular speaker on Open Source topics at conferences worldwide, her work beyond OpenStack includes contributions to the Ubuntu project and serving on the board of a non-profit that puts Linux-based computers in public schools.

Matthew Fischer has worked as a software developer for over 15 years in roles ranging from UNIX kernel to mobile phone development to DevOps. Matt currently works on a team deploying and running OpenStack and has been using Puppet to deploy OpenStack since 2013. When not solving automation problems, Matt enjoys hiking, camping, skiing, craft beer, and spending time with his family in Fort Collins, Colorado.

What Is OpenStack?

If I could remember the name of all these particles,
I would have been a botanist.
Enrico Fermi

As an infrastructure project that has a variety of options available for various types of deployments, answering the question "What is OpenStack?" can take some time. Simply put, OpenStack is a series of independent, yet related, software pieces that can be used to build an infrastructure for deploying and managing servers and storage arrays of various types. These software pieces include projects for web- or API-based control, compute, networking, object storage, block storage and more.

Whole books can and have been written covering each of these various components. In this chapter, we talk about some of the basics around cloud, and you are provided with an overview that will serve as a reference for the various components as you begin working on sample deployments in the next several chapters. Further detail about each component, and how it relates to the deployment you're working on, will be provided as you go through each deployment scenario.

The Preface explained that the target operating system for this book is Ubuntu. The chapter will conclude by talking about the Ubuntu Cloud Archive, which always provides the latest version of OpenStack to each supported Ubuntu Long Term Support release as well as the Puppet modules we will use for the deployment scenarios.

The Cloud

The term "cloud" has become very overloaded in recent years. To the layperson it may mean the place where all of their music and photos are kept when they use syncing and storage applications for their phones. A developer working for a payroll accountant may view the cloud as a platform against which applications for the financial department can be written. To a systems administrator it may specifically mean where a virtual machine, able to be scaled and deployed on demand but otherwise almost indistinguishable from any other basic server to which they've deployed applications, resides. This is where we get to the distinction of different "as a Service" models.

In the first example of a user uploading photos and music, this is typically known as Software as a Service (SaaS). The user may have a local application to accomplish the task of syncing the data, but it's then uploaded to a centralized location and the user has no view into or any control over how this works. When the user shuts off the device, the software in "the cloud" still runs. This is in contrast to how users may have stored all of their files on their desktop computers in the past and synced to their phones from there.

The second example takes advantage of Platform as a Service (PaaS). A development team may select a specific PaaS provider that has the required back end, support for their tools and focus for their organization. In the case of a payroll department, they may choose a PaaS provider that specializes in finances but which allows them to build their own applications to support and augment the default features. Now, instead of having servers in-house for the accountants to interact with, they are using a service online that has a framework supported by the PaaS company, with features provided by their own developers. Again, there is no view or control over how this works on the customer side.

The third example of deploying scalable virtual machines is the lowest level Infrastructure as a Service (IaaS). If you purchase this from a vendor, you typically still don't have control over the underlying hardware, like how background networking works or view into when a hard drive dies. However, you do get access to the full operating system on each virtual machine you create, enabling freedom to tackle software decisions and problems without having to worry about the hardware that is keeping everything running.

This growing world of "as a Service" models is where OpenStack was born in mid-2010.

OpenStack Joins the Cloud

The mission statement for OpenStack is as follows: "to produce the ubiquitous Open Source Cloud Computing platform that enables building interoperable public and private clouds regardless of size, by being simple to implement and massively scalable while serving the cloud users' needs." This statement gives you a view into the environment that OpenStack entered into when it was founded. There were some open source options for cloud, but it was never the comprehensive solution that OpenStack has ultimately provided.

Since it was founded in 2010, OpenStack is a relative newcomer to the cloud technology scene. It was initially a collaboration of components due to be made open source by Rackspace and NASA around the same time, and so was launched with much fanfare by these organizations. They were quickly joined by other major technology companies who were interested in collaborating on a centralized core for open cloud technology, rather than building their own in house. In 2012 the formal OpenStack Foundation was created with the support of several founding organizations in order to provide an organization-independent body. The foundation serves to protect respective trademarks and handle legal issues that could arise within OpenStack, organize the participation of the various organizations involved and to make sure a healthy development, user and operator community is promoted and maintained. To this end, the OpenStack Foundation is the leader in organizing the OpenStack Summits every six months, handles trademark disputes and even hires development talent to address specific concerns within the community.

The commitment to open source (along with the other three "opens": design, development and community) is key to the success of OpenStack. Many of the organizations who now put development resources into OpenStack do not necessarily want to give control to and pay a vendor for their infrastructure stack or are hoping to compete in that market. By using OpenStack, your organization can build their own cloud platform, offering everything from the basic Infrastructure as a Service with a cloud computing offering, to building a comprehensive object storage cloud where users can easily store their files on your scalable storage back end.

Building Your Cloud

Managing systems is a lot like baking a cake. There are plenty of options to choose from: pay a friend (contractor) to make it, get it pre-made from a bakery (commercial solutions), go to a bake sale (third-party vendors) and so on. However, in order to get the best possible cake to suit all of your needs, you'll want to bake it yourself. Unfortunately baking it yourself (building in-house) is very time-consuming and can be just as expensive as buying one.

What if instead you were able to buy each component of the cake pre-made, but to your specifications? You would have a cake suited to your particular tastes and methods but instead of having to bake it from scratch, all you have to do is assemble the components and bake. This is the approach that OpenStack takes. OpenStack provides a fully functioning cloud in its open source offering, but your organization can then extend and expand upon it as you see fit. In the most basic implementation, only a handful of services are required and you can add, mix and remove components as is most appropriate for your environment.

Uses

Progressing in your OpenStack learning experience, you will learn about several common uses, from organizations wishing to build a collection of computational-driven server instances for their researchers to those looking for an object storage solution for files belonging to their customers. Organizations that have found OpenStack to be useful include for-profit companies across various markets, governments, educational institutions and non-profit organizations. Deployments can be used entirely in-house to service applications run within an organization or be used to give computing and other resources to users paying them directly. There's also a hybrid cloud approach where an organization leverages a mixture of their own in-house constructed OpenStack alongside a hosted solution. Learn more about the hybrid approach in Chapter 14, "Vendors and Hybrid Clouds."

As we walk through deployment scenarios in the following chapters, specific uses will be detailed to provide examples and a taste for the flexibility of OpenStack.

Key Components

OpenStack is built from a series of components that are developed as their own projects within the OpenStack community. The following is a quick summary of each of the terms that will be referenced in the deployments throughout this book.

Instances

With the exception of storage and bare-metal focused deployments, you will need to be familiar with instances in OpenStack. Instances are typically Virtual Machines (VMs) using an underlying VM technology that you may be familiar with such as KVM or qemu, VMware or Hyper-V. However, as you will learn in Chapter 11, "Controlling Containers," there has been a push to provide stronger support of containers in OpenStack. Whether they are VMs or containers, they are referred to as instances in OpenStack.

Queuing

Before getting into specific OpenStack project components, it's important to talk about how the services interact with each other. At the most basic level, OpenStack services interact through a series of APIs that each project supports. Calls to these APIs are handled by a messaging queue that is installed early in an OpenStack installation. All interactions go through the queue so that processing can be reliable and predictable, happening in the order in which they were issued and providing a buffer when there is a spike in usage so that none of the commands issued get lost. In order to interact with this queuing system, most post requests directly, but you will notice that a small subset of the OpenStack components also run with a scheduling daemon.

Dashboard (Horizon)

Horizon is the web-based dashboard for OpenStack that provides an interface for both OpenStack administrators and users of the platform. It enables administrators and operators to manipulate various settings related to users, servers, quotas and more. The dashboard is also easily customizable by organizations and cloud operators who wish to add their own branding to the dashboard. The capabilities of Horizon expand as OpenStack continues to grow and add features with each release.

The interface for administrators provides the capability to manipulate users, view system information and adjust defaults and much more (see Figure 1.1).

By contrast, the user dashboard shown in Figure 1.2 is a user-facing view that enables individual users to control their virtual machines, networking configuration and components made available to them by an administrator.

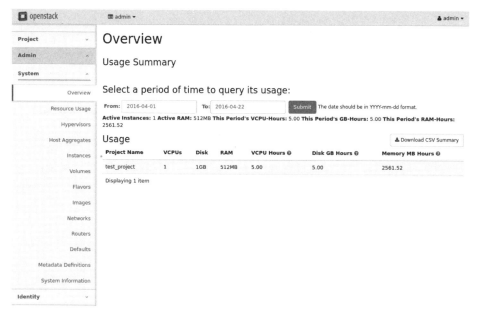

Figure 1.1   Administrative Dashboard. The Administrative dashboard enables configuration of OpenStack users and system-wide setting.

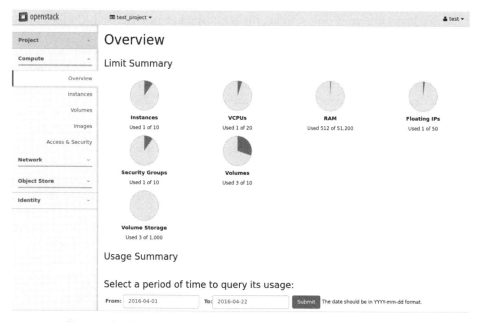

Figure 1.2   User Dashboard. The User dashboard is provided to manage virtual machines and configurations on a per-user basis.

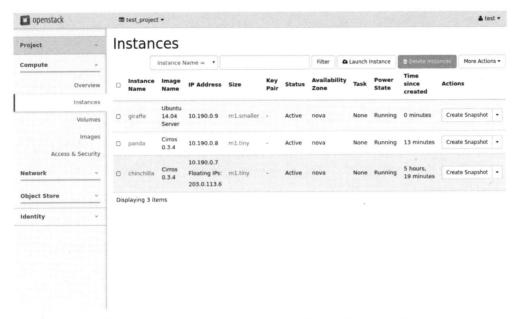

Figure 1.3   Several compute instances. The dashboard provides various simple tools for instance manipulation.

While many operators choose to use the command line interface and API for automated control of large fleets, the Horizon dashboard page for managing instances (see Figure 1.3) enables quick and simple deployment of individual instances without having to have a highly sophisticated background in OpenStack. This enables it to be presented to users who have simple needs when it comes to small deployments of instances and provides a clean interface for completing various tasks.

Another component in Horizon is the networking screen (see Figure 1.4). The OpenStack Networking component, Neutron, is now widely used for the flexibility it provides operators in handling networks. An administrator may grant a lot of flexibility to users when it comes to how they use networks, from providing simple access that give instances direct Internet access, to allowing a whole series of instances created by the user to privately interact with each other without being on the public Internet.

The plethora of tools provided by Horizon make it a valuable tool for administrators and operators. However, note that given the way that OpenStack itself is developed, the command line interface will always have more features than Horizon. Additionally, everything that can be done in Horizon can also be done with the command line tools.

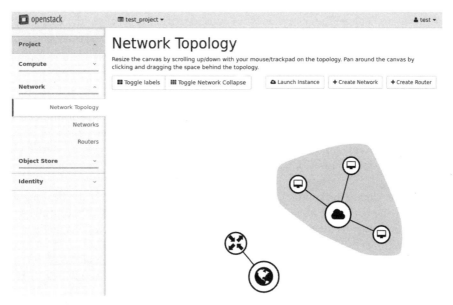

Figure 1.4   A simple Internet-facing network in the dashboard. This view shows a private network connecting to a public network where an instance can get a routable IP address. These networks are connected with a configured router, which is represented by the icon that connects the two networks.

Compute (Nova)

Nova is the compute component of OpenStack. Along with being one of the most well-known projects in OpenStack, it is also one of the two projects launched when OpenStack was announced as a project in 2010 (the other was Swift for object storage). The compute component handles provisioning and control over the compute servers in OpenStack. As noted earlier, Nova has a variety of drivers that enable it to talk to a variety of VM and container technologies, including: libvirt (supporting qemu/KVM), Xen, VMware, Hyper-V and Docker.

This component consists of the following core daemons and services that most installations will have:

- **nova-compute:** Accepts actions from the queue in order to perform common actions on an instance, like starting and terminating.
- **nova-conductor:** In order to avoid nova-compute having risky direct access to a database that can cause irregular data, the conductor controls interactions between the compute daemon and the database.
- **nova-scheduler:** Controls interactions with the messaging queue, picking up requests from the queue, determining which Nova compute instance to send it to and passing it along.

- nova-api: The API service that Nova runs so that other services, the CLI and Horizon can interact with Nova.
- nova-api-metadata: The API service that responds to metadata requests that returns data about specific instances.

Unless you're running a single-server instance of OpenStack (typically only for testing or development), some of these services will be divided across servers. For instance, to provide sufficient isolation, the nova-compute daemon should be on a different server than the database and conductor. As we explore our first few deployments, starting in Chapter 6, "Private Compute Cloud," you will see more examples of how these services are split up.

If you're seeking to use console-based access to the instances, you may also be using some of the following daemons: nova-consoleauth, nova-novncproxy, nova-spicehtml5proxy or nova-xvpvncproxy. Console-based access can be in the form of access via the Horizon interface as shown in Figure 1.5.

You can also gain direct VNC-type access through your VNC client of choice. For small deployments and when you are testing you can also use an interface like libvirt's Virtual Machine Manager (https://virt-manager.org/) graphical interface as seen in Figure 1.6. You will notice that this tool only provides basic support for connecting to compute nodes one by one and so is not a sufficient console tool as you scale your infrastructure.

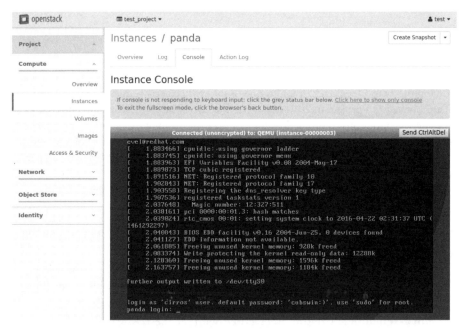

Figure 1.5   Console access via Horizon Dashboard. A console daemon is required for console access to be enabled in the Horizon Dashboard.

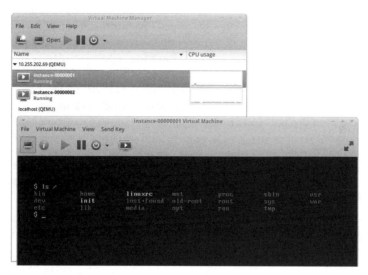

Figure 1.6   Accessing OpenStack with Virtual Machine Manager. Virtual Machine Manager
can be used for accessing qemu/KVM-based OpenStack instances.

Identity (Keystone)

Keystone is the identity service for OpenStack. It is used by other services to confirm the identity of a user. Confirmation of identity can be done through various mechanisms, from a simple user name and password or API key combination to an authentication token provided by Keystone itself. Once authenticated, Keystone has a concept of Projects, Domains and Roles that control what a User or User Group can do. Each of these and how they interact are explored further in Chapter 4, "Your First OpenStack."

Rather than running as a standalone daemon, today Keystone instead uses a Web Server Gateway Interface (WSGI). By default, Apache with mod_wsgi is used to serve up the Keystone service.

Note

Keystone used to run a standalone daemon, so you may see reference to it if you find documentation prior to the Kilo release. This standalone daemon method is no longer supported. All Keystone deployments now use the WSGI method.

Networking (Neutron)

Neutron is the networking component of OpenStack. It provides a variety of networking options for your OpenStack cloud. Defaults will set up a private network that instances live directly on and an Internet routable (or public) network that you will need to connect instances to in order for them to get a public address.

The project began as a subset of Nova called nova-network and eventually branched off into its own project that was previously named Quantum. The previous project name, Quantum, is why you may see q- in some of the log names when we deploy DevStack in Chapter 2, "DevStack." Neutron has been built to support a vast array of network configurations made available through a series of plug-ins. More plug-ins are added each release but currently include various network bridge types, virtual local area networks (VLANs) and subnets and plug-ins for several proprietary networking switches and other network tools, both physical and virtual.

Neutron requires a daemon to process requests, and you need to run plug-ins and agents to complete specific tasks depending on your deployment.

- neutron-server: A daemon that accepts and sends requests via the API to the appropriate Neutron plug-in.
- plug-ins and agents: Neutron ships with several for port, bridge and address handling as well as more vendor-specific plug-ins for various virtual and physical switches.

Basic configuration of Neutron will be covered as we work through sample deployments. Neutron is very flexible, so much more complex deployments are also possible as your needs and environment change.

Image Service (Glance)

Glance is the image service for OpenStack. An image will typically be a qcow2, ISO or img file that contains an operating system you wish to use on an OpenStack instance.

- glance-api: This daemon runs the API that is used to submit requests for image discovery, retrieval and storage in tandem with the registry. All interactions from the outside go through this API.
- glance-registry: An internal Glance registry that does the work of storing, processing and retrieving metadata about the images loaded via the API.

You also need storage space to hold the actual images and a database for the image metadata.

Block Storage (Cinder)

Cinder provides the block storage component to OpenStack. Block storage volumes can provide persistent base storage to compute instances or to add additional storage to a running instance.

- cinder-api: The API daemon that accepts requests and passes them on to the volume daemon for processing.
- cinder-backup: A service that provides backing up of volumes to a storage provider.
- cinder-scheduler: The daemon that does the work of selecting which storage node to create a volume on.

- cinder-volume: Using input from the API daemon and the scheduler, this daemon actually does the work of interacting with various storage providers.

Cinder supports several different types of storage back ends, both open source and proprietary, that are provided by a plug-in infrastructure. More about how Cinder works and how you can use it to attach volumes to instances in Chapter 8, "Block Storage Cloud."

Object Storage (Swift)

Swift is built to manage *object* storage for OpenStack. In contrast to direct file and block storage, object storage is built to be a highly scalable and available storage mechanism for storing files that are then accessible via a RESTful HTTP API. Note that all user-created files being loaded into Swift are called objects.

- **periodic processes:** There are various periodic processes (replicators, updaters, auditors, reapers and more) run by Swift to do housekeeping on the data store itself.

- **swift-account-server:** Handles management of accounts.

- **swift-container-server:** Handles management of the mapping of containers or folders.

- **swift-object-server:** Handles management of the objects on the storage nodes.

- **swift-proxy-server:** A service that accepts requests via API and HTTP in order to upload objects, change meta-data, and create containers.

It's also worthy to note, that unlike many of the other OpenStack components, Swift can be run with an identity service other than Keystone. For all types of identity services Swift uses specially tuned middleware provided by Python WSGI middleware. A more comprehensive overview of how Swift works, along with the basic overview of key concepts like the ring system which is used for the indexing of objects, can be found in Chapter 9, "Object Storage Cloud."

Telemetry (Ceilometer)

Ceilometer is the telemetry module for OpenStack, meaning it provides the following functions:

- Polls for metering data on a defined set of OpenStack services
- Collects metering data and events by monitoring notifications
- Publishes collected data to specified targets, including messaging queues and traditional data stores

These functions make it so Ceilometer is not a light-weight addition to your OpenStack deployment. The benefit that Ceilometer brings to your deployment is monitoring that is integrated, which you won't necessarily find in third part alerting systems.

To accomplish the collection, metering and more, a large number of services are used, and, unless otherwise specified, they run on a centralized management server:

- **ceilometer-agent-central:** A horizontally scalable component to poll for statistics from various resources being tracked.
- **ceilometer-agent-compute:** A service that runs on each compute node to poll it for usage statistics.
- **ceilometer-agent-notification:** A service to consume messages from the queue to build event and metering data.
- **ceilometer-api:** The API that is polled to provide data that is used by the administrator or customer to examine usage.
- **ceilometer-collector:** After consuming data from agents and other OpenStack services, this service is used to dispatch the data to whatever is used for metering data storage.

These services mean that Ceilometer can track usage of services for the purposes of billing or other accountability of users. Ceilometer can be used on its own or in collaboration with the Gnocchi project.

Bare Metal (Ironic)

As organizations moved to using OpenStack to manage everything from their virtual machines and containers to their object storage array, it became clear that there was a desire to control physical machines as well. This began with a nova-baremetal project but was quickly moved into its own project, Ironic. Ironic serves as the Bare Metal Service, provisioning physical machines rather than virtual machines and providing a series of drivers that support the most common management tools like Preboot Execution Environment (PXE) and Intelligent Platform Management Interface (IPMI). Additionally,

- **ironic-api:** The API that processes requests and sends them to the ironic-conductor.
- **ironic-conductor:** This service completes the tasks of adding, editing and deleting nodes, handling power state, typically with IPMI, and the provisioning, deployment and decommissioning of bare metal nodes.
- **ironic-python-agent:** A python service that is run in a temporary ram disk to provide ironic-conductor service(s) with remote access and in-band hardware control.

Ironic also has a python-ironicclient, which is a command line tool for interacting with the service. More about Ironic, along with a sample deployment, is explored in Chapter 10, "Bare Metal Provisioning."

Orchestration (Heat)

Heat is the orchestration service specifically built for OpenStack. By using a series of text-based templates, Heat enables you to spin up a collection of resources in what Heat calls a stack, which may include instances, network components and security rules, and more. Templates can either be in the OpenStack-specific Heat Orchestration Template (HOT) or AWS CloudFormation Template (CFN) formats.

Like the others, Heat is comprised of a series of daemons and services:

- **heat-api:** A RESTful API that is used to interact with the Heat service.
- **heat-api-cfn:** Used if you wish to support the CFN template.
- **heat-engine:** The core of the product that provides the actual orchestration service.

There is also a Heat command line tool that is strictly used to communicate with the heat-api if CFN is being used.

A guide for using HOT templates can be found at http://docs.openstack.org/developer/heat/template_guide/.

Containers (Magnum)

Magnum is specifically built for managing the orchestration around *containers* like Docker and Kubernetes. As mentioned in the section about Nova, there is a virtualization driver that enables Nova to control Docker, but this treats the container like a VM and takes advantage of very few features that make containers really valuable. Magnum seeks to take advantage of container features provided in the orchestration tools that come with Kubernetes or Docker Swarm, including the bays and pods structure you may already be familiar with if you use these container tools.

More about containers and using Magnum can be found in Chapter 11, "Controlling Containers."

Other Projects

During the OpenStack Kilo release cycle in 2015, the OpenStack project began supporting an initiative called "Big Tent," where they sought to be more inclusive of other projects within the OpenStack ecosystem. With Big Tent, there is less bureaucracy around the inclusion of projects in the OpenStack name space, and there could now be competing technologies existing alongside each other. This new approach to accepting projects into OpenStack has led to an ever-growing number of projects approved for inclusion by the OpenStack Technical Committee. The full list is maintained by the OpenStack Technical Committee (TC) at http://governance.openstack.org/reference/projects/.

Release Cycle

OpenStack releases occur every six months, around April and October of each year (see Figure 1.7). The release names are in alphabetical order, so recent names include Juno, Kilo, Liberty and Mitaka. These are names of places near where the OpenStack Summit occurred to begin planning for that version's release cycle. For instance, the summit for Liberty was held in Vancouver, Canada and Liberty is a village in the nearby Canadian province of Saskatchewan. Mitaka is a city located near Tokyo.

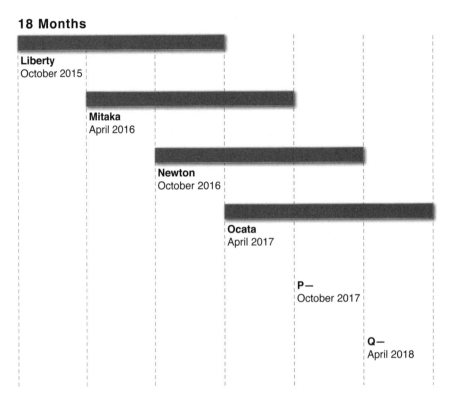

Figure 1.7   OpenStack release and support schedule

These releases are supported for a minimum of 18 months, but only release to imme-diate release upgrades are supported. For instance, if you install OpenStack Kilo, you can upgrade directly to Liberty and from Liberty you can upgrade to Mitaka, but you will not be able to upgrade directly from Kilo to Mitaka.

In this book we're using the OpenStack release Mitaka, which came out in April 2016.

Ubuntu Long Term Support

Every two years, the Ubuntu community releases a Long Term Support (LTS) release of Ubuntu. These releases are supported for five years, whereas the intermediary six-month releases are only supported for nine months. Using Ubuntu LTS releases as the base for server-based deployments is extremely common.

We have chosen to use Ubuntu 14.04 LTS as the base of all the installations in this book, rather than the newly released 16.04 LTS. We made this decision for a number of reasons:

- Though 16.04 ships Mitaka by default, the upstream OpenStack development team used 14.04 for testing for the entire Mitaka development cycle.

- 16.04 introduces significant changes from 14.04. Particularly of note is the init system switch from Upstart to systemd, and we use some Upstart scripts in our scenarios.
- Using 16.04 would not have given us the opportunity to demonstrate use of the Ubuntu Cloud Archive (UCA), which we'll discuss in a moment, since it has Mitaka by default. The UCA is an important tool in using OpenStack with Ubuntu and is used more often than not as new releases come out during the life of an Ubuntu LTS release.
- For most of the time spent preparing this book, 14.04 was the only supported LTS release available to us and our reviewers. We could not spend a satisfying amount of time testing it with 16.04 without significant delays in release.
- Mitaka will still be supported by the Ubuntu community through the life of 14.04, which is a respectable three years from the release of 16.04. This makes it a satisfactory choice for our scenarios.

Using Ubuntu 16.04 with this book is not something we can recommend. If you wish to try anyway, make sure you have developed a firm understanding Puppet so you can make the inevitable adjustments that will be needed. Both the DevStack install in Chapter 2 and the manual install in Chapter 4 will also need some adjustments that are not yet documented at the time of writing.

Ubuntu Cloud Archive

Much of the software in an Ubuntu release is pinned to a specific version, except in the cases of major bug fixes or security vulnerabilities. Due to the infrastructure nature of the project, pace of development and desire for users to have newer versions, the Ubuntu Server Team maintains a special archive for support of OpenStack in Ubuntu LTS releases called the Ubuntu Cloud Archive.

Each Ubuntu LTS release ships with a version of OpenStack, so Ubuntu 14.04 includes OpenStack Icehouse. Icehouse was the first of two named releases in 2015 and came out just before Ubuntu 14.04.

The cloud archive is used to support OpenStack releases not shipped with the Ubuntu LTS release. It is only activated for an LTS release once the version that shipped with the LTS release is no longer the current stable release of OpenStack. For example, shortly after the next version of OpenStack came out, in October of 2014, the Ubuntu Cloud Archive for 14.04 was activated and users could now enable the archive and install or upgrade to the next version of OpenStack, Juno and later Kilo, Liberty and Mitaka. Support for Mitaka will continue in the Ubuntu Cloud Archive for 14.04, but is shipped by default without need for the archive in the 16.04 release of Ubuntu.

The goal is for versions of OpenStack that are made available without the Ubuntu Cloud Archive to be supported for 5 years and for all versions provided by the Ubuntu Cloud Archive to be supported for 18 months. See Figure 1.8 for details about the current releases.

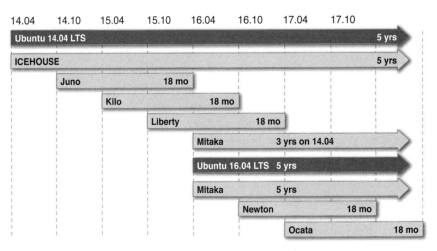

OpenStack on Ubuntu Support Model

LTS support 5 years, non-LTS support 18 months.

Figure 1.8   Ubuntu Cloud Archive support schedule

Puppet Modules

Like we've chosen to use Ubuntu as the operating system, we've made a decision to use Puppet as the configuration management system. Puppet uses a series of modules in order to build a working system. In the case of the OpenStack Puppet modules, this means there is a module for each mature component of OpenStack, including Nova, Neutron and Keystone. These modules enable you to define preferences for each of these services inside the configuration management system, which will keep your configurations in a centralized place as you deploy your servers.

Like much of OpenStack, the official Puppet modules for OpenStack are maintained by a team of contributors from various organizations. Many of these contributors use these modules in-house for their own deployments. As such, they've been tested with production-level loads and varying levels of complexity. The infrastructure used for development also provides varying levels of unit and integration testing to make sure no commits break deployments.

The Puppet modules for any given release are typically released shortly *after* the release of that version of OpenStack. This enables the team to complete more tests and confirm that everything is working with the new stable release.

In Chapter 5, "Foundations for Deployments," you will learn about the details of how Puppet is used for our deployment scenarios. While our deployment scenarios are very basic, the key components and use of Puppet can be scaled up to a production-level deployment. Learn more about decisions you will have to make about scaling up in Appendix C, "Long-lived Puppet."

Summary

We have just completed a tour of the key components of OpenStack. It's unlikely that you'll remember all of the service names when you're just starting out, so you can refer back to refresh your memory about the key daemons, plug-ins, agents and other components that support each component. In subsequent chapters we explore many of these in more depth.

OpenStack is an ever-expanding ecosystem of projects, so you are also now familiar with the location of all projects governed by the OpenStack Technical Committee and can explore other projects there. Finally, we've covered the support model for the LTS versions of Ubuntu with various versions of OpenStack by way of the Ubuntu Cloud Archive.

First Deployments

To hit the ground running, the following two chapters will get you going with some quick and easy demonstration deployments. These will give you a feel for OpenStack and some of its features. However, they are not meant for production use.

2

DevStack

Quality is never an accident.
It is always the result of intelligent effort.
John Ruskin

The OpenStack project uses a tool called DevStack to help developers get a development version of OpenStack running to test their patches against. In this chapter we explore how it can be used by an OpenStack newcomer to explore basic concepts and get OpenStack running on a single machine.

What Is DevStack?

DevStack, found at http://docs.openstack.org/developer/devstack/, began as an independent project to provide developers a single machine installation of the latest development version of OpenStack. The core of the project is a shell script called stack.sh, which can take a series of arguments to define a basic OpenStack environment on a host system. The script is made to be somewhat self-documenting, with a variety of options for using configurations and services that are not the default.

Over the years it has become a vital part of the development workflow and infrastructure for the OpenStack project. The project also is being used for training administrators in the basics of OpenStack and as an essential part of the continuous integration tests performed on every change to OpenStack.

As a single machine install of OpenStack, DevStack is not meant for production use. In addition to deploying the development version of OpenStack by default, it is not built to be maintainable and breaks best practices for separation of services (like nova-compute and nova-conductor discussed in Chapter 1, "What Is OpenStack?").

> **Caution**
>
> Don't run DevStack on any important or production machines. The script makes changes to your software repositories, networking setup and more, which leaves the system in a poor state for continued maintenance.
>
> Instead, use a Virtual Machine (VM) or spare system that you can reinstall at a later date.

Developer Usage

DevStack was created by developers, and developer utilization remains one of its most common usages. Developers in the OpenStack project have a fondness for DevStack because while it does not provide a real-world OpenStack deployment, it enables them to quickly get a development framework up to test their patches against. DevStack also offers a version to spin up supported releases so that developers can also test how their changes impact upgrades and assist when writing security patches and major bug fixes for previous releases.

Typically, developers using DevStack will have a system for deploying these test environments quickly so they can run their tests. Many also maintain local mirrors of some repositories for their operating system of choice so that the DevStack installation runs more quickly.

Training Usage

Some training programs have taken to using DevStack as a training tool for students to get up to speed with OpenStack quickly. The goal is to go from a base Linux install to running OpenStack as quickly as possible so they have an opportunity to work with a live system that is running the basics of what an OpenStack deployment requires.

Once you have learned some of the basics of OpenStack from your DevStack install, you have confidence about how things are supposed to work. At that point you can dive deeper into how to deploy OpenStack in a production environment in a maintainable fashion.

Continuous Integration Usage

DevStack is an integral part of the continuous integration system within the OpenStack project itself. The project prepares DevStack-based images for testing OpenStack changes in development and deploys the images on hundreds of systems per day in order to do testing. As such, DevStack is used for everything from integration tests to upgrade tests using the Grenade test harness.

All changes to OpenStack must pass all changes in the continuous integration system before being merged, so development code pulled in by DevStack has already been automatically tested with a default DevStack environment. Several companies in the OpenStack ecosystem also use DevStack as part of their quality assurance system.

DevStack Requirements

In order to get started with DevStack, you will need a Virtual Machine (VM) or spare system available with at least 4GB of RAM, but note that DevStack runs better with 6-8GB of RAM. For best performance, you will also need to be using a 64-bit CPU with hardware virtualization support.

You have several options for a base operating system, as Ubuntu LTS, Fedora and RHEL/CentOS currently maintain support for DevStack, with several other distributions having semi-maintained support for specific versions.

Finally, if you are using a VM and wish to use the web-based Horizon dashboard as described later in this chapter, you will need to either install the Desktop version of your chosen base operating system or provide access to port 80 to that machine from another machine. This is so you can use the web browser on localhost or install the server version with a bridged interface so the server is accessible from the outside. If you're using physical hardware, make sure the system is accessible via the network.

Deploying DevStack

Now that you have the required resources to run DevStack, you have some configuration decisions to make.

DevStack is designed to be run out of the box, with no configuration changes, with a series of simple commands, the last of which will take some time:

```
$ sudo apt-get install git
$ git clone https://git.openstack.org/openstack-dev/devstack.git
$ cd devstack
$ ./stack.sh
```

The first few steps will ask you for a series of passwords for each component. You will want to take note of what you put in for these passwords. Once it has the passwords, it will take some time as it modifies your software sources and networks and then downloads requirements and the latest development version of OpenStack components used in DevStack. The script will also pause at some points in the beginning to ask you for service passwords (see the section "Customizing DevStack" later in this chapter for tips on how to use a local.conf file with these variables instead).

The DevStack project provides a commented version of the stack.sh script for perusal while the default install takes place; you can view it locally in the devstack directory or online at http://docs.openstack.org/developer/devstack/stack.sh.html.

Common Failures

If your permissions are not correct, you will have problems running DevStack. Here are a few tips:

- Do not use root or sudo when running any of the commands outlined above.
- While you shouldn't run the commands as root or sudo, the user you're running stack.sh with must have sudo access, preferably passwordless.
- When you are running stack.sh, confirm the devstack/ directory is owned by the user you are attempting to run it with.
- If you wish to create a "stack" user specifically designed for running DevStack, you can use the tools/create-stack-user.sh script that ships with DevStack. This script needs to be run with sudo from an account with sudo access.

Networking is the root cause of many failures. The following are some of the most common problems:

- Your local network conflicts with the default setup of DevStack's internal network (10.0.0.1/24).
- The VM or physical system cannot access the Internet. Internet access is required to run stack.sh. This can manifest as anything from name resolution errors to timeouts to the operating system repositories.

Sometimes DevStack is broken. As explained, DevStack pulls down a development version of OpenStack. In spite of the plethora of testing that happens before code is merged, there are some days when the current state of DevStack does not allow for deployments. See later in this chapter for details about DevStack "stable" if you're struggling to get pure DevStack to run.

Once the install has completed successfully, it should end with something like the following before returning you to your command prompt:

```
=========================
DevStack Components Timed
=========================

run_process - 46 secs
apt-get-update - 12 secs
pip_install - 377 secs
restart_apache_server - 9 secs
wait_for_service - 13 secs
git_timed - 248 secs
apt-get - 258 secs
```

```
This is your host IP address: 192.168.122.216
This is your host IPv6 address: ::1
Horizon is now available at http://192.168.122.216/dashboard
Keystone is serving at http://192.168.122.216:5000/
The default users are: admin and demo
The password: 12345
2016-04-20 21:51:40.175 | stack.sh completed in 1466 seconds.
```

The first link is Horizon, which is the web-based dashboard for OpenStack. This is a valuable place to begin as it provides a graphical overview of your deployment with both user and administrative logins.

The second link is to Keystone's API endpoint, which is the service that anything needing to manipulate OpenStack via the API will need to authenticate with, such as the Nova, compute, command line client. This typically will need to go into an environment variable or configuration file when executing commands against DevStack.

Warning

Did you reboot? Since DevStack is not designed to be a persistent installation, it won't automatically bring back your deployment when you boot back up.

You will need to run ./unstack.sh and ./stack.sh again to create a new DevStack environment. Unfortunately this will start again with a fresh install, none of your instances, volumes or anything else will be retained.

Dashboard: Log In as a User

We will begin with the Horizon interface. Navigate to the URL given previously, and first you can log in as a regular user. By default, you will have a user called "demo" set

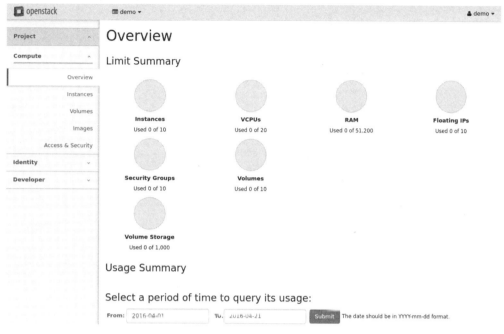

Figure 2.1   Horizon dashboard (user view)

up for this purpose with the password you specified during installation. Once logged in, you are presented with the user-facing view of the dashboard (see Figure 2.1).

> **Tip**
>
> Having trouble loading the Horizon login screen? It is sometimes slow when it first starts up, so give it a few seconds and try again.

As a user you can explore the options you have, but as a first task you can experiment with bringing up an instance.

First, you will need to set up user credentials that will be passed along to any instance that you launch. To do this, you want to choose Access & Security on the left hand menu in the Compute section. The first screen you will see is for Security Groups, which control the ports that are accessible on your instances, both inbound and outbound. You want to select the Key Pairs tab as shown in Figure 2.2. From this screen you can either upload an existing public SSH key that you already have on your system or create a key pair. If you choose to create a key pair through the interface, it will download the associated .pem file, which you will then use with your SSH client to log into instances once they have started.

The next step is creating your first instance through the Horizon dashboard. You do this by selecting Instances on the left-hand menu and clicking on the Launch Instance button. This will bring up a dialog as seen in Figure 2.3 where you be walked through putting in all the information required for your first instance.

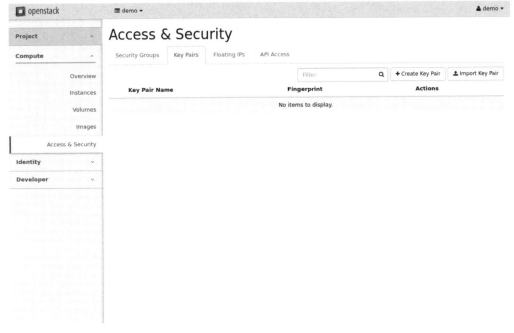

Figure 2.2   Horizon dashboard (Key Pairs)

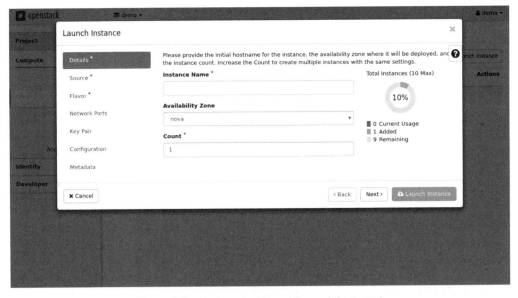

Figure 2.3   Horizon dashboard (Launch Instance)

The dialog choices include the following in the Details screen:

- **Instance Name:** This will be the name of the instance as referenced within OpenStack. This can later be used to reference the instance in the Horizon interface, but note that these names do not have to be unique, so you will likely want to reference this by UUID if you later wish to access this instance.

  For this demonstration, you can use whatever name you wish here.

- **Availability Zone:** Since this is a DevStack install, the only Availability Zone (AZ) available is the default—nova. If you were using a public OpenStack cloud or had a distributed cloud, you would have more options.

- **Count:** Defines how many of this kind of instance you wish to launch.

  For now, we just want one.

With these sections filled out, click Next to go to the Source screen.

- **Instance Boot Source:** The source is flexible, enabling you to use predefined images already uploaded to OpenStack, existing volumes or snapshots, or to upload your own image. Depending on what you select, the dialog will change to further describe the boot source.

  1. In the Select Boot Source dropdown, Image should be selected. If not, select it.
  2. DevStack ships with a very basic cloud-focused Linux image called CirrOS. Click the plus sign on the far right on the Available section of the dialog to move it up to Allocated.

Click Next again to select your Flavor. A flavor describes the resources to be allocated to the instance, including number of CPUs, amount of RAM, and disk space. Just like the Source screen, click the plus sign to the right of the flavor you wish to select. Since I tend to have resource constraints when using DevStack, I typically select m1.nano.

Since you've set up your SSH key, you'll now want to click on Key Pair in the menu on the left. Like with the previous two screens, you'll see the key you created earlier and can click the plus sign to add it to Allocated. With that complete, you can now finally click the Launch Instance button.

The build status of the instance will be shown in Horizon. Launching should be pretty quick with CirrOs, and soon after seeing a local IP assigned, you can ssh into it using the SSH key you either created or already use. Using the default networking configuration, this is a local-only IP. You will need to ssh in from the DevStack host, for instance:

```
$ ssh -i .ssh/elizabeth.pem cirros@10.0.0.2
The authenticity of host '10.0.0.2 (10.0.0.2)' can't be established.
RSA key fingerprint is 4e:51:73:48:0f:5d:e5:20:80:11:17:e3:b3:44:75:e6.
Are you sure you want to continue connecting (yes/no)? yes
Warning: Permanently added '10.0.0.2' (RSA) to the list of known hosts.
$
```

A single $ sign is the indication that you're on the CirrOS image. You can confirm with:

```
$ cat /etc/cirros/version
0.3.4
```

If you did not set up an SSH key earlier or are having trouble with your key, you can still log in with the password "cubswin:)":

```
$ ssh cirros@10.0.0.2
cirros@10.0.0.3's password:
$
```

If you poke around in the instance, you will notice that it's a pretty simple Linux install. There may not be much to do there. You can log out at any time.

Now, back in the Horizon interface, if you navigate back to Overview in the left-hand menu, you will see your new instance show up in the summary.

> **Tip**
>
> Modifying instances through the Horizon interface is great for learning and for organiza-
> tions with smaller deployments, but the power of OpenStack really comes from the APIs
> and Command Line Interface (CLI)-based tools. See Chapter 4, "Your First OpenStack," for
> the first discussion about manipulation of your instances from the command line using the
> OpenStack CLI.

Dashboard: Log In as an Administrator

Now that you know what the user side of the Horizon dashboard looks like, we will explore the administrative side. You will use the same URL for logging in as you did with the demo account, but this time you will log in as admin with the admin password you defined when you ran stack.sh. You will likely arrive at what is shown in Figure 2.4.

In this view of Horizon, you will have the Identity Projects screen, but you will also have an Admin section of the menu that enables you to view and change several things about your DevStack install.

> **Tip**
>
> The default admin screen for OpenStack has changed over time, you may also end up on
> the Project screen like you did with the demo user. To navigate to the default screen we've
> identified here, click on Identity and then Projects in the left-hand menu.

There are two sections of this menu dealing with System and Identity. The following are a sampling of the key sections you will want to be aware of from the System Panel:

- **Instances:** View all instances run by various users in your system. You also have the capability to edit and manipulate them from this screen.
- **Flavors:** Change the flavors offered to meet your operating requirements, delete and add new ones.

- **System Information:** See an overview of what is currently enabled in your DevStack instance.

Next you'll want to explore the Identity Panel, which has the following:

- **Projects:** An organizational unit in the OpenStack cloud that may be shared between users with varying permissions. By default, each user comes with a single project that only they belong to.
- **Users:** Allows you to manipulate the users that exist on the system. Note that some of these users are system users (such as the ones that control Glance and Nova) and are required for the operation of OpenStack. These system users should not be deleted. Also be mindful that care should be taken in changing passwords while running DevStack, since some of these are hard-coded in configuration files.
- **Groups:** A collection of users who are assigned to a specific project or domain.
- **Roles:** A defined series of permitted actions that you can assign to a specific project or domain.

You can learn more about using Horizon in Chapter 6, "Private Compute Cloud."

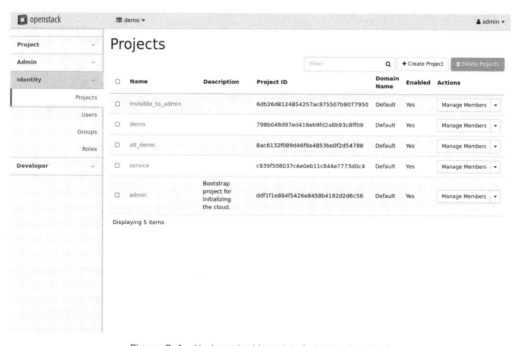

Figure 2.4   Horizon dashboard (administrative view)

Working with the Host on the Command Line

Now that you have explored some of the interface, you can attach to the screen session on the command line to begin exploring the specific processes that are being run in the foreground running daemon mode.

To attach to the screen you issue the standard screen reattach command:

```
screen -r
```

The initial screen session should look something like Figure 2.5.

Since DevStack does not create log files by default, all information about the running services is spread out over a couple dozen child screens within a screen process. An interesting one to navigate to is a screen called n-api, which shows you the output from the nova-api daemon. You can also browse through the calls you just made in the Horizon dashboard.

Navigating Screen

DevStack uses a tool called screen to manage the daemons running in the foreground. The following commands will help you navigate this screen session so you can interact with the daemons and see what they're doing.

Connect to the running screen session:

```
screen -r
```

Once you're inside the screen session, the following key combination will get you a listing of all the child screens running:

```
ctrl + a + "
```

You can then navigate through the screens by using your up and down arrows. Later, if you wish to go to a specific screen and know the number you can use the following:

```
ctrl + a + '
```

That will bring up a prompt where you can type in the screen number to which you want to go.

If you're just looking to get an overview of what's showing in all the screens, you can navigate through them one by one by using the following:

```
ctrl + a + n
ctrl + a + p
```

These will get you to the next and previous screens, respectively.

Finally, to detach from this screen session and go back to your terminal, type the following:

```
ctrl + a + d
```

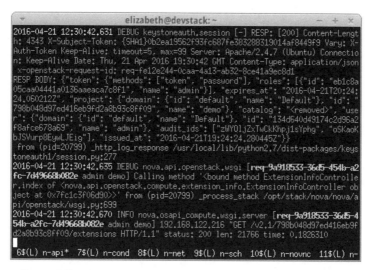

Figure 2.5   The nova-api window of a screen session for DevStack

Now that you're familiar with what is being run on the system, you can also start using the OpenStack command line client to launch instances, view the status of instances and more. You will first need to load the credentials by sourcing the openrc file in the devstack directory. The following commands are some simple ones to get you started,

```
$ source ~/devstack/openrc
$ openstack flavor list
$ openstack server list --all-projects
```

You will learn more about OpenStack Client commands in later chapters, and a basic reference is available in Appendix E, "OpenStack Client (OSC)."

DevStack Options

The preceding section of this chapter covered launching DevStack without any customization. However, customization is recommended for testing out different aspects of the development version of OpenStack.

DevStack "Stable"

One of the perhaps lesser-known features of DevStack is the capability to launch a stable version of OpenStack with the DevStack scripts. This is heavily used by developers and the OpenStack Continuous Integration stack to test upgrades. However, it can also help newcomers get a feel for a specific, released version of OpenStack rather than using a development version. Using this version can also be valuable for getting started with OpenStack if you're having trouble getting the DevStack version from master running.

> **Caution**
>
> Even though this installs a stable version of OpenStack, this is still not a maintainable or recommended way to run OpenStack in a production environment. You should continue to use a Virtual Machine or spare system that you can reinstall at a later date and learn proper separation and high availability procedures for maintaining a production system.

The procedure for running a stable version of OpenStack using DevStack is a slightly modified version of the three steps mentioned earlier, adding another step to switch to one of the supported stable branches in the cloned git repository:

```
$ git clone git://git.openstack.org/openstack-dev/devstack.git
$ cd devstack
$ git checkout stable/mitaka
$ ./stack.sh
```

> **Tip**
>
> Want to list the available stable branches in DevStack you have to select from? While in the devstack directory, type:
>
> ```
> git branch -a
> ```
>
> OpenStack releases are alphabetical, so the last listing in the branch list will be the most recent stable release.

Just like running standard DevStack, this will take some time as it downloads dependencies and sets up your environment. Instead of pulling from the development version, it will pull from the requested stable environment.

The demonstrations shown earlier in this chapter for logging in as a user and administrator can also be done with this stable version, but you will instead have a version that has been released and is more like the one you would find shipped with your distribution.

Customizing DevStack

There are many customizations you can make in order to adjust your DevStack environment to do everything from pre-seed passwords and networks, to enabling additional services.

> **Tip**
>
> If you want to make customizations, it is recommended that you don't use one of the stable branches of DevStack. The development version is always adding new options and is actively being maintained and tested, where it may be less likely for the stable versions to be updated.

Changes are made to a local.conf file in the main devstack directory. You can find a sample configuration file at samples/local.conf.

At minimum, it's recommended that you write a local.conf to match your environment and make the script non-interactive. This will include setting default passwords for the admin user and services like database and queue server and network configuration.

Learn more about minimal configuration by reading the documentation for the version of DevStack you're running, stored in configuration.rst of the doc/source directory of the source code. The latest development version is available online at: http://docs.openstack.org/developer/devstack/configuration.html#minimal-configuration.

Beyond these basic environment variables, there are also several notable ones:

- Changing of the DevStack directory:

```
DEST=/opt/stack (default, change this to what you wish to use)
```

- Enable logging:

```
LOGFILE=$DEST/logs/stack.sh.log
```

You can also manipulate the number of days stored for logs (default 7 days) and settings concerned with where the logs go (their own logs or unified syslog).

Enabling other services is one of the more powerful things you can do when customizing DevStack. By enabling other services in this development environment you can test out the latest features, or deploy a DevStack that has components that look more like what your own future deployment will look like. For example, if you want to focus on storage you may wish to enable Swift, the object store component for OpenStack. Enabling additional services is typically done by defining variables in your local.conf file. The supported services in DevStack change routinely in the development version as new services enter the OpenStack ecosystem. In addition to shipped documentation mentioned earlier, to learn more about how the available services, as well as the default services, work and are called within DevStack, you can browse files in the lib/ directory of the DevStack source. These libraries contain extensive documentation in the comments along with exports and functions needed to deploy them.

You can set up a DevStack install that uses multiple hosts, like you will later when we install OpenStack in a more maintainable way. However, this is poorly supported and DevStack developers warn that it is only tested with very basic configurations.

As mentioned earlier, you can read the heavily commented stack.sh script for more customizations that can be made via environment variables or in the local.conf script.

Summary

We have now covered some of the most basic uses for DevStack and got you going with a real, non-production install of OpenStack. With this, you were able to begin to get familiar with the interface and basic navigation of foreground daemonized processes to get a glimpse of the internals of several services. We then reviewed some of the ways you can extend DevStack to run a stable version of OpenStack and enable some of the other OpenStack services that are not enabled by default.

3

Networking

If there is magic in this planet, it is contained in the water.
Loren Eiseley

Before we launch into the deployment scenarios, it's important to pause to discuss networking. Networking is a major consideration when configuring OpenStack. It will influence the hardware and environment choices you make and naturally has a significant role in the choices made for you and the deployment scenarios in this book.

Networking in OpenStack is also a complicated topic that trips up systems and network administrators alike who are working to deploy OpenStack. Additionally, the physical network and equipment you have in your environment, such as a data center, will determine what you can do with the networking tooling that OpenStack supports.

Key Concepts

The first thing you should know about networking on OpenStack is that there is no standard deployment. Needs of organizations, the environments they have to work in and the hardware being used will vary greatly. The concepts outlined in this chapter are generalized, and not all deployments will obey the same rules. The goal here is to give you a glimpse into what you may encounter when deploying OpenStack yourself so you have a starting point to understand how it all works.

Planes of Operation

It is useful to consider traffic flows throughout an OpenStack environment using the same terminology found in general networking. Specifically, network engineering conceptualizes traffic flows as occurring on one of the management, control or data planes. OpenStack has a very similar division of network types, but these networks are sometimes combined. For the sake of simplicity, our deployment scenarios will be using a single private network for the control, management and data traffic, but we should still explain each.

Management Plane

Administrators need a way to maintain, update and interrogate their servers and network elements, and this is done over the management plane.

OpenStack also has a concept of a management network. It's one of several private networks in an OpenStack deployment and is used by the administrators to log into the machine to complete systems administration tasks. This network is also available for monitoring. Splitting out this network prevents system administration and system access monitoring from being impacted by traffic being used elsewhere in the deployment, such as bursts of API and compute instance traffic.

In the deployment scenarios in this book, we give our OpenStack nodes firewalled access to the Internet in order to allow for the installation of packages, Puppet modules and other sources required by the scenarios. This may also be what you do in production, but in a more secure environment access to all of your installation resources would be restricted to the local network. In this secure environment, you may host a local distribution package mirror, configuration management repositories, and netboot or system installation servers on your local management network. Doing so also allows you to stage and thoroughly test all the changes in packages and other resources stored on local mirrors before putting them into production.

Control Plane

In networking terms, the control plane carries signaling traffic between network elements.

In OpenStack you may consider using a very similar control network. It would be the network where your messaging queue for interaction between services would live and any other traffic related to service interaction. In lieu of a dedicated management network, it's common for management traffic to share the same private network as control traffic.

Data Plane

Finally, there's the data plane. This is where all of your actual network payload going to users and customers will be running. In OpenStack you can think of this as where instance traffic and public services like access to files in the Swift object storage are served up.

Provider Network

A Provider Network is simply the logical representation of a network that is provided to OpenStack for use. This is not necessarily a different type of network from those mentioned above, but it has the distinction of being provided by a source outside of OpenStack and is marked as such. This source may be a switch or other network hardware or software that has control over the network you're connected to. A provider network may map to a physical network, which may be a network that is routable within a data center or a network that is accessible to the Internet. It's common to have multiple provider networks. Since provider networks are externally provided, configuring them in OpenStack is simply a matter of informing Neutron about basic data center network topology so it can use this information for the compute instances.

Tenant Networking

An OpenStack deployment will typically have a series of *Tenant Networks*, which run on top of the data plane. Each instance connects to one or more tenant networks, where they will get their native IP address(es), which can be seen within the instance. By default, this address will only be locally routable between instances that exist in that tenant network and to specific services, such as the DHCP server used to assign those addresses and the router that may pass along that traffic to an external provider network.

Tenant networking for instances is where things get complicated. Traffic on tenant networks needs to be appropriately forwarded between instances; you generally want some kind of isolation, and in many deployments there is an allowance for overlapping subnets to be used as internal networks. OpenStack Neutron offers three options for handling traffic in the tenant network: flat, virtual local area network (VLAN) and tunneled.

Flat Network

In a flat network, everyone shares the same network segment. No network segregation is applied nor any kind of tagging. This means that tenants can see the traffic from other tenants and the controller, plus address space cannot overlap. This decreases the amount of flexibility considerably, and if these are instances controlled by different parties, this is not an ideal situation. Use of flat networking is typically not advisable unless you fully understand the implications and limitations but could be reasonable in a small enterprise environment controlled by a single team and when external hardware resources are used extensively.

Segmented Network

With flat networking behind us, we're left with the other two options for handling traffic to focus on: VLANs and tunneling. In both of these scenarios, separation is provided, which also means that tenants can overlap in network subnet range, using the same local IP addresses without conflict. Whichever one you decide to use, it will be implemented via the Modular Layer 2 (ML2) plug-in with Open vSwitch (OVS) or Linux Bridge.

In this book we'll be using the OVS model. OVS is often easier to use and more flexible than Linux Bridging. Neutron creates bridges within OVS, as well as internal VLANs. These internal VLANs that are created are entirely local to the node and use VLAN numbering that is distinct from the external segmentation IDs (such as VLANs outside the node). These internal VLANs exist even if you are not using external VLANs, such as if you are deploying a VXLAN-based topology.

VLAN

In a VLAN network, each tenant is assigned to a VLAN. To support this environment, you must have hardware switches in your infrastructure that supports VLANs for each tenant network. This typically would be set up by using the tooling that comes with the switch or, if supported, allowing OpenStack to use a plug-in from that vendor (see the "Exploring the Possibilities with Neutron" sidebar in Chapter 5, "Foundations for Deployments"). This is particularly useful in a data center where VLANs are already used. It's also useful if you have other hardware, such as a storage device, that you wish to include in your VLANs. You can also make use of external firewalls and routers to intelligently handle tenant traffic.

Tunneling

In a tunnel-driven network, encapsulation of traffic is used to provide separation. The most common encapsulation protocols are Generic Routing Encapsulation (GRE) and Virtual Extensible Local Area Networking (VXLAN). GRE and VXLAN are very similar, but VXLAN is more commonly used in cloud deployments because of its greater flexibility and efficiency. Using Neutron with OVS, a mesh of tunnels is set up between the OpenStack nodes in your environment. As traffic is sent along these tunnels, the Ethernet frame will be encapsulated in a new IP packet, which is routed to the destination node. The packet is then decapsulated and delivered into the appropriate instance (running on a compute node), control process (like DHCP running on the control node) or routed out of the tenant network (via a virtual router on the controller node or a physical router). See Figure 3.1 for an example of what a packet coming from an instance would look like.

Although the traffic is carried over the physical network, because it's encapsulated there is no visibility to the specific tenant network traffic from the perspective of the data center hardware. It just appears to be traffic between two OpenStack nodes.

It's worth noting that, in practice, it has generally been found that tunneling (such as GRE and VXLAN) scales better than VLANs. VLANs are more commonly found in an enterprise environment where the number of tenant networks is finite and the data center uses a common layer-2 switch fabric throughout. VLANs also require configuration of all your networking hardware to support each tenant and can run into limitations with regard to the number of VLANs that can exist on a given switch or link. Tunneling instead pushes complexity and scaling concerns into OpenStack, so it is not required on the data center network equipment. Using tunneling can also be easier to deploy and debug. When you go into production, you'll need to do an analysis of your own environment with your networking team to determine which method to use.

Maximum Transmission Unit (MTU)

Before going any further, it's also important to take a moment to discuss Maximum Transmission Units (MTUs). If you refer to Figure 3.1, you will notice that this

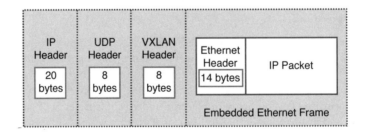

Figure 3.1   VXLAN-encapsulated instance traffic packet

encapsulated packet has a lot in it that is not in a typical Ethernet frame. As an encapsulated frame, we're adding the VXLAN data. This causes the frame held within to be restricted to a certain size in order for traffic to flow reliably on a typical network.

Most networks will default to accepting an MTU size of 1500 bytes. That's the size that many systems assume packets should be when transmitting them onto an Ethernet network. In the deployment scenarios in this book we're setting an MTU size of 1450 bytes, referring back to Figure 3.1. Each header can take up to a certain amount of space:

- **IP header:** usually 20 bytes
- **UDP header:** 8 bytes
- **VXLAN header:** 8 bytes
- **Embedded Ethernet header:** usually 14 bytes

When you add all of these up you get 50. So the biggest packet you can send must be restricted to 1500 bytes of total space minus that 50 bytes, so 1450 bytes.

> **Tip**
>
> How do you know if you're having an MTU problem? The first few symptoms will be that you may be able to ping an instance but not SSH into it. Or your SSH command starts, but can't complete the handshake. See the Networking section of Chapter 13, "Troubleshooting," to learn more about what you can do to debug MTU problems.

When you move your deployment into a data center and start running real services on it, you will likely find this restricted size inadequate. There are many applications that perform poorly when restricted to the smaller packet size. At this point it becomes necessary to start using jumbo frames. Jumbo frames are Ethernet frames with more than 1500 bytes of payload, conventionally supporting up to around 9000 bytes. Using jumbo frames on the underlying data plane networks is almost universally done in production cloud deployments. This is achieved by ensuring that all nodes are running with physical Ethernet interface MTUs greater than 1550 so that no reduction to the MTU size is needed for instance and tunneled interfaces.

Deployment Requirements

For the deployment scenarios in this book, we will be using two nodes. The first node will be a controller that's used to run the OpenStack services for each deployment scenario. The second will be a compute node that will only be used for running your compute instances. Full specifications for what each server needs will be covered in detail in Chapter 4, "Your First OpenStack," but for now you only need to know that on your controller node you will need two NICs and for the compute node you will need one NIC.

We will be using OVS and VXLAN to create a mesh of tunnels for us to pass along traffic to instances that live on the compute node. This is configured manually in Chapter 4, but in later chapters will all automatically be configured with Puppet. It's important to understand how the traffic flows so you can debug any problems with your deployment scenarios and make informed decisions about your own production deployment moving forward.

The networks we will be using in our deployment scenarios are as follows:

- **Example external network:** 203.0.113.0/24
- **Example tenant network:** 10.190.0.0/24
- **Example network used for accessing your nodes, API endpoints, control traffic and encapsulated tenant traffic:** 192.168.122.0/24

Tip

The external network 203.0.113.0/24 may look real, but it is an RFC 5735 test net block that has been assigned to look like a public address but be used for testing.

By using this default external network, your instances will not have Internet access, but we can place example resources on the 203.0.113.0/24 network to emulate Internet endpoints. For instance, in our deployment scenarios, a web browser on this network will be used to access a web page running on one of your instances.

If you have an external network connected to the Internet that you wish to use as the external provider network, you may want to use this instead.

Deployment examples in this book were designed to be flexible enough to be used on physical hardware or with your choice of virtualization technology. However, the requirements remain quite strict, and you may struggle with our configuration decisions if there are deviations from the switches and bridges we outline. If you have any trouble setting up a deployment, refer to Appendix A, "Reference Deployment," to give that example a try. The reference deployment has been fully tested.

Physical Hardware

We'll begin by talking about the physical hardware scenario, since that may help with conceptually understanding the layout. If you're using physical hardware, you'll want two physical networks, each with a switch. Follow along with Figure 3.2 as we dive into how this should be set up.

The first switch, at the top of Figure 3.2, will connect your controller server and your compute server. This network will carry the management, control and data plane traffic. As mentioned, we're focusing on the network right now, so see Chapter 4 for full specification details of the hardware you'll need for these servers. You will need to have access to both of these servers, whether they are connected to a monitor, keyboard and mouse, over a serial console, through SSH from another computer connected to

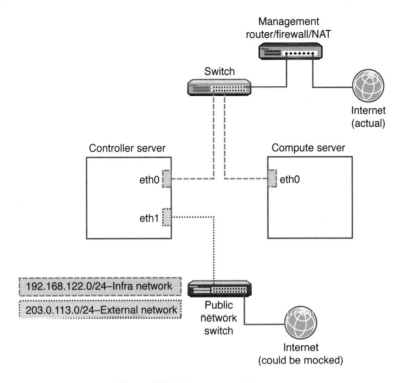

Figure 3.2   Physical machine setup

this first switch or via IPMI. This switch will be the one that all of your administrative duties can be completed through as you work with your servers in the deployment scenarios.

This first switch is also connected to a router/firewall/NAT device which ultimately provides access to the real Internet. This provides Internet access to your nodes so you can install the Ubuntu packages, git repositories, Puppet modules and other installation resources we need throughout our configuration of OpenStack.

The second switch, at the bottom of Figure 3.2, is your "Public network switch," which in a production deployment would connect the gateway functions on the controller node to an Internet- or intranet-connected network in your data center. If you're using our example "public" addresses it will not actually be routable online. The "Internet (could be mocked)" in Figure 3.2 would likely be replaced with a laptop or other computer where you can do tests to check for connectivity once you have instances deployed and floating IP addresses assigned from the external network.

Virtual Machines

Using virtual machines for these deployment examples will likely be significantly easier as you start out. In the reference deployment in Appendix A, we're using a virtualized environment powered by KVM running on Ubuntu 14.04. If you understand the architecture we're aiming for, you're welcome to use an alternate virtualization technology that you're comfortable with.

Host, Node and Instance

It's easy to get confused when we start talking about the components of an environment where you have a single physical machine with a whole bunch of virtualization on top. The following will define what we mean when we use each term.

- **Host:** This is the hardware where all your virtual machines will run. It can be a laptop, a desktop or a server, but it should be something you can sit in front of and run commands on. This host will need to run some form of Linux and you will be setting up Linux Bridges on it for use by the nodes.
- **Node:** A node is a component of OpenStack that runs OpenStack services. In our examples you'll have a controller node and a compute node. Other OpenStack deployments may have their own network nodes, storage nodes and more. This would normally be its own physical machine.
- **Instance:** This is the server you use OpenStack to launch and on which you do all your organization's work. It'll be where you host your web site or the server for the latest game your company you released. It will typically be a virtual machine, but may also be bare metal as we will discuss in Chapter 10, "Bare Metal Provisioning," or a container, which is covered in Chapter 11, "Controlling Containers."

The virtual machine setup will be identical to the physical machine setup, but you will be replicating the scenario virtually. Instead of switches you will be using bridges on the host for each node, so the machine hosting them will need to be configured with two bridges. Other than that, Figure 3.3 should look very similar to Figure 3.2, and comparing the two may help you conceptualize the configuration.

When you create your controller node, one NIC should be associated with virbr0 and the second NIC with virbr1. The NIC connected to the virbr0 network will be how you access the system to configure and interact with OpenStack. Management traffic on this bridge will need access to the Internet through eth0 (shown in dotted lines in Figure 3.3), so iptables NAT rules will typically be put in place to allow for this.

The second bridge (virbr1) will be used for the example external provider network, which is meant to give your instances access beyond their default tenant networks.

Your single NIC compute node must only be associated with the virbr0 bridge.

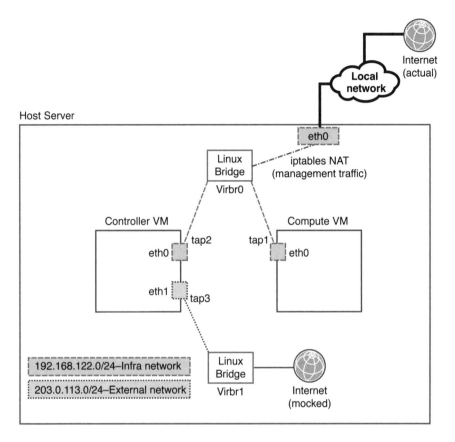

Figure 3.3   Virtual machine setup

Traffic Flow

You now have some switches or bridges to handle traffic, but this only scratches the surface of the routing that's happening inside of an OpenStack deployment. Many of the issues you'll find with networking will be related to internal interfaces that are passing along the traffic, so being aware of what these are for is important. Once you have a deployment scenario up and running, you can explore what's happening yourself. Figure 3.4 gives a detailed overview of how traffic is flowing that you'll likely wish to come back to frequently later on.

For the sake of explanation, this diagram shows a controller and two compute nodes (our deployment scenarios only have a single compute node). As you can see, traffic between compute nodes is handled directly between the nodes. This would be the instance traffic going over VXLAN tunnels. In order to leave the tenant network, traffic must

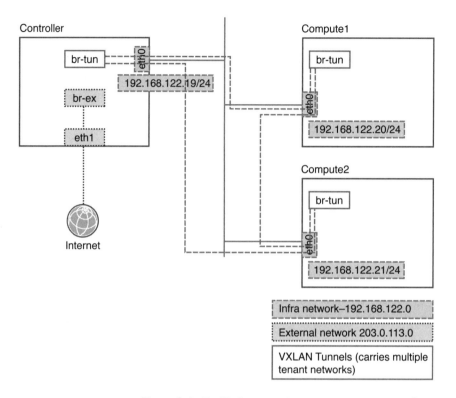

Figure 3.4   Traffic flow overview

go through the controller. The controller runs the common network services, like DHCP for the tenant networks, and also handles the routing of traffic to external networks.

This view is not complete though. It's time to dive a bit deeper to look at exactly what's happening inside your controller and compute nodes in order to handle your network traffic.

Controller Node

As you know from the setup requirements, you will have the following interfaces on your controller node: eth0 and eth1. These two interfaces end up handling a lot, so we'll take a look inside to see what OVS is doing to route traffic, run a DHCP server and use iptables.

First, have a look at Figure 3.5 for a detailed view of what's going on inside your controller node. This can be a bit overwhelming at first, but being familiar with the concepts is important when you start debugging.

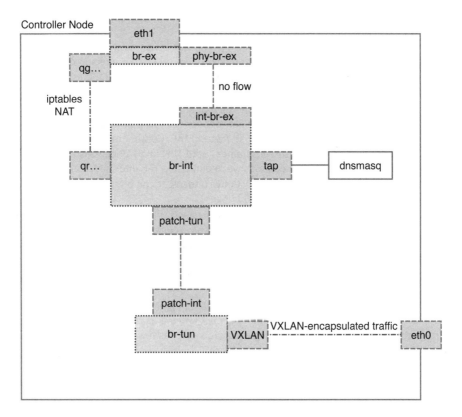

Figure 3.5   Traffic flow on the controller node

Figure 3.5 is a complicated diagram, but the easiest way to describe it is by reviewing each of the OVS bridges.

Starting with br-int, we have your internal bridge around which much of your activity happens. On br-int we have the following:

- An OVS virtual tap interface that runs dnsmasq as a DHCP server for your instances. This runs in its own network name space.

- For each tenant network, an OVS virtual tap interface qr-★ which connects to the qrouter-★ name space for NATed external traffic.

- A patch named patch-tun, which connects to the br-tun bridge and is used to pass traffic directly between the two bridges.

- A patch named int-br-ex, which connects to the br-ex bridge. This patch is automatically configured in our setup but is not used in our deployment scenarios.

Linux Networking Terms Quickstart

We have thrown out a lot of terms as we've begun to discuss networking on the controller. Some of these are standard networking terms, others are specific to OVS. You
can learn more about all of them using networking-specific resources, but for now,
here is a quick rundown to get you started:

- **TUN/TAP**—Virtual kernel network devices that are created and manipulated in userland, allowing a program to act as a network device. TUN (network TUNnel) simulates
  a network layer device operating on IP frames. TAP (network tap) simulates a link
  layer device working with Ethernet frames. Both TUN and TAP devices are provided
  by the same driver. In our scenarios we're only using TAP interfaces.
- **Patch**—An OVS concept that connects two bridges. It can be thought of as running
  an Ethernet cable between two OVS bridges.
- **Bridge**—Behaving much like a network switch, a software bridge (whether you're using
  OVS or Linux bridge) connects multiple network segments by enslaving physical or
  logical network interfaces as ports on the bridge.
- **Name spaces**—Viewed and manipulated with ip netns commands, network name
  spaces represent a copy of the network stack with their own network interfaces,
  routing tables and ability to use iptables.
- **NAT**—Network Address Translation, provides remapping of IP address space as
  traffic moves into another network. A simple example is traffic moving from a local
  network out to the Internet having its source address rewritten as it is routed onto
  the Internet.
- **iptables**—A userland program for configuring the kernel-based Linux firewall.

In order to make configuration of tunneling more modular, tunneling interfaces are
not added directly to the br-int bridge. Instead, a dedicated OVS bridge called br-tun
bridge is created to handle the tunneling activity, which in our case is the VXLAN
traffic. This bridge has only two ports:

- The other end of the patch-tun patch, patch-int for passing traffic to and from
  the br-int bridge.
- The VXLAN tunnel interface, which uses the controller's host networking
  stack for routing and forwarding, resulting in traffic flowing through its main
  interface—eth0.

Finally, look at the br-ex bridge, which exists on the other side of NAT rules for
passing traffic to the public network:

- The eth1 external interface is attached to this bridge.
- For each tenant network, an OVS virtual tap interface qg-★, which connects
  to the qrouter-★ name space for NATed external traffic.
- The other end of the unused int-br-ex patch—phy-br-ex.

It's important to take a moment to talk about the qrouter-* network name space. As described above, it sits between the br-int and br-ex bridges via a pair of OVS virtual tap interfaces. Normal Linux kernel-based IP forwarding within this name space is used to route traffic between the two tap interfaces (and thus between the two OVS bridges). Additionally, iptables rules within the namespace act on packets flowing between the two tap interfaces. Along with filtering rules, the iptables config also includes NAT rules to translate addresses between the tenant network addressing and the external network addressing, such as the floating IPs assigned from the external provider network.

To view all of these on your controller, you'll want to keep a few commands handy. The first is an OVS command that shows all of your OVS bridges, patches and interfaces:

```
$ sudo ovs-vsctl show
f8356299-3562-4303-a217-c2049cd0b5e2
    Bridge br-int
        fail_mode: secure
        Port patch-tun
            Interface patch-tun
                type: patch
                options: {peer=patch-int}
        Port br-int
            Interface br-int
                type: internal
        Port "qr-0ed92e71-46"
            tag: 1
            Interface "qr-0ed92e71-46"
                type: internal
        Port "tapb35f58ac-3e"
            tag: 1
            Interface "tapb35f58ac-3e"
                type: internal
        Port int-br-ex
            Interface int-br-ex
                type: patch
                options: {peer=phy-br-ex}
    Bridge br-tun
        fail_mode: secure
        Port patch-int
            Interface patch-int
                type: patch
                options: {peer=patch-tun}
        Port "vxlan-c0a87a20"
            Interface "vxlan-c0a87a20"
                type: vxlan
                options: {df_default="true", in_key=flow, local_ip="192.168.122.38",
out_key=flow, remote_ip="192.168.122.32"}
        Port br-tun
            Interface br-tun
                type: internal
    Bridge br-ex
        Port "eth1"
            Interface "eth1"
        Port "qg-dd1efdc1-6a"
            Interface "qg-dd1efdc1-6a"
                type: internal
```

```
        Port phy-br-ex
            Interface phy-br-ex
                type: patch
                options: {peer=int-br-ex}
        Port br-ex
            Interface br-ex
                type: internal
    ovs_version: "2.5.0"
```

The second will show you the two network name spaces used for the instance dhcp server and tenant traffic from your instances:

```
$ sudo ip netns
qrouter-9bc585a7-5cc6-4a59-92f5-b0648f6adab0
qdhcp-a7897e45-0d16-4e8f-8b8a-846ce504b766
```

Between these two commands, you can start exploring how the output from these commands maps to Figure 3.5. Your standard ip addr and ip -d link commands can also help you drill down into details about your configuration and understand the types of devices being used.

Compute Node

The compute node is a bit simpler, but it does add a couple new concepts to the mix. Figure 3.6 provides the overview of how traffic flows within a compute node.

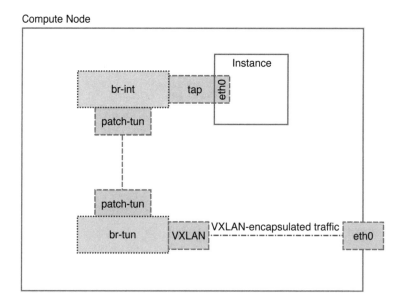

Figure 3.6   Traffic flow on the compute node

Just like with the controller, the easiest way to view this diagram is by starting with the internal bridge (br-int) and moving outwards. From br-int, you have:

- A tap interface for each instance, representing the other side of the Ethernet interface within the instance.
- A patch named patch-tun, which connects to the br-tun bridge and is used to pass traffic directly between the two bridges. The br-tun OVS bridge is constructed and utilized on the compute nodes in the same manner as it is constructed and utilized on the controller node.

Just like with the controller, you can run the `ovs-vsctl show` command to see the OVS configuration of these virtual interfaces tunnels and more. By using the `ip -d link` command, you will be able to see your interfaces, as well as the tap interfaces for each instance you're running.

Other Resources

The OpenStack community maintains a Networking Guide that provides an introduction to important networking terms, a tour of networking with regard to OpenStack specifically and a tour of various scenarios using Flat, VLAN and VXLAN/GRE: http://docs.openstack.org/mitaka/networking-guide.

The installation guides maintained by the OpenStack community also have sections about networking that can be referenced.

You can also see the extensive Networking section of Chapter 13, "Troubleshooting," for tips on fixing a deployment and Appendix F, "Finding Help with OpenStack," to learn how to ask for advice and assistance from the OpenStack community.

Summary

Decisions you make with networking will impact everything else in your OpenStack deployment, and they're also the hardest to change after you've deployed. It's important to have a discussion with your networking team to design a network topology that best addresses the needs of your users and the constraints of your environment. To assist with these decisions, we've walked through key concepts of networking and Neutron itself in OpenStack.

For the deployment scenarios used in this book, we defined the physical and virtual networking requirements. With the basic configuration explained, you also learned how traffic will flow at a high level, and how it is broken down on the controller and compute nodes.

4

Your First OpenStack

The journey of a thousand miles begins with one step.

Lao-tzu

In Chapter 2, "DevStack," you got your feet wet with an initial deployment of OpenStack using DevStack on a single server. Now we are moving on to the basics involved in creating a more realistic install of the core components of OpenStack on a single system with the Mitaka release of OpenStack on two servers.

While these steps will produce a system that is more reflective of how OpenStack will look in a real-world deployment, it still will not be production-ready. Steps we complete here are manual, resulting in an install that is not very maintainable, and we're not taking scaling into consideration. In production, you will also want to use some kind of configuration management system, such as Puppet, which we use in later chapters.

Since configuration management abstracts away so much of the configuration, the instructions in this chapter are intended to get you more familiar with the components on their own. Understanding the interactions between OpenStack components, MySQL, and the message queueing system and how services are added to the Keystone identity service are important. This understanding will help you with making architecture decisions, debugging and, ultimately, scaling your OpenStack deployment and adding new services.

Requirements

For this demonstration of OpenStack, and all subsequent ones in this book, you will want two servers. The first is a controller node, and the second is a compute node. These servers will need the following specifications, also show in Figure 4.1:

- Controller Node—1 x 64-bit processor, 4GB of memory, 30GB of storage and two Network Interface Cards (NICs)
- Compute Node—1 x 64-bit processor, 2GB of memory, 20GB of storage and one NIC

If you're using physical hardware, you will also want two physical switches, as described in Chapter 3, "Networking." If you're using a series of Virtual Machines (VMs), you will be creating bridges on the host system rather than using physical switches, also outlined in Chapter 3.

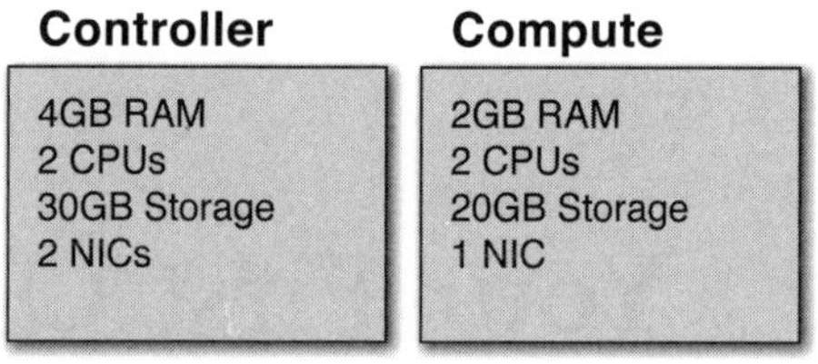

Controller

4GB RAM
2 CPUs
30GB Storage
2 NICs

Compute

2GB RAM
2 CPUs
20GB Storage
1 NIC

Figure 4.1   Minimum requirements for the simple, two node deployment

If you're using VMs for this setup, adding a second NIC should be simple. See the documentation for your VM technology for how to do this. As in Chapter 2, for best performance you also will need to use a 64-bit CPU with hardware virtualization support and, preferably, at least four cores, so you can launch an instance.

Reference Deployment

The examples in this book are intended to be flexible enough to work with your choice of virtualization technology or hardware setup. However, if you are satisfied with using a deployment example prepared and tested by the authors, see Appendix A, "Reference Deployment." This reference deployment walks you through using an Ubuntu 14.04 system as a host with Linux Bridges, the libvirt toolkit with KVM (Kernel-based Virtual Machine) for the OpenStack nodes and QEMU for compute instances.

Use of the reference deployment is also recommended if you're struggling to get the configurations working on your own choice of setup. Nuances regarding networking defaults, in particular, vary between virtualization technologies and can easily put you in a situation that is difficult to debug while you're also learning OpenStack fundamentals.

Initial Setup

You will begin by satisfying the prerequisites needed for a working network. Once your network is set up, we'll then complete an installation of the operating system on your system and install the key components of OpenStack. As discussed in Chapter 1, "What is OpenStack?" the operating system we'll be using is Ubuntu 14.04 LTS Server, and we'll be installing the Mitaka release of OpenStack. This chapter leads you through creating a fully manual network to get you familiar with the specific components. In the next chapter you'll be introduced to how we do this with Puppet.

Networking

In Chapter 3 you learned about the internals of how networking works in OpenStack and, specifically, how it works for the deployments we're working on. If you're using a physical network set up according to Figure 3.2 in Chapter 3, the virtualized networking we'll be talking about in this section is instead handled by the hardware on your network. With your physical network in place, you can skip to the next section, "Operating System."

If you're using a virtualization technology other than our reference deployment in Appendix A to run through these deployment scenarios, you will need to do a bit of configuration on the host system where your OpenStack virtual machines are running.

Both VMs, controller and compute, will need to be configured to use a bridge with NAT. This is likely an option in the configuration of your virtualization technology. A basic NAT, in which all of the VMs' outbound traffic is automatically translated, will not work for this environment.

The following is an example of how you would set up your bridges on the virtual machine host if it's not being done automatically by your virtualization technology. You will need the bridge-utils and iptables packages installed.

```
$ sudo brctl addbr virbr0
$ sudo ip addr add 192.168.122.1/24 dev virbr0
$ sudo ip link set up dev virbr0
$ sudo iptables -t nat -A POSTROUTING -s 192.168.222.0/24 \
    \! -d 192.168.222.0/24 -j MASQUERADE
$ sudo brctl addbr virbr1
$ sudo ip addr add 203.0.113.1/24 dev virbr1
$ sudo ip link set up dev virbr1
```

When you launch your controller node, one NIC should be associated with virbr0 and the second NIC with virbr1. The NIC connected to the virbr0 network will be how you access the system to configure and interact with OpenStack. The second bridge (virbr1) will be used for the example external network, which will be used to give your instances access beyond their default tenant networks.

Your single NIC compute node needs to be associated with virbr0.

Operating System

Now that you understand how networking needs to be set up, install Ubuntu 14.04 LTS Server on your OpenStack nodes. During the installation most defaults will be fine, but you can use the "Guided - use entire disk" in the "Partition disks" screen option, since you don't need LVM. Also, when you come to a screen that says Software selection, which allows you to select additional components for installation, make sure everything is unselected except OpenSSH server. This option will install the SSH daemon on the servers and start it when you first boot up so you can access it remotely over SSH.

If you didn't choose to do software updates during installation, do them after you have installed and booted your nodes so you have an up-to-date Ubuntu system:

```
$ sudo apt-get update
$ sudo apt-get dist-upgrade
$ sudo reboot
```

This may take some time, but Ubuntu will give you a package count and status on downloads and configuration. This upgrade will likely include a new kernel, so we reboot the systems before moving forward so that they come up in the new kernel. Once you have rebooted, you're ready to move on to manual system configuration.

From this point forward, everything covered in this chapter is automatically done by Puppet in later chapters. Again, this chapter walks you through how to do a basic installation of OpenStack without Puppet so you can gain an understanding of how the pieces fit together.

System Configuration

When the system boots, you will want to enable the Ubuntu Cloud Archive for the latest version of OpenStack with the following command and update the package lists as well as any packages that the cloud archive brings in that are newer than what comes with Ubuntu 14.04 by default:

```
$ sudo add-apt-repository cloud-archive:mitaka
$ sudo apt-get update
$ sudo apt-get dist-upgrade
```

Note mitaka in the first command. As explained previously, at the time of writing Mitaka is the name of the latest stable release of OpenStack. The update command is also important. Without running it you will not get all the packages you need, and it will install a much older version of OpenStack that is not compatible with some of the options explained in this book.

You'll now move into configuring the network and installing the packages required for the OpenStack components running on each of your nodes.

> **Tip**
>
> A git repository called scripts-and-configs is part of the DeploymentsBook project on GitHub at https://github.com/DeploymentsBook. This repository contains the contents of many of the configuration files and more detailed in this chapter. You can use this repository to copy and paste any of the examples into your systems rather than copying them character by character from this book.

We'll begin with the controller node.

Controller Node

The controller node is the heart of your OpenStack deployment. It runs all of the OpenStack services, your database, the queuing server and more. The other node, compute, is reserved only for running compute instances.

Networking

The networking specifications for our deployments were discussed in detail in Chapter 3. The first modification to your configuration that you'll need to make is to your /etc/network/interfaces file, which configures your networks. In the following example, the assumption is that you have your local loopback interface, lo, and your two NICS defined as the eth0 and eth1 interfaces.

> **Remember**
>
> The eth0 interface is the one connected to virbr0 or the switch that connects to the compute server.
>
> The eth1 interface is either connected to virbr1 or is the one that connects out to your other switch, into our example provider network for "public" addresses.

Open /etc/network/interfaces using sudo and your preferred text editor and make changes so it looks something like the following:

```
# The loopback network interface
auto lo
iface lo inet loopback

# The primary/maintenance network interface
auto eth0
iface eth0 inet static
      address 192.168.122.2
      netmask 255.255.255.0
      network 192.168.122.0
      broadcast 192.168.122.255
      gateway 192.168.122.1
      dns-nameservers 8.8.8.8 8.8.4.4

# Tenant network (no address directly assigned)
auto eth1
iface eth1 inet manual
```

In this example, the IP address of your controller server is 192.168.122.2. Adjust this to be consistent with your own network and the address of your controller server that was served from DHCP.

Now you'll want to bring up your eth1 network. This will not have an address directly assigned but will need to be in the UP state for the networking service to use it later:

```
$ sudo ifup eth1
```

The next time you reboot, this interface will come up automatically. You can test this now if you like and then confirm that eth1 is in the UP state.

```
$ ip link show eth1
3: eth1: <BROADCAST,MULTICAST,UP,LOWER_UP> mtu 1500 qdisc pfifo_fast state UP mode DEFAULT
group default qlen 1000
    link/ether 52:54:00:7b:95:83 brd ff:ff:ff:ff:ff:ff
```

Finally, add the controller host and the compute host to your /etc/hosts file. This is not necessarily a change you'd use in production, but it will make subsequent steps in this chapter easier by resolving your IP addresses for you in places where a name will suffice. In this example, your compute server has the address of 192.168.122.5. The following can be added to the bottom of the file:

```
192.168.122.2    controller
192.168.122.5    compute
```

Keep this change in mind as you continue going through this chapter. In place of the IPs for each server, we will be using the names "controller" and "compute" to refer to them in the configurations.

Packages

The OpenStack controller requires several packages to prepare your environment. These will often come from the regular Ubuntu repositories, but sometimes the Ubuntu Cloud Archive team will include a newer version of a piece of software in the repository for use with a newer version of OpenStack. Use the following command to install these prerequisite packages on your controller server:

```
$ sudo apt-get install ntp rabbitmq-server mysql-server \
  python-pymysql python-openstackclient openvswitch-switch
```

This will install the Network Time Protocol (ntp) daemon to make sure your time stays properly synced between nodes. No configuration is required for ntp. Services for the back end of OpenStack to function will also be installed with the command, including the queue service RabbitMQ, the MySQL server and related python connector for MySQL. During installation you will be prompted to set a root password for MySQL. Make sure this is a unique and secure password that you will remember. The python-openstackclient tool will be what is used to make most queries to your OpenStack services. The Open vSwitch package is needed for networking, configured later in this chapter.

> **Tip**
>
> Did you get an "E: Unable to locate package python-pymysql" message? This package is only included in the Ubuntu Cloud Archive (UCA). Make sure you followed the earlier step to enable the UCA and ran apt-get update to make sure your sources are current.

RabbitMQ does not prompt you to create a user and set up permissions, so we'll want to do that now. In the following command and subsequent responses, we are creating a user called "openstack" and you will replace RABBIT_PASSWORD with a password you wish to use.

```
$ sudo rabbitmqctl add_user openstack RABBIT_PASSWORD
Creating user "openstack" ...
$ sudo rabbitmqctl set_permissions openstack ".*" ".*" ".*"
Setting permissions for user "openstack" in vhost "/" ...
```

Remember the password set. You will need it later when configuring Nova and Neutron.

> **Tip**
>
> We're using the same RabbitMQ password for all services. In production it's recommended that you use different Rabbit credentials for every service.

Finally, a couple of changes will need to be made to the MySQL configuration. Create a new file called /etc/mysql/conf.d/openstack.cnf that will contain the following, replacing the 192.168.122.2 example with your own controller address:

```
[mysqld]
bind-address = 192.168.122.2
default-storage-engine = innodb
innodb_file_per_table
collation-server = utf8_general_ci
character-set-server = utf8
```

With that file in place, restart the MySQL server to apply the changes:

```
$ sudo service mysql restart
```

Your controller now has a basic configuration. After you do the basic configuration of your compute node, we'll be able to start installing OpenStack packages for services you'll be running on your node.

Compute Node

Since the compute node is only used for running OpenStack instances, the requirements here are considerably simpler.

Networking

The only change you should need to make in your compute system regarding networking is to the /etc/hosts file, just like you did for the controller node. As before, in this example we're assuming your controller has the address of 192.168.122.2 and the compute server has the address of 192.168.122.5. Again, update all the examples to reflect the real addresses of your systems.

The following can be added to the bottom of your /etc/hosts file:

```
192.168.122.2   controller
192.168.122.5   compute
```

You'll want to keep this change in mind. This is not something you'd necessarily do in production, but for our purposes, using the names "controller" and "compute" to refer to each system as we set up services makes explaining everything easier.

Packages

At this stage of the install, you only need two packages:

```
$ sudo apt-get install ntp python-openstackclient
```

The Network Time Protocol (ntp) daemon, which makes sure time stays properly synced between nodes and the python-openstackclient tool, will be what you use on the command line to make most queries to your OpenStack services. We install the client on your compute node just in case you need to use it for debugging later.

OpenStack Components

Now that your core systems have been prepared, you will go ahead and set up the typical standard services for OpenStack for a simple configuration. On the controller, you will have the following key services with their various supporting agents, daemons and plug-ins:

- Keystone (Identity)
- Nova (Compute)
- Neutron (Network)
- Glance (Image)

On the compute node, you will simply be running the Nova compute service for running instances and the openvswitch agent for Neutron to handle the tunnels. We'll begin with the configuration of the controller node.

Controller Node

Again, your controller node is what will run the core services of OpenStack. It runs most of the services, the database and queuing servers, and is the host for the API end-points. This server also has the two NICs for handling networking traffic that comes from the compute server.

Keystone

As described in Chapter 1, "What Is OpenStack?" Keystone is the Identity Service for OpenStack that provides identity, token, catalog and policy (such as roles) services for OpenStack. For users and services, Keystone can be used to provide user-based authentication with passwords or more service-focused interactions between OpenStack services through APIs using tokens. Keystone also tracks policy for users and stores the API endpoints for each OpenStack service. Each of the services you deploy for OpenStack must register with Keystone or an alternate identity service providing the same function, so we want to install this first.

We configured the Ubuntu Cloud Archive for Mitaka earlier in the chapter, which means we can now install the latest OpenStack stable release packages using apt-get. However, we'll first create a MySQL database and user with access to that database to use with Keystone. You may do this with a MySQL tool that you are already familiar with or via the command line with the following commands, where KEYSTONE_DBPASSWORD is replaced with a database password for the Keystone user:

```
$ mysql -u root -p
mysql> CREATE DATABASE keystone;
mysql> GRANT ALL PRIVILEGES ON keystone.* TO 'keystone'@'%' IDENTIFIED BY
  'KEYSTONE_DBPASSWORD';
mysql> quit
```

Before we install Keystone itself, we want to make sure it doesn't start any legacy daemons upon launch. Run the following (this command has no output):

```
$ sudo sh -c 'echo "manual" > /etc/init/keystone.override'
```

Now you can install Keystone, the Apache web server with WSGI (Web Server Gateway Interface), which is used in lieu of a Keystone daemon:

```
$ sudo apt-get install keystone apache2 libapache2-mod-wsgi
```

With these packages installed, you will now have a configuration file for Keystone located at /etc/keystone/keystone.conf. You will need to use sudo to edit this file.

> **Warning**
>
> The directories containing OpenStack configurations such as /etc/keystone are owned and only read-accessible by the root user. The files contained within include important secret data that other users on the system should not be able to access.
>
> Do not change these permissions.

This Keystone configuration file will need a few edits. We'll begin by adding an admin_token. The admin_token is an important piece of data that gives you a considerable amount of access to Keystone—and so your whole OpenStack deployment. It is used temporarily for our initial configuration and should not be a simple password. Official OpenStack documentation recommends that you use the following command to generate your admin token:

```
$ openssl rand -hex 10
```

Take the result of this command, and add it to the configuration. This is also under the [DEFAULT] section. Here is an example:

```
admin_token=975ec8ac7c7718d3ba57
```

Next you'll want to update the [database] section to use your new MySQL database rather than the SQLite database that the Ubuntu package creates. If a sqlite connection stanza exists, you will need to comment it out, since you cannot have two connection types defined. Then add the following:

```
connection = mysql+pymysql://keystone:KEYSTONE_DBPASSWORD@controller/keystone
```

Finally, we want to use Fernet tokens with our Keystone install, so add the following to the [token] section:

```
provider = fernet
```

An example keystone.conf file with these changes made can be found in the scripts-and-configs repository for this book mentioned earlier.

Fernet Tokens

Fernet is an implementation of Symmetric Key Encryption used to encrypt plaintext and the same cryptographic key to decrypt ciphertext. Using this implementation, Fernet tokens were released as a supported token format in OpenStack Kilo and have undergone improvements in performance and reliability in the releases since. Fernet's main advantage over UUID is that tokens don't need to be persistent; that is, they don't need to be stored in a database. This solves problems of database replication lag for tokens and also means that no cronjobs are needed to prune expired tokens. Although UUID tokens are still more widely used, including in our deployment scenarios later in this book, the Keystone community is working towards making Fernet the default token format.

Fernet tokens are cryptographically signed by Fernet keys. Fernet signing keys are typically located in /etc/keystone/fernet-keys and are rotated, typically weekly or monthly, to prevent brute force attacks on the encryption. Although you can have more, you need to have a minimum of three Fernet keys available: a primary, secondary and staged.

Key rotation may take some more explanation in order to become clear, but the main thing to remember is that if you run Keystone in a cluster you do not need to perform simultaneous key rotations. If you need more information, various members of the OpenStack community have written blog posts and given conference talks about their usage and implementation. To learn more you may start with the FAQ in the OpenStack Administrators Guide at http://docs.openstack.org/admin-guide/keystone_fernet_token_faq.html and search online for more.

The next step is adding the schema to your Keystone database. There is a keystone-manage command that can help with this, which needs to be run as the root user:

```
$ sudo -u root /bin/sh -c "keystone-manage db_sync" keystone
```

Now we'll want to set up Fernet.

```
$ sudo keystone-manage fernet_setup --keystone-user keystone \
  --keystone-group keystone
2016-05-15 16:52:25.128 10350 INFO keystone.token.providers.fernet.utils [-] [fernet_tokens]
key_repository does not appear to exist; attempting to create it
2016-05-15 16:52:25.129 10350 INFO keystone.token.providers.fernet.utils [-] Created a new
key: /etc/keystone/fernet-keys/0
2016-05-15 16:52:25.129 10350 INFO keystone.token.providers.fernet.utils [-] Starting key
rotation with 1 key files: ['/etc/keystone/fernet-keys/0']
2016-05-15 16:52:25.129 10350 INFO keystone.token.providers.fernet.utils [-] Current primary
key is: 0
2016-05-15 16:52:25.130 10350 INFO keystone.token.providers.fernet.utils [-] Next primary key
will be: 1
2016-05-15 16:52:25.130 10350 INFO keystone.token.providers.fernet.utils [-] Promoted key 0
to be the primary: 1
2016-05-15 16:52:25.130 10350 INFO keystone.token.providers.fernet.utils [-] Created a new
key: /etc/keystone/fernet-keys/0
```

The final component to configure for Keystone is the Apache web server. First, you will set the ServerName in /etc/apache2/apache2.conf to be the following:

```
ServerName controller
```

Next, create a file at /etc/apache2/sites-available/wsgi-keystone.conf and add the following:

```
Listen 5000
Listen 35357

<VirtualHost *:5000>
    WSGIDaemonProcess keystone-public processes=5 threads=1 user=keystone group=keystone
display-name=%{GROUP}
    WSGIProcessGroup keystone-public
    WSGIScriptAlias / /usr/bin/keystone-wsgi-public
    WSGIApplicationGroup %{GLOBAL}
    WSGIPassAuthorization On
    <IfVersion >= 2.4>
      ErrorLogFormat "%{cu}t %M"
    </IfVersion>
    ErrorLog /var/log/apache2/keystone.log
    CustomLog /var/log/apache2/keystone_access.log combined

    <Directory /usr/bin>
        <IfVersion >= 2.4>
            Require all granted
        </IfVersion>
        <IfVersion < 2.4>
            Order allow,deny
            Allow from all
        </IfVersion>
    </Directory>
</VirtualHost>

<VirtualHost *:35357>
    WSGIDaemonProcess keystone-admin processes=5 threads=1 user=keystone group=keystone
display-name=%{GROUP}
    WSGIProcessGroup keystone-admin
    WSGIScriptAlias / /usr/bin/keystone-wsgi-admin
```

```
WSGIApplicationGroup %{GLOBAL}
WSGIPassAuthorization On
<IfVersion >= 2.4>
  ErrorLogFormat "%{cu}t %M"
</IfVersion>
ErrorLog /var/log/apache2/keystone.log
CustomLog /var/log/apache2/keystone_access.log combined

<Directory /usr/bin>
    <IfVersion >= 2.4>
        Require all granted
    </IfVersion>
    <IfVersion < 2.4>
        Order allow,deny
        Allow from all
    </IfVersion>
</Directory>
</VirtualHost>
```

Reminder

This Apache configuration file is one of the many included in the scripts-and-configs repository for this book at https://github.com/DeploymentsBook/scripts-and-configs. You can easily copy it or use git to clone it from there.

Then enable that site in Apache and reload:

```
$ sudo a2ensite wsgi-keystone
$ sudo service apache2 reload
```

Now that the configuration file options, database and web server are configured, you'll want to interact with the service to configure the command line level specifics. First, prepare your environment with a series of exported variables. The OS_TOKEN is the admin_token you set in your keystone.conf earlier, generated from the provided openssl command. The following is an example. Remember, as discussed earlier, "controller" was added to your /etc/hosts file and is associated with your controller host IP address.

```
export OS_TOKEN=975ec8ac7c7718d3ba57
export OS_URL=http://controller:35357/v3
export OS_IDENTITY_API_VERSION=3
```

Tip

Remember, exports don't preserve across shells or sessions. Every time you open a new shell or SSH in to your server, you will need to run your export commands again. Later we will put the export commands you will be using long-term in a text file and then run source /etc/openrc.admin to make things easier.

With these environment variables set, you can now create the basic set of services and endpoints that Keystone expects:

```
$ openstack service create --name keystone --description \
  "OpenStack Identity" identity
+-------------+----------------------------------+
| Field       | Value                            |
+-------------+----------------------------------+
| description | OpenStack Identity               |
| enabled     | True                             |
| id          | 23b87169d1c541568021936c7cde9636 |
| name        | keystone                         |
| type        | identity                         |
+-------------+----------------------------------+
$ openstack endpoint create --region RegionOne identity public \
  http://controller:5000/v3
+--------------+----------------------------------+
| Field        | Value                            |
+--------------+----------------------------------+
| enabled      | True                             |
| id           | c4ffbd93f5e94b9cb49d764f6cb359a3 |
| interface    | public                           |
| region       | RegionOne                        |
| region_id    | RegionOne                        |
| service_id   | d2027a47cf854adf951fa55aeefee8d6 |
| service_name | keystone                         |
| service_type | identity                         |
| url          | http://controller:5000/v3        |
+--------------+----------------------------------+
$ openstack endpoint create --region RegionOne identity internal \
  http://controller:5000/v3
+--------------+----------------------------------+
| Field        | Value                            |
+--------------+----------------------------------+
| enabled      | True                             |
| id           | 36ac8356c7464135910bea3a7c64a291 |
| interface    | internal                         |
| region       | RegionOne                        |
| region_id    | RegionOne                        |
| service_id   | d2027a47cf854adf951fa55aeefee8d6 |
| service_name | keystone                         |
| service_type | identity                         |
| url          | http://controller:5000/v3        |
+--------------+----------------------------------+
$ openstack endpoint create --region RegionOne identity \
  admin http://controller:35357/v3
+--------------+----------------------------------+
| Field        | Value                            |
+--------------+----------------------------------+
| enabled      | True                             |
| id           | e753685c682b4918a0aea53d3c8eaf49 |
| interface    | admin                            |
| region       | RegionOne                        |
| region_id    | RegionOne                        |
| service_id   | d2027a47cf854adf951fa55aeefee8d6 |
| service_name | keystone                         |
| service_type | identity                         |
| url          | http://controller:35357/v3       |
+--------------+----------------------------------+
```

Next, we'll add the default domain, along with projects, users, roles and services expected. When prompted for passwords, make sure you remember the passwords you entered.

```
$ openstack domain create --description "Default Domain" default
+-------------+----------------------------------+
| Field       | Value                            |
+-------------+----------------------------------+
| description | Default Domain                   |
| enabled     | True                             |
| id          | f26f2b8ab0694a3cbbf4373486bcc3ae |
| name        | default                          |
+-------------+----------------------------------+
$ openstack project create --domain default --description \
  "Admin Project" admin
+-------------+----------------------------------+
| Field       | Value                            |
+-------------+----------------------------------+
| description | Admin Project                    |
| domain_id   | f26f2b8ab0694a3cbbf4373486bcc3ae |
| enabled     | True                             |
| id          | 716e41286e1b46e68238508349e944fd |
| is_domain   | False                            |
| name        | admin                            |
| parent_id   | f26f2b8ab0694a3cbbf4373486bcc3ae |
+-------------+----------------------------------+
$ openstack user create --domain default --password-prompt admin
User Password:
Repeat User Password:
+-----------+----------------------------------+
| Field     | Value                            |
+-----------+----------------------------------+
| domain_id | f26f2b8ab0694a3cbbf4373486bcc3ae |
| enabled   | True                             |
| id        | a316cc1e27e74e79a66555dea8e1b951 |
| name      | admin                            |
+-----------+----------------------------------+
$ openstack role create admin
+-----------+----------------------------------+
| Field     | Value                            |
+-----------+----------------------------------+
| domain_id | None                             |
| id        | bdfce39d3a334108aabdcd0c0b9191c9 |
| name      | admin                            |
+-----------+----------------------------------+
$ openstack role add --project admin --user admin admin
$ openstack project create --domain default --description \
  "Service Project" service
+-------------+----------------------------------+
| Field       | Value                            |
+-------------+----------------------------------+
| description | Service Project                  |
| domain_id   | f26f2b8ab0694a3cbbf4373486bcc3ae |
| enabled     | True                             |
| id          | 91e8d3828c2a4d77b8415611a0b2bc77 |
| is_domain   | False                            |
| name        | service                          |
| parent_id   | f26f2b8ab0694a3cbbf4373486bcc3ae |
+-------------+----------------------------------+
```

```
$ openstack project create --domain default --description \
  "Test Project" test
+-------------+--------------------------------+
| Field       | Value                          |
+-------------+--------------------------------+
| description | Test Project                   |
| domain_id   | f26f2b8ab0694a3cbbf4373486bcc3ae |
| enabled     | True                           |
| id          | 225bf2e6c9de4a93b89635e57cb42cec |
| is_domain   | False                          |
| name        | test                           |
| parent_id   | f26f2b8ab0694a3cbbf4373486bcc3ae |
+-------------+--------------------------------+
$ openstack user create --domain default --password-prompt test
User Password:
Repeat User Password:
+-----------+--------------------------------+
| Field     | Value                          |
+-----------+--------------------------------+
| domain_id | f26f2b8ab0694a3cbbf4373486bcc3ae |
| enabled   | True                           |
| id        | 4d2950b731ba45e290a485ecf3affcfb |
| name      | test                           |
+-----------+--------------------------------+
$ openstack role create user
+-----------+--------------------------------+
| Field     | value                          |
+-----------+--------------------------------+
| domain_id | None                           |
| id        | cd4d42f8c7ef461cb6954ea70483c38d |
| name      | user                           |
+-----------+--------------------------------+
$ openstack role add --project test --user test user
```

You now have an administrative (admin) account project, user and role associated with each other, a service project that will be used later when we create other OpenStack services that belong to this and a test user that is part of the test project. You have also created a test user, the user you use to do non-administrative tasks, such as creating compute Instances. If you recall back to using DevStack, similar admin and demo users were created in that configuration.

Projects, Domains, Roles, Users and User Groups

OpenStack is built to be a flexible infrastructure for a variety of different types of consumers of the cloud. However, the existence of projects, domains, roles, users and user groups within an OpenStack installation can be confusing at first. With that in mind, welcome to your crash course in what exactly each of them are.

- **Projects**—Previously called a "Tenant," projects are a group of users that have the same quotas and share resources such as cores, memory and storage. An administrative tenant is configured to isolate the administrative user from other users on the system. A project is typically created for each segment of your organization that will share resources.

- **Domains**—High-level account containers for projects, users and groups, separate domains can use different authentication back ends.
- **Roles**—Define the operations in the form of rights and privileges that a user can perform in particular projects.
- **Users**—Individual accounts used to interface with Keystone for access to OpenStack services.
- **User Groups**—A collection of users.

A user is a member of one or more projects and is assigned roles. Roles exist within projects. There is no way to have a role outside of one, with the exception of admin. While it's granted within a project, once granted it's global.

Finally, you will need to unset your token-based authentication environment variable and set the new password-based authentication credentials that you just set up to test that Keystone is working as expected. The OS_PASSWORD will be the custom password you were prompted for when creating the admin user.

```
$ unset OS_TOKEN OS_URL
$ export OS_PROJECT_DOMAIN_NAME=default
$ export OS_USER_DOMAIN_NAME=default
$ export OS_PROJECT_NAME=admin
$ export OS_USERNAME=admin
$ export OS_PASSWORD=ADMIN_PASSWORD
$ export OS_AUTH_URL=http://controller:5000/v3
$ export OS_IDENTITY_API_VERSION=3
```

To make using these exported variables in the future easier, we'll talk later about adding them to an /etc/openrc.admin file that you will source later to perform administrative functions.

You now want to run the `token issue` command to confirm that it returns four lines of token data and the `user list` command, which will show you a table with the admin and test users (some output truncated):

```
$ openstack token issue
+------------+---------------------------------+
| Field      | Value                           |
+------------+---------------------------------+
| expires    | 2016-05-16T01:54:40.942971Z     |
| id         | gAAAAABXORpRX00APYtIm5q1oMQ-b... |
| project_id | 716e41286e1b46e68238508349e944fd |
| user_id    | a316cc1e27e74e79a66555dea8e1b951 |
+------------+---------------------------------+
$ openstack user list
+----------------------------------+-------+
| ID                               | Name  |
+----------------------------------+-------+
| 8b1fe57aa6e64ad9add7cfc4d9504def | test  |
| bc2d151a86394372a5fa4c50055f7a58 | admin |
+----------------------------------+-------+
```

If this all works, congratulations! Keystone is configured.

> **Tip**
>
> Tired of environment variables? You can also pass this data into your environment within
> the openstack command with the following (when prompted for a password, it is the admin
> password you set):
>
> ```
> $ openstack --os-auth-url http://controller:5000/v3 --os-project-domain-name default \
> --os-user-domain-name default --os-project-name admin --os-username admin \
> --os-auth-type password token issue
> ```

OpenStack Client

At this point we can pause and complete the creation of the openrc files mentioned earlier
that will contain the echo statements we used above. First, let's create /etc/openrc.admin
with the following contents. We're using ADMIN_PASSWORD as a placeholder for the admin
user password you set earlier:

```
export OS_PROJECT_DOMAIN_NAME=default
export OS_USER_DOMAIN_NAME=default
export OS_PROJECT_NAME=admin
export OS_USERNAME=admin
export OS_PASSWORD=ADMIN_PASSWORD
export OS_AUTH_URL=http://controller:5000/v3
export OS_IDENTITY_API_VERSION=3
export OS_IMAGE_API_VERSION=2
```

Now we'll create /etc/openrc.test with similar information. Here, TEST_PASSWORD
should be replaced with what you specified when creating the test user.

```
export OS_PROJECT_DOMAIN_NAME=default
export OS_USER_DOMAIN_NAME=default
export OS_PROJECT_NAME=test
export OS_USERNAME=test
export OS_PASSWORD=TEST_PASSWORD
export OS_AUTH_URL=http://controller:5000/v3
export OS_IDENTITY_API_VERSION=3
export OS_IMAGE_API_VERSION=2
```

> **Warning**
>
> All components depend upon Keystone. If you ran into any problems configuring Keystone,
> debug the commands and configuration before moving forward with configuring other
> components.

Glance

Glance is the image service for OpenStack. It provides a mechanism for uploading and
indexing disk images that will be used to launch instances in OpenStack. The OpenStack
API can then read the index of images in order to retrieve information about each so that
it can be deployed later by Nova, the compute service.

Just like for Keystone, the Glance image service will be installed via the Ubuntu Cloud
Archive, and we will need to create an empty database in MySQL for Glance to use. Once
again, you may create this empty database with a tool you like or with the following

commands on the command line. Make sure you replace GLANCE_DBPASSWORD with something of your own choosing:

```
$ mysql -u root -p
> CREATE DATABASE glance;
> GRANT ALL PRIVILEGES ON glance.* TO 'glance'@'%' IDENTIFIED BY
  'GLANCE_DBPASSWORD';
> quit
```

Now you'll want to add a Glance user into the service project and create the service and endpoint with Keystone. Take note of the password you enter when prompted:

```
$ source /etc/openrc.admin
$ openstack user create --domain default --password-prompt glance
User Password:
Repeat User Password:
+-----------+----------------------------------+
| Field     | Value                            |
+-----------+----------------------------------+
| domain_id | f26f2b8ab0694a3cbbf4373486bcc3ae |
| enabled   | True                             |
| id        | 7c5e8824acfa4126bbef0f17ccd4db74 |
| name      | glance                           |
+-----------+----------------------------------+
$ openstack role add --project service --user glance admin
$ openstack service create --name glance --description \
  "OpenStack Image service" image
+-------------+----------------------------------+
| Field       | Value                            |
+-------------+----------------------------------+
| description | OpenStack Image service          |
| enabled     | True                             |
| id          | 4168f8427e8b4b1ca762b8f2ebc39e5a |
| name        | glance                           |
| type        | image                            |
+-------------+----------------------------------+
$ openstack endpoint create --region RegionOne image \
  public http://controller:9292
+--------------+----------------------------------+
| Field        | Value                            |
+--------------+----------------------------------+
| enabled      | True                             |
| id           | 936e7c2cbbf0485197c95a8217dd031e |
| interface    | public                           |
| region       | RegionOne                        |
| region_id    | RegionOne                        |
| service_id   | 4168f8427e8b4b1ca762b8f2ebc39e5a |
| service_name | glance                           |
| service_type | image                            |
| url          | http://controller:9292           |
+--------------+----------------------------------+
$ openstack endpoint create --region RegionOne image \
  internal http://controller:9292
+--------------+----------------------------------+
| Field        | Value                            |
+--------------+----------------------------------+
| enabled      | True                             |
| id           | 0e8474f2001a4c179822a3e1af565ee4 |
```

```
| interface    | internal                         |
| region       | RegionOne                        |
| region_id    | RegionOne                        |
| service_id   | 4168f8427e8b4b1ca762b8f2ebc39e5a |
| service_name | glance                           |
| service_type | image                            |
| url          | http://controller:9292           |
+--------------+----------------------------------+
$ openstack endpoint create --region RegionOne image \
  admin http://controller:9292
+--------------+----------------------------------+
| Field        | Value                            |
+--------------+----------------------------------+
| enabled      | True                             |
| id           | 171c0fef25cb4b37ad5277a9d043f0f1 |
| interface    | admin                            |
| region       | RegionOne                        |
| region_id    | RegionOne                        |
| service_id   | 4168f8427e8b4b1ca762b8f2ebc39e5a |
| service_name | glance                           |
| service_type | image                            |
| url          | http://controller:9292           |
+--------------+----------------------------------+
```

> **Tip**
>
> Make a mistake? The OpenStack Client commands that enable you to add and create things also have analogous remove and delete commands. For instance, if your `user create` command was malformed, you can delete the entry you made by using `user delete` instead. Not sure if you made a mistake? There are also list commands, such as `user list` that enable you to see what you've entered already.

You now have an empty MySQL database and details for Glance registered with Keystone. The next step is installing the Glance package and editing the configuration file.

```
$ sudo apt-get install glance
```

Glance has two major configuration files, one for the API and another for the registry. The Glance API is what clients use to directly interface with Glance, and the registry is the service that actually stores the metadata about the services that the API references.

Just like the Keystone configuration file, permissions are restricted on these files because they contain sensitive authentication data. You don't want to change these permissions. You will need sudo to edit these files.

The configuration file for Glance API is located at /etc/glance/glance-api.conf. The first change you'll want to make is switching from using SQLite to using MySQL by commenting out the `sqlite_db=` line in the [database] section and replacing it with the following (remember GLANCE_DBPASSWORD should be replaced with the value you used when you created the Glance user in MySQL):

```
connection=mysql+pymysql://glance:GLANCE_DBPASSWORD@controller/glance
```

The following lines under the [keystone_authtoken] section will also need to be changed to set the API endpoint, tell it where Keystone resides and configure the details you set earlier with the OpenStack Client commands. Remember, the password will be the one you were prompted for in the user create section:

```
auth_uri = http://controller:5000
auth_url = http://controller:35357
auth_type = password
project_domain_name = default
user_domain_name = default
project_name = service
username = glance
password = GLANCE_PASSWORD
```

And under [paste_deploy] add the flavor keystone:

```
flavor = keystone
```

You can now save this file.

Next, edit the /etc/glance/glance-registry.conf file to make similar changes, under [database], commenting out the sqlite_db= line and adding a connection line for MySQL:

```
connection = mysql://glance:GLANCE_DBPASSWORD@controller/glance
```

And edit the [keystone_authtoken] with the same data as earlier in the api config file:

```
auth_uri = http://controller:5000
auth_url = http://controller:35357
auth_type = password
project_domain_name = default
user_domain_name = default
project_name = service
username = glance
password = GLANCE_PASSWORD
```

And under [paste_deploy] you'll again add the flavor keystone:

```
flavor = keystone
```

With these changes made to the configuration file, you will now want to restart both the api and registry services:

```
$ sudo service glance-api restart
$ sudo service glance-registry restart
```

Now you want to create the default schema for the MySQL database that was created earlier, much like you did with Keystone. This will take a few moments to run:

```
$ sudo -u root /bin/sh -c "glance-manage db_sync" glance
```

Finally, test! First we will want to get a simple image, called CirrOS, to load into Glance:

```
wget http://download.cirros-cloud.net/0.3.4/cirros-0.3.4-x86_64-disk.img
```

You may also browse http://download.cirros-cloud.net/ to see if a newer version of CirrOS is available.

Now you want to load the image into Glance. If you haven't logged out of your shell, your previously exported variables will still be available. Otherwise you will need to run source /etc/openrc.admin again before running the following commands:

```
$ export OS_IMAGE_API_VERSION=2
$ openstack image create --name "CirrOS 0.3.4" --file \
  cirros-0.3.4-x86_64-disk.img --disk-format qcow2 \
  --container-format bare --public
+------------------+------------------------------------------------------+
| Field            | Value                                                |
+------------------+------------------------------------------------------+
| checksum         | ee1eca47dc88f4879d8a229cc70a07c6                     |
| container_format | bare                                                 |
| created_at       | 2016-05-19T01:07:28Z                                 |
| disk_format      | qcow2                                                |
| file             | /v2/images/b74a4190-b9ef-4fdd-88c8-3e8e9262a6e0/file |
| id               | b74a4190-b9ef-4fdd-88c8-3e8e9262a6e0                 |
| min_disk         | 0                                                    |
| min_ram          | 0                                                    |
| name             | CirrOS 0.3.4                                         |
| owner            | d936682232ed4bfc820fc825f0737b89                     |
| protected        | False                                                |
| schema           | /v2/schemas/image                                    |
| size             | 13287936                                             |
| status           | active                                               |
| tags             |                                                      |
| updated_at       | 2016-05-19T01:07:29Z                                 |
| virtual_size     | None                                                 |
| visibility       | public                                               |
+------------------+------------------------------------------------------+
```

As you can see, this loads your qcow2 format CirrOS image into Glance. Now you can confirm the file has been added to the Glance registry by running:

```
$ openstack image list
+--------------------------------------+--------------+--------+
| ID                                   | Name         | Status |
+--------------------------------------+--------------+--------+
| e17a02c3-b776-4bf7-8255-633519e47aa7 | CirrOS 0.3.4 | active |
+--------------------------------------+--------------+--------+
```

Congratulations, Glance has been configured!

> **Tip**
>
> You're using environment variables with administrative credentials loaded throughout this process to interface with the Glance API, whether you're creating an image or listing images or anything else. If you wish to make an image that is only available to your test user, use the /etc/openrc.test file for the test user.
>
> Also, note that these administrative credentials are not the same as Linux system credentials. You should not use sudo for any of these commands, since it will likely cause the commands to fail. The environment variables are not passed along to the execution of the sudo command.

Nova

Installation of Nova on the controller will closely mirror the previous instructions for Glance, with registration with Keystone and configuration file changes prior to testing. However, this time we'll be creating two MySQL databases: nova and nova_api. Use your favorite MySQL tool, or create them via the command line.

```
$ mysql -u root -p
> CREATE DATABASE nova;
> GRANT ALL PRIVILEGES ON nova.* TO 'nova'@'%' IDENTIFIED BY
  'NOVA_DBPASSWORD';
> CREATE DATABASE nova_api;
> GRANT ALL PRIVILEGES ON nova_api.* TO 'nova'@'%' IDENTIFIED BY
  'NOVA_DBPASSWORD';
> quit
```

Create the credentials in Keystone for the Nova user and service and add the API endpoints. As before, remember the value you enter when prompted for a nova password, since it will need to be used in the configuration files.

```
$ source /etc/openrc.admin
$ openstack user create --domain default --password-prompt nova
User Password:
Repeat User Password:
+-----------+----------------------------------+
| Field     | Value                            |
+-----------+----------------------------------+
| domain_id | f26f2b8ab0694a3cbbf4373486bcc3ae |
| enabled   | True                             |
| id        | 3e3df83ce01549799bbb9e4af7e30931 |
| name      | nova                             |
+-----------+----------------------------------+
$ openstack role add --project service --user nova admin
$ openstack service create --name nova --description \
  "OpenStack Compute" compute
+-------------+----------------------------------+
| Field       | Value                            |
+-------------+----------------------------------+
| description | OpenStack Compute                |
| enabled     | True                             |
| id          | 6d8da6185a234ed08203931e0e8eca75 |
| name        | nova                             |
| type        | compute                          |
+-------------+----------------------------------+
$ openstack endpoint create --region RegionOne compute \
  public http://controller:8774/v2.1/%\(tenant_id\)s
+--------------+-------------------------------------------+
| Field        | Value                                     |
+--------------+-------------------------------------------+
| enabled      | True                                      |
| id           | f0f82d91d7b04d59a024ebd6c5acedb1          |
| interface    | public                                    |
| region       | RegionOne                                 |
| region_id    | RegionOne                                 |
| service_id   | aee3db3dfc5741d7b92f44678c8b8a9d          |
| service_name | nova                                      |
| service_type | compute                                   |
| url          | http://controller:8774/v2.1/%(tenant_id)s |
+--------------+-------------------------------------------+
```

```
$ openstack endpoint create --region RegionOne compute \
  internal http://controller:8774/v2.1/%\(tenant_id\)s
+--------------+------------------------------------------+
| Field        | Value                                    |
+--------------+------------------------------------------+
| enabled      | True                                     |
| id           | f879688639174ad698e45143f9ee8be8         |
| interface    | internal                                 |
| region       | RegionOne                                |
| region_id    | RegionOne                                |
| service_id   | aee3db3dfc5741d7b92f44678c8b8a9d         |
| service_name | nova                                     |
| service_type | compute                                  |
| url          | http://controller:8774/v2.1/%(tenant_id)s |
+--------------+------------------------------------------+
$ openstack endpoint create --region RegionOne compute \
  admin http://controller:8774/v2.1/%\(tenant_id\)s
+--------------+------------------------------------------+
| Field        | Value                                    |
+--------------+------------------------------------------+
| enabled      | True                                     |
| id           | 476096b7ad4b4888b6d5c9b7170bb6d1         |
| interface    | admin                                    |
| region       | RegionOne                                |
| region_id    | RegionOne                                |
| service_id   | aee3db3dfc5741d7b92f44678c8b8a9d         |
| service_name | nova                                     |
| service_type | compute                                  |
| url          | http://controller:8774/v2.1/%(tenant_id)s |
+--------------+------------------------------------------+
```

With the service user and endpoints created, now install the packages. For Nova there are several more that you need to install than for Keystone and Glance:

```
$ sudo apt-get install nova-api nova-conductor nova-consoleauth \
  nova-novncproxy nova-scheduler
```

Basic Pieces of Nova

Glance just had a couple services, but Nova has a whole lot of them. The following is a quick rundown of the services you are installing now:

- API—Just like with other OpenStack services, the API is how you interact with the service, including activities such as launching a new instance or asking for details about one already running.
- **Conductor**—A daemon that enables OpenStack to function in an isolated manner so that compute nodes don't need to directly access the database.
- **Consoleauth**—Provides access via a VNC-style console in an instance, either from the outside or directly via something like Horizon, the OpenStack dashboard.
- **Novncproxy**—As with consoleauth, this proxy daemon is also required for access to the console on an instance.
- **Scheduler**—A daemon that takes an instance creation request from the queue and determines which compute server a host should run on.

With these packages installed, you will now have an /etc/nova/nova.conf configuration file that will need several changes. The [DEFAULT] section will need the following (remember to replace 192.168.122.2 with the actual IP address of your controller):

```
my_ip = 192.168.122.2
rpc_backend = rabbit
auth_strategy = keystone
use_neutron = True
firewall_driver = nova.virt.firewall.NoopFirewallDriver
```

Next, remove ec2 from the enabled_apis line, so it only has the following:

```
enabled_apis=osapi_compute,metadata
```

Now, switch from SQLite to MySQL in new [database] and [api_database] sections by adding:

```
[database]
connection = mysql://nova:NOVA_DBPASSWORD@controller/nova
[api_database]
connection = mysql://nova:NOVA_DBPASSWORD@controller/nova_api
```

In a new [oslo_messaging_rabbit] section put the following, where RABBIT_PASSWORD is the password you set up when installing the rabbitmq-server package earlier in the chapter:

```
[oslo_messaging_rabbit]
rabbit_host = controller
rabbit_userid = openstack
rabbit_password = RABBIT_PASSWORD
```

Oslo

We're using this oslo_messaging_rabbit section here. What's Oslo?

Named after the Oslo Peace Accord with the intent to "bring peace" to the OpenStack project, the Oslo project was created to develop a series of shared libraries for common solutions that many OpenStack projects need. For instance, most need to parse configuration files, generate log files and use a messaging queue. Rather than each project solving these in different ways with their own code, projects are encouraged to use Oslo.

As the OpenStack project has grown, so has Oslo. It now also includes solutions for caching, concurrency, policy enforcement, internationalization (i18n) features, database connectivity and more. For a full listing of all the shared libraries now provided, see http://governance.openstack.org/reference/projects/oslo.html.

And in a new [keystone_authtoken] section add the following, using the password you were prompted for while setting up the nova user in place of NOVA_PASSWORD:

```
[keystone_authtoken]
auth_uri = http://controller:5000
auth_url = http://controller:35357
```

```
auth_type = password
project_domain_name = default
user_domain_name = default
project_name = service
username = nova
password = NOVA_PASSWORD
```

Create a [vnc] section that has the following:

```
[vnc]
vncserver_listen = $my_ip
vncserver_proxyclient_address = $my_ip
```

In a new [glance] section you'll want to tell it where to find the Image Service, which in our case is on this system:

```
[glance]
api_servers = http://controller:9292
```

Finally, add an [oslo_concurrency] section that has the following:

```
[oslo_concurrency]
lock_path = /var/run/nova
```

Now you will want to apply the default schema for your MySQL databases as we've done with the earlier OpenStack components:

```
$ sudo -u root /bin/sh -c "nova-manage db sync" nova
$ sudo -u root /bin/sh -c "nova-manage api_db sync" nova_api
```

With these changes completed, restart all of the nova services for your changes to be picked up:

```
$ sudo service nova-api restart
$ sudo service nova-consoleauth restart
$ sudo service nova-scheduler restart
$ sudo service nova-conductor restart
$ sudo service nova-novncproxy restart
```

In order to test that Nova is working, run the following:

```
$ openstack compute service list
+------------------+------------+----------+---------+-------+
| Binary           | Host       | Zone     | Status  | State |
+------------------+------------+----------+---------+-------+
| nova-consoleauth | controller | internal | enabled | up    |
| nova-scheduler   | controller | internal | enabled | up    |
| nova-conductor   | controller | internal | enabled | up    |
+------------------+------------+----------+---------+-------+
```

You may also want to run openstack endpoint list --service nova to view the endpoints you created.

If this all works, your controller node for Nova has now been configured! Later, you'll set up the compute node side of Nova on your other server.

Neutron

Perhaps one of the most complicated sections of an OpenStack deployment to configure is the networking service, Neutron. Earlier in the chapter we configured several Open vSwitch bridges and virtual connectors that will be important here. First, we'll need to create a MySQL database and user like we've done for all the other services:

```
$ mysql -u root -p
> CREATE DATABASE neutron;
> GRANT ALL PRIVILEGES ON neutron.* TO 'neutron'@'%' IDENTIFIED BY
  'NEUTRON_DBPASSWORD';
> quit
```

Configure Neutron with the Keystone identity server. Remember the password you put in when prompted; you'll need this later for the configuration file.

```
$ source /etc/openrc.admin
$ openstack user create --domain default --password-prompt neutron
User Password:
Repeat User Password:
+-----------+----------------------------------+
| Field     | Value                            |
+-----------+----------------------------------+
| domain_id | f26f2b8ab0694a3cbbf4373486bcc3ae |
| enabled   | True                             |
| id        | fbee1a7ba7834432acdbf6675c8b4f54 |
| name      | neutron                          |
+-----------+----------------------------------+
$ openstack role add --project service --user neutron admin
$ openstack service create --name neutron --description \
  "OpenStack Networking" network
+-------------+----------------------------------+
| Field       | Value                            |
+-------------+----------------------------------+
| description | OpenStack Networking             |
| enabled     | True                             |
| id          | 213edd8459684ea1872ddb4c56040a0d |
| name        | neutron                          |
| type        | network                          |
+-------------+----------------------------------+
$ openstack endpoint create --region RegionOne network \
  public http://controller:9696
+--------------+----------------------------------+
| Field        | Value                            |
+--------------+----------------------------------+
| enabled      | True                             |
| id           | 01e6628811c84583acf8010115a0210e |
| interface    | public                           |
| region       | RegionOne                        |
| region_id    | RegionOne                        |
| service_id   | 213edd8459684ea1872ddb4c56040a0d |
| service_name | neutron                          |
| service_type | network                          |
| url          | http://controller:9696           |
+--------------+----------------------------------+
```

```
$ openstack endpoint create --region RegionOne network \
  internal http://controller:9696
+--------------+---------------------------------+
| Field        | Value                           |
+--------------+---------------------------------+
| enabled      | True                            |
| id           | fa7d9be4e9394756b33fa05429874312 |
| interface    | internal                        |
| region       | RegionOne                       |
| region_id    | RegionOne                       |
| service_id   | 213edd8459684ea1872ddb4c56040a0d |
| service_name | neutron                         |
| service_type | network                         |
| url          | http://controller:9696          |
+--------------+---------------------------------+
$ openstack endpoint create --region RegionOne network \
  admin http://controller:9696
+--------------+---------------------------------+
| Field        | Value                           |
+--------------+---------------------------------+
| enabled      | True                            |
| id           | 9fb5225b96a943189215a7dcfbbf992f |
| interface    | admin                           |
| region       | RegionOne                       |
| region_id    | RegionOne                       |
| service_id   | 213edd8459684ea1872ddb4c56040a0d |
| service_name | neutron                         |
| service_type | network                         |
| url          | http://controller:9696          |
+--------------+---------------------------------+
```

Then you will install the Neutron packages. Like Nova, there are several things you'll need to install:

```
$ sudo apt-get install neutron-server neutron-dhcp-agent \
  neutron-13-agent neutron-metadata-agent neutron-plugin-ml2 \
  neutron-plugin-openvswitch-agent
```

Basic Pieces of Neutron

Just like Nova, Neutron has several services in a standard install. The following is a quick rundown of the services you are installing:

- **Agents**—Typically run on your controller node and communicated directly to the Neutron server to provide certain functions, like DHCP or IP forwarding and NAT. They can also work as an agent for a plug-in.
- **Plug-ins**—Often interface with an agent and provide support for specific components, such as the virtual networking solutions like Open vSwitch, or support for specific networking hardware, which may be open source or proprietary.
- **Server**—The actual server that listens for API requests from the queue and completes them or routes them to the appropriate agent or plug-in for dispensation and then completes them.

Once again, you'll need to edit the configuration files. This time the main configuration file is located at /etc/neutron/neutron.conf, and you'll want to make the following changes or additions under the [DEFAULT] section:

```
service_plugins = router
allow_overlapping_ips = true
api_workers = 2
rpc_workers = 2
router_scheduler_driver = neutron.scheduler.l3_agent_scheduler.ChanceScheduler
log_dir =/var/log/neutron
```

Like the others, you'll also need to disable the connection line that references sqlite and replace it with details for MySQL under [database]:

```
connection = mysql://neutron:NEUTRON_DBPASSWORD@controller/neutron
```

Now, in the [keystone_authtoken] section, you'll want to make some edits so it looks like the following (replace NEUTRON_PASSWORD with the value you set when running the openstack client command earlier):

```
auth_uri = http://controller:5000
auth_url = http://controller:35357
project_domain_name = default
user_domain_name = default
project_name = service
username = neutron
password = NEUTRON_PASSWORD
auth_type = password
```

In the [nova] section you'll want to set an auth_type, and also the following where NOVA_PASSWORD is the password you were prompted for when setting up the nova user earlier:

```
auth_url = http://controller:35357
auth_type = password
project_domain_name = default
user_domain_name = default
region_name = RegionOne
project_name = service
username = nova
password = NOVA_PASSWORD
```

In the [oslo_messaging_rabbit] section you'll want to update it to point to your controller's address and inform it of the Rabbit user and password:

```
rabbit_host = controller
rabbit_userid = openstack
rabbit_password = RABBIT_PASSWORD
```

Next, you'll want to edit /etc/neutron/l3_agent.ini to set the interface_driver to OVS:

```
interface_driver = neutron.agent.linux.interface.OVSInterfaceDriver
```

Now edit /etc/neutron/plugins/ml2/openvswitch_agent.ini and add the following to the [agent] section:

```
tunnel_types = vxlan
```

In the [ovs] section, update the local_ip to be its own IP, set up a bridge mapping and enable tunneling:

```
local_ip = 192.168.122.2
bridge_mappings = external:br-ex
enable_tunneling = true
```

The final change to make to this file is to specify the firewall driver to use for the security groups:

```
firewall_driver = neutron.agent.linux.iptables_firewall.OVSHybridIptablesFirewallDriver
```

You now need to make a couple edits to the /etc/neutron/dhcp_agent.ini:

```
interface_driver = neutron.agent.linux.interface.OVSInterfaceDriver
dnsmasq_config_file = /etc/neutron/dnsmasq.conf
```

Create the /etc/neutron/dnsmasq.conf file with a couple options set by using the following command:

```
$ echo "dhcp-option-force=26,1450" | sudo tee /etc/neutron/dnsmasq.conf
```

Next, edit /etc/neutron/metadata_agent.ini to add a metadata_proxy_shared_secret. This secret will also be used by Nova. Replace something_secret with something you wish to use:

```
metadata_proxy_shared_secret = something_secret
```

Finally, the last Neutron file you'll want to edit is for the ml2 plug-in at /etc/neutron/plugins/ml2/ml2_conf.ini. This file will need the following customizations in the [ml2] section:

```
type_drivers = vxlan,flat
tenant_network_types = vxlan
mechanism_drivers = openvswitch
```

Under [ml2_type_vxlan], set the vni_ranges and the vxlan_group:

```
vni_ranges = 10:100
vxlan_group = 224.0.0.1
```

Before restarting the services, you'll need to set up the Neutron database schema:

```
$ sudo -u root /bin/sh -c "neutron-db-manage --config-file \
  /etc/neutron/neutron.conf --config-file \
  /etc/neutron/plugins/ml2/ml2_conf.ini upgrade mitaka" neutron
```

Now you'll want to restart all of the Neutron services by running the following:

```
$ sudo service neutron-l3-agent restart
$ sudo service neutron-metadata-agent restart
$ sudo service neutron-openvswitch-agent restart
$ sudo service neutron-dhcp-agent restart
$ sudo service neutron-server restart
```

We'll now move away from Neutron configuration files and back over to Nova. We need to add a [neutron] section in our /etc/nova/nova.conf that contains the following (remember, the metadata_proxy_shared_secret from the metadata_agent.ini earlier):

```
[neutron]
auth_url = http://controller:35357/v3
url = http://controller:9696
auth_plugin = v3password
project_domain_name = default
project_name = service
user_domain_name = default
username = neutron
password = NEUTRON_PASSWORD
ovs_bridge = br-int
region_name = RegionOne
timeout = 30
extension_sync_interval = 600
service_metadata_proxy = True
metadata_proxy_shared_secret = something_secret
```

Restart your nova services to be sure all your configuration changes have been picked up:

```
$ sudo service nova-api restart
$ sudo service nova-consoleauth restart
$ sudo service nova-scheduler restart
$ sudo service nova-conductor restart
$ sudo service nova-novncproxy restart
```

As discussed in Chapter 3, we'll be using a series of OVS bridges for the deployment. Most of these are set up automatically by Neutron, but we do need to manually add the address for your external bridge, br-ex:

```
$ sudo ovs-vsctl add-br br-ex
$ sudo ovs-vsctl add-port br-ex eth1
```

The final step is adding details to Neutron about your networks. As we go through these commands, you may want to refer back to Figures 3.5 and 3.6 from Chapter 3, which give you a detailed view into these interfaces and networks.

```
$ neutron net-create ext-net --router:external \
  --provider:physical_network br-ex --provider:network_type flat \
  --shared
Created a new network:
+--------------------------+--------------------------------------+
| Field                    | Value                                |
+--------------------------+--------------------------------------+
| admin_state_up           | True                                 |
| availability_zone_hints  |                                      |
| availability_zones       |                                      |
| created_at               | 2016-05-17T02:56:07                  |
| description              |                                      |
| id                       | 3016c117-052d-44e8-8115-ce9290ccd2e6 |
| ipv4_address_scope       |                                      |
| ipv6_address_scope       |                                      |
| is_default               | False                                |
```

```
| mtu                        | 1500                                  |
| name                       | ext-net                               |
| provider:network_type      | flat                                  |
| provider:physical_network  | br-ex                                 |
| provider:segmentation_id   |                                       |
| router:external            | True                                  |
| shared                     | True                                  |
| status                     | ACTIVE                                |
| subnets                    |                                       |
| tags                       |                                       |
| tenant_id                  | 716e41286e1b46e68238508349e944fd      |
| updated_at                 | 2016-05-17T02:56:07                   |
+----------------------------+---------------------------------------+
$ neutron subnet-create ext-net 203.0.113.0/24 --name ext-subnet \
  --allocation-pool start=203.0.113.5,end=203.0.113.200 --disable-dhcp \
  --gateway 203.0.113.1
+-------------------+-----------------------------------------------+
| Field             | Value                                         |
+-------------------+-----------------------------------------------+
| allocation_pools  | {"start": "203.0.113.5", "end": "203.0.113.200"} |
| cidr              | 203.0.113.0/24                                |
| created_at        | 2016-05-17T02:57:39                           |
| description       |                                               |
| dns_nameservers   |                                               |
| enable_dhcp       | False                                         |
| gateway_ip        | 203.0.113.1                                   |
| host_routes       |                                               |
| id                | 0329b04b-2ebf-4cf3-be96-4a00f87f1160          |
| ip_version        | 4                                             |
| ipv6_address_mode |                                               |
| ipv6_ra_mode      |                                               |
| name              | ext-subnet                                    |
| network_id        | 3016c117-052d-44e8-8115-ce9290ccd2e6          |
| subnetpool_id     |                                               |
| tenant_id         | 716e41286e1b46e68238508349e944fd              |
| updated_at        | 2016-05-17T02:57:39                           |
+-------------------+-----------------------------------------------+
$ neutron net-create Network1 --provider:network_type vxlan --shared
Created a new network:
+---------------------------+------------------------------------------+
| Field                     | Value                                    |
+---------------------------+------------------------------------------+
| admin_state_up            | True                                     |
| availability_zone_hints   |                                          |
| availability_zones        |                                          |
| created_at                | 2016-05-17T02:58:45                      |
| description               |                                          |
| id                        | 94d79735-dd56-4f5f-bf4e-131a3b7c76dc     |
| ipv4_address_scope        |                                          |
| ipv6_address_scope        |                                          |
| mtu                       | 1450                                     |
| name                      | Network1                                 |
| provider:network_type     | vxlan                                    |
| provider:physical_network |                                          |
| provider:segmentation_id  | 93                                       |
| router:external           | False                                    |
| shared                    | True                                     |
```

```
| status                      | ACTIVE                                      |
| subnets                     |                                             |
| tags                        |                                             |
| tenant_id                   | 716e41286e1b46e68238508349e944fd            |
| updated_at                  | 2016-05-17T02:58:45                         |
+-----------------------------+---------------------------------------------+
$ neutron subnet-create Network1 10.190.0.0/24 --name Subnet1 \
  --allocation-pool start=10.190.0.5,end=10.190.0.254 --enable-dhcp \
  --gateway 10.190.0.1 --dns-nameserver 8.8.8.8 --dns-nameserver 8.8.4.4
Created a new subnet:
+-------------------+-----------------------------------------------+
| Field             | Value                                         |
+-------------------+-----------------------------------------------+
| allocation_pools  | {"start": "10.190.0.5", "end": "10.190.0.254"}|
| cidr              | 10.190.0.0/24                                 |
| created_at        | 2016-05-17T03:00:12                           |
| description       |                                               |
| dns_nameservers   | 8.8.8.8                                       |
|                   | 8.8.4.4                                       |
| enable_dhcp       | True                                          |
| gateway_ip        | 10.190.0.1                                    |
| host_routes       |                                               |
| id                | ed04966e-2f43-4fe1-9741-1e727ec2e9ef          |
| ip_version        | 4                                             |
| ipv6_address_mode |                                               |
| ipv6_ra_mode      |                                               |
| name              | Subnet1                                       |
| network_id        | 94d79735-dd56-4f5f-bf4e-131a3b7c76dc          |
| subnetpool_id     |                                               |
| tenant_id         | 716e41286e1b46e68238508349e944fd              |
| updated_at        | 2016-05-17T03:00:12                           |
+-------------------+-----------------------------------------------+
```

Next, set up a router (Router1) in Neutron to connect your tenant network (Subnet1) to the provider network (ext-net).

```
$ neutron router-create Router1
Created a new router:
+-------------------------+-------------------------------------------+
| Field                   | Value                                     |
+-------------------------+-------------------------------------------+
| admin_state_up          | True                                      |
| availability_zone_hints |                                           |
| availability_zones      |                                           |
| description             |                                           |
| distributed             | False                                     |
| external_gateway_info   |                                           |
| ha                      | False                                     |
| id                      | 7fe37ec8-a038-43a6-812c-22b3b02f87ac      |
| name                    | Router1                                   |
| routes                  |                                           |
| status                  | ACTIVE                                    |
| tenant_id               | 716e41286e1b46e68238508349e944fd          |
+-------------------------+-------------------------------------------+
$ neutron router-interface-add Router1 Subnet1
Added interface 2e355d24-fbe5-4186-80cc-e25a5478b6e7 to router Router1.
$ neutron router-gateway-set Router1 ext-net
Set gateway for router Router1
```

Now let's make sure all your neutron agents are running as we expect:

```
$ neutron agent-list -c agent_type -c alive -c admin_state_up
+--------------------+-------+----------------+
| agent_type         | alive | admin_state_up |
+--------------------+-------+----------------+
| DHCP agent         | :-)   | True           |
| L3 agent           | :-)   | True           |
| Metadata agent     | :-)   | True           |
| Open vSwitch agent | :-)   | True           |
+--------------------+-------+----------------+
```

Now test that the networks have been created:

```
$ neutron net-list -c name -c subnets
+----------+------------------------------------------------------+
| name     | subnets                                              |
+----------+------------------------------------------------------+
| ext-net  | 0329b04b-2ebf-4cf3-be96-4a00f87f1160 203.0.113.0/24  |
| Network1 | ed04966e-2f43-4fe1-9741-1e727ec2e9ef 10.190.0.0/24   |
+----------+------------------------------------------------------+
```

With this, Neutron has been successfully installed, and configuration of your controller node is complete!

Compute Node

The compute node is much simpler than the controller node, requiring just a handful of services to be installed. This configuration is used exclusively for the management of instances and takes instructions via the services running on the controller.

Nova

First we'll install the nova-compute package and sysfsutils, which though not necessarily being used for the original purpose, does enable us to easily pull in the required virtualization tooling that we'll need to run compute instances.

```
$ sudo apt-get install nova-compute sysfsutils
```

Once the installation completes, we're going to once again edit /etc/nova/nova.conf, making the following changes. Remember to update the password to the Nova user password you were prompted for earlier, set my_ip to this compute node IP (using 192.168.122.5 as an example again) and the rabbit_password to the one you set when first setting up the openstack rabbit user. For the enabled_apis line in the following, remove ec2 from the list.

```
[DEFAULT]
my_ip = 192.168.122.5
enabled_apis=osapi_compute,metadata
rpc_backend = rabbit
auth_strategy = keystone
use_neutron = True
firewall_driver = nova.virt.firewall.NoopFirewallDriver
[oslo_messaging_rabbit]
```

```
rabbit_host = controller
rabbit_userid = openstack
rabbit_password = RABBIT_PASSWORD
[keystone_authtoken]
auth_uri = http://controller:5000
auth_url = http://controller:35357
auth_type = password
project_domain_name = default
user_domain_name = default
project_name = service
username = nova
password = NOVA_PASSWORD
[vnc]
enabled = True
vncserver_listen = 0.0.0.0
vncserver_proxyclient_address = $my_ip
novncproxy_base_url = http://controller:6080/vnc_auto.html
[glance]
api_servers = http://controller:9292
[oslo_concurrency]
lock_path = /var/run/nova
[libvirt]
virt_type = qemu
```

With these changes in place, restart nova-compute:

```
$ sudo service nova-compute restart
```

Back on the control node, you should be able to run the service list command again
and see that there is now a compute service available on your compute host (output
truncated):

```
$ openstack compute service list
+----+------------------+----------+----------+---------+-------+------------+
| Id | Binary           | Host     | Zone     | Status  | State | Updated At |
+----+------------------+----------+----------+---------+-------+------------+
|  3 | nova-conductor   | control1 | internal | enabled | up    | 2016-05... |
|  4 | nova-consoleauth | control1 | internal | enabled | up    | 2016-05... |
|  5 | nova-scheduler   | control1 | internal | enabled | up    | 2016-05... |
|  7 | nova-compute     | compute1 | nova     | enabled | up    | 2016-05... |
+----+------------------+----------+----------+---------+-------+------------+
```

You're now ready to finalize the networking configuration on this node by configuring the Neutron OVS agent.

Neutron

The compute node does not have a Neutron database. It only has a couple of plug-ins
that interact with the networking services on the controller. So first we'll install these
plug-ins:

```
$ sudo apt-get install neutron-openvswitch-agent
```

In the /etc/neutron/neutron.conf file, make the following edit in the [DEFAULT] section:

```
service_plugins = router
```

In the `[oslo_messaging_rabbit]` section you'll want to update it to point to your controller's address and inform it of the Rabbit user and password:

```
rabbit_host = controller
rabbit_userid = openstack
rabbit_password = RABBIT_PASSWORD
```

Next, edit /etc/neutron/plugins/ml2/openvswitch_agent.ini and add the following to the [agent] section:

```
tunnel_types = vxlan
```

In the [ovs] section, update the `local_ip` to be its own IP and enable tunneling:

```
local_ip = 192.168.122.5
enable_tunneling = true
```

The final change to make to this file will be to specify the iptables firewall driver to use for the security groups:

```
firewall_driver = neutron.agent.linux.iptables_firewall.OVSHybridIptablesFirewallDriver
```

Next you'll want to edit your /etc/nova/nova.conf file to add the [neutron] section to your configuration:

```
[neutron]
auth_url = http://controller:35357/v3
url = http://controller:9696
auth_plugin = v3password
project_domain_name = default
user_domain_name = default
project_name = service
username = neutron
password = NEUTRON_PASSWORD
ovs_bridge = br-int
region_name = RegionOne
timeout = 30
extension_sync_interval = 600
```

Restart the Neutron OVS agent and the compute services to apply your changes.

```
$ sudo service nova-compute restart
$ sudo service neutron-openvswitch-agent restart
```

Manage an Instance

Congratulations, your system is now running a bare bones OpenStack configuration with Keystone, Glance, Nova and Neutron, which you can interact with through the command line. We've completed small tests for each component to confirm they are working, and now it's time to test that everything has come together to create instances on your new OpenStack installation. Up until now we've been using an openrc.admin file to load up the administrative credentials for your cloud, but now you'll want to create a testrc file that uses the test user we configured earlier. The test user cannot run some commands that the admin user can, such as `openstack user list` or `openstack endpoint list`, but is the appropriate account to use as we start launching instances and using OpenStack as a user. With that in mind, we'll load up the test user environment variables:

```
$ source /etc/openrc.test
```

Now you will want to adjust the default security group for test user so that you can use SSH and ping in your new instances.

```
$ openstack security group rule create --proto tcp \
  --src-ip 0.0.0.0/0 --dst-port 22 default
+----------------------+--------------------------------------+
| Field                | Value                                |
+----------------------+--------------------------------------+
| id                   | 9ed63108-dbc4-46fd-beaf-e1c1ddf71c14 |
| ip_protocol          | tcp                                  |
| ip_range             | 0.0.0.0/0                            |
| parent_group_id      | a861046e-9cba-4f1a-ab2c-833d7e27c122 |
| port_range           | 22:22                                |
| remote_security_group|                                      |
+----------------------+--------------------------------------+
$ openstack security group rule create --proto icmp \
  --src-ip 0.0.0.0/0 --dst-port -1 default
+----------------------+--------------------------------------+
| Field                | Value                                |
+----------------------+--------------------------------------+
| id                   | 6acfea29-5ad4-4e4d-b8f1-8f2a13cf1aa7 |
| ip_protocol          | icmp                                 |
| ip_range             | 0.0.0.0/0                            |
| parent_group_id      | a861046e-9cba-4f1a-ab2c-833d7e27c122 |
| port_range           |                                      |
| remote_security_group|                                      |
+----------------------+--------------------------------------+
```

Finally, you can launch your first instance with the name `my_first_instance` with the following command:

```
$ openstack server create --flavor m1.tiny --image "CirrOS 0.3.4" \
  --security-group default --nic net-id=Network1 \
  --availability-zone nova my_first_instance
```

This will launch your instance. To see details about it you can use the following command to show it in a list of instances running:

```
$ openstack server list
+-----------------+-------------------+--------+---------------------+
| ID              | Name              | Status | Networks            |
+-----------------+-------------------+--------+---------------------+
| 4d3f9633-fbff...| my_first_instance | ACTIVE | Network1=10.190.0.6 |
+-----------------+-------------------+--------+---------------------+
```

For more details, including information about the instance failing to launch for any reason, you can use the following:

```
$ openstack server show my_first_instance
```

You can also replace the name of the instance with the instance ID if you somehow end up with more than one instance with the same name.

Finally, you should try to log in to the instance via SSH. The address of the machine will be in a different network name space than your server, so you will have to SSH from a network name space shared by the instance. Get a list of name spaces with:

```
$ sudo ip netns
qdhcp-94d79735-dd56-4f5f-bf4e-131a3b7c76dc
qrouter-7fe37ec8-a038-43a6-812c-22b3b02f87ac
```

Now using the netns exec command, we'll use the qrouter network space to SSH into the server. Looking at the Networks column from the openstack server list command and SSH to that address as the cirros user. When it prompts for a password, use the default of cubswin:) (the closing parenthesis is part of the password).

```
$ sudo ip netns exec qrouter-7fe37ec8-a038-43a6-812c-22b3b02f87ac \
  ssh cirros@10.190.0.6
cirros@10.190.0.6's password:
$
```

This prompt, with just the $, will be on the CirrOS instance you launched. You can poke around this filesystem to see what's running—not much! In Chapter 6, "Private Compute Cloud," you'll learn more about what you can do with an instance, like assigning floating IP addresses and running services. Everything that works there will work here as well. We have a floating IP address pool and the resources to upload more images.

To wrap up, delete the instance. This action cannot be undone:

```
openstack server delete my_first_instance
```

Summary

In this chapter, you learned how to configure a non-production deployment of OpenStack on a controller and compute node. Going through these commands manually provided you with a greater understanding of how OpenStack services fit together but which is abstracted away when you use DevStack or configuration management tools like Puppet.

II

Deployments

In the following chapters, you are given examples of several types of OpenStack deployments to consider. Each deployment is based on a series of real-world scenarios that will be described in detail and followed up with instructions for how the deployment can be constructed in a small scale.

5

Foundations for Deployments

Enter these enchanted woods,
You who dare.
George Meredith, *The Woods of Westermain*

As has been discussed, an OpenStack deployment is made up of a series of components that come together, and of these components, there are key services that are used in most installations. All installations will require identity services provided by Keystone. Most deployments, including those demonstrated in subsequent chapters, will require networking services provided by Neutron, compute services provided by Nova and the RabbitMQ queuing service.

This chapter covers how to get your foundation of identity, networking, compute and queuing configured so that you can move on to build the rest of your infrastructure using Puppet.

Requirements

For configuration of your systems you will need to satisfy the same requirements as you needed to for Chapter 4, "Your First OpenStack." You need a single system (virtual or physical) as a controller node and a single system as a compute node.

Our recommended minimum specifications for a basic two-system setup of OpenStack are as follows:

- Controller Node—1 x 64-bit processor, 4GB of memory, 30GB of storage and two Network Interface Cards (NICs)

You will also want to prepare a compute node now:

- Compute Node—1 x 64-bit processor, 2GB of memory, 20GB of storage and one NIC

Why Do I Need Two Nodes?

You have read here, and perhaps elsewhere, that the bare minimum for a production OpenStack cloud is two nodes. But why?

- **Scalability**—It's very natural for some portions of your OpenStack deployment to scale beyond a single machine, like the Compute Node. Your Compute Node is the host to the virtual machines so that can often be the first node that you'll want to have more of as your pool of users grow and you need to offer more resources. The Controller node can easily handle the functions for these additional Compute nodes.
- **High-availability**—In a mature, production OpenStack environment, you want your machines to be highly available (HA). By starting your first deployment as a two-node deployment, you are already making logical splits in your architecture which lend themselves to being made highly available. You may learn that you want nearly identical Controller Nodes for redundancy, but may not want or need the same in some of your other nodes at the same rate.
- **Security**—While service isolation is not the panacea for security, it does help. Privilege escalation from within instances of all types is a sadly common vulnerability and protecting your other services from this by keeping them on separate machines is important.

If you are configuring the Compute Node and wish to launch more than a couple small compute instances, you will want to give it more resources. Keep in mind, in the case of virtualization, you will also need to leave some resources for the host system.

Caution

The default configuration we're using in this book for OpenStack makes the HTTP-accessible dashboard (Horizon) accessible from any address. Many of the API endpoints are also accessible. While you do need authentication, the default passwords that we ask you to change are simple.

For the sake of security, when you're setting this up initially as a demonstration consider using a local area network (LAN) for these systems and don't allow SSH or HTTP access from the outside world. Networking can get complicated for newcomers to OpenStack, and you want to make sure you're working in a trusted environment.

If you do choose to use cloud-based systems or other publicly accessible servers rather than local Virtual Machines or hardware, please keep security in mind as you work with OpenStack and take appropriate precautions with standard Linux access controls and firewalls. Remember, it's very common for these providers to leave SSH and HTTP access available by default, and that's precisely what you want to protect.

Reference Deployment

As we covered in Chapter 4, this book provides a reference deployment using a pair of virtualized nodes using KVM. This can be found in Appendix A, "Reference Deployment."

If you don't have a preference as to virtualization technology or are struggling to get any of the components working with our scenarios, it's recommended that you start with this reference deployment.

Networking

The networking will be the same as we set up in Chapter 4, and as explained in depth in Chapter 3, "Networking." In this chapter, most of the configuration will now be handled through Puppet. The exception is if you're using a virtualized environment, you will still need to set up the bridges on the host machine where your VMs run from. Again, see Chapter 4 for a reminder on how to do this.

As a quick general refresher, you will be using two networks for the controller node, one for your "public" addresses that are assigned to instances, and one for everything else. Your compute node will only be on the latter network.

Select Deployment Mechanism

As you saw in Chapter 2, "DevStack," it is technically possible to write a shell script to deploy OpenStack. However, this is not a supported way to run OpenStack for anything other than development work. It is very difficult to use and maintain this type of install because of how many interconnected components OpenStack has. Even as a development tool, maintaining the DevStack project takes a full team of contributors.

The OpenStack community provides several solutions for deploying OpenStack, including Puppet, Chef and Ansible.

Common Deployment Mechanisms

The following open source resources are available to operators for deployment of OpenStack. Each is maintained by a team whose focus and expertise is the deployment technology. Several also maintain add-ons to these basic deployment tools in both open source and proprietary versions.

Official deployments for these configuration management tools can be found in the OpenStack software repositories at https://git.openstack.org/cgit/openstack.

- **Puppet**—Puppet is what we will be using for all the exercises in this book. The Puppet community within OpenStack manages modules for each component of OpenStack. Puppet repositories are prefixed with "puppet-".
- **Chef**—Contributors to the Chef community in OpenStack maintain cookbooks for the components of OpenStack. Chef repositories are all prefixed with "chef-".
- **Ansible**—Ansible playbooks for OpenStack, collectively known as OpenStack Ansible Deployment (OSAD), are located within the openstack-ansible project. Several related projects are prefixed with "openstack-ansible-".

See Appendix B, "Other Deployment Mechanisms," to learn more about doing OpenStack deployments with these and other tools.

Many vendors offer deployment mechanisms as their "value add" when you hire them to deploy your infrastructure. These custom solutions range from being fully open source to being fully proprietary, so it's important to understand the licensing agreement when you work with a vendor.

This and the following chapters will show you how to deploy OpenStack using Puppet, leveraging the community-maintained OpenStack Puppet modules and OpenStack packages in the Ubuntu Cloud Archive. This is done to help you learn about the types of deployments that exist and how the pieces move. Your organization can select a different deployment and maintenance mechanism when you're ready for production. Again, learn more about some of the other options available for configuration and orchestration with OpenStack in Appendix B.

Initial Setup

Now that the appropriate hardware or virtual resources have been made available, you will want to do some initial configuration of your servers. This includes installation of Ubuntu 14.04 and setup of the Puppet configuration.

You should begin by installing the Server edition of Ubuntu 14.04 LTS on both servers.

> **Tip**
>
> When installing, use the most basic configuration possible. We recommend using most defaults in the installer, with two exceptions. On the Partition disks screen, you should select Guided - use entire disk since you don't need LVM (Linux Volume Management). Second, on the Software selection screen, you probably want to select OpenSSH server so you can log into your system over SSH.

Once your two Ubuntu 14.04 systems are installed, complete all upgrades and reboot the systems. When the server comes back up after the reboot, you'll also want to install git in order to download the files we need to set up and configure Puppet.

```
$ sudo apt-get update
$ sudo apt-get dist-upgrade
$ sudo reboot
$ sudo apt-get install git
```

Configuration of Puppet on both servers is done through the contents of a GitHub repository crafted specifically for this book. The GitHub repositories used in this book can be browsed here at https://github.com/DeploymentsBook.

There is a script in this repository that installs the required Puppet components and uses the r10k Puppet deployment tool to install additional dependencies. In order to see this in action, we'll want to clone this puppet-data repository and then run the setup script:

```
$ git clone https://github.com/DeploymentsBook/puppet-data.git
$ cd puppet-data/
```

The following is the contents of the setup.sh script that you want to run next. This will set up your Puppet environment:

```
#!/bin/bash

sudo apt-get update
sudo apt-get install -y puppet
sudo gem install --no-rdoc r10k

sudo cp -a * /etc/puppet
sudo service puppet restart

cd /etc/puppet
sudo r10k puppetfile install -v info
```

Let's run this script now. This should be run as your user, since it will invoke sudo as needed:

```
$ ./setup.sh
```

Running the setup script will take several minutes as it downloads the Ruby gems and required packages from the Ubuntu repositories. Once complete, you will have a Puppet-driven environment that you can then start running scenarios on.

Select Components

In Chapter 1, "What is OpenStack?" the components of OpenStack presented in this book were summarized. The following will explain how each are used with respect to our scenarios.

Identity (Keystone)

Used for every scenario in this book, the Keystone identity service provides authentication and access management in OpenStack. A Keystone component will be added to every project your users interact with so that access controls can be set and enforced. Refer back to Chapter 4 for a detailed outline of how this is handled through Projects, Domains, Roles, Users and User Groups.

As an identity service, Keystone provides integration with popular authentication mechanisms such as various LDAP implementations, including Active Directory.

Identity versus Authentication

An important and often confused component of Keystone are the concepts of "Identity" and "Authentication" when handling users.

Identity refers to identifying *who* is accessing specific cloud resources. This is typically a user.

Authentication refers to the act of verifying that a user is who they say they are. This is typically done through some sort of login by the user which is either managed by Keystone itself or passed on to a back end such as LDAP.

These components work together to fold into Access Management, or authorization, to determine what authenticated identities have access to each component.

Database (MySQL)

Most components of OpenStack, and all of those in scenarios used in this book, use a database in order to store many of the configuration values for your deployment and more. It is highly recommended that you use something like MySQL or MariaDB, which most production deployments do.

MySQL is used for every scenario in this book.

Message Queuing (RabbitMQ)

RabbitMQ is the default selection and most popular choice of operators as the Advanced Message Queuing Protocol (AMQP) framework in OpenStack. Just like MySQL, this component is not part of OpenStack but instead is an independent open source project. Learn more about RabbitMQ at http://www.rabbitmq.com/.

Queues in OpenStack are used so that services can properly communicate with each other. Actions are scheduled, dependencies are managed and tasks can be stored safely if there are delays or if load balancing between requests is required. For instance, when you make a request to add a floating IP address to a running instance, your request is put into a queue. Several OpenStack services will then interact with this request, including Neutron and Nova in order to authorize, allocate and apply the change to your instance. Also note that multiple services from the same project use this message bus to talk to each other, but between project boundaries services use the REST APIs.

Queuing is required for all of the OpenStack scenarios presented in this book except for Swift object storage.

Networking (Neutron)

In order to prepare networking for most of the nodes defined in our scenarios, our examples will be using Neutron's "networking as a service" to configure the networks. As discussed in the Chapter 1 description of Neutron and continued in depth in Chapter 3, there are a variety of setups that are supported by Neutron to cover a vast array of networking options, but for our scenarios we will only be doing a basic deployment.

Neutron-driven networking is required for all of the OpenStack scenarios presented in this book.

Exploring the Possibilities with Neutron

As nova-networking was phased out of the OpenStack project, Neutron promised a variety of options for operators with regard to networking, built right into OpenStack. Today, a variety of plug-ins, both open source and proprietary, provide for this, including:

- **Firewall, Load Balancer and VPN as a Service**—Three distinct components, these are extensions to Neutron that bring in some of the most popularly asked for services. The future development of these components is currently up for discussion.

- **Open Source, vendor-specific drivers and agents**—From Cisco to vSphere VMware drivers, a variety of open source drivers and agents that are being tested by the vendors are available in the open source repositories from. Each determines what features to support, but give you the most direct support for the networking ecosystem that you may be working in.

- **Proprietary, vendor-specific**—Many vendors who charge for OpenStack deployments also have their own drivers and agents. You may run into these if you pay for a deployment.

When considering drivers, note that some of these are shipped with Neutron and others are packaged separately. Learn more about drivers for OpenStack at http://www.openstack.org/marketplace/drivers

Compute (Nova)

For the purpose of our scenarios, the compute components outlined in Chapter 1 are broken up between two servers to offer service isolation.

On the controller node, you will have the nova-conductor, scheduler, api and api-metadata daemons. On the compute node where instances run, you will only have nova-compute. This isolation is to keep the privileged controller isolated from the Instances that users run, and any privilege escalation vulnerabilities that may crop up with the virtualization technology being used.

Like Queuing and Networking, this compute node is used for all of our scenarios.

Image (Glance)

When you want to boot an instance in OpenStack, one of the first things you need to do is select what operating system you wish to use. Glance is what holds those images and makes them available to the user, storing both metadata and images themselves on your local disk or a storage backplane.

The image service in our scenarios will serve up a default CirrOS image from the local disk. In a later chapter, you will be adding Ubuntu Server 14.04 as well (at the time of writing, Ubuntu 16.04 had just been released and we were unable to make time to test it).

Dashboard (Horizon)

The Horizon dashboard offers a friendly, web-based interface for interacting with your OpenStack deployment, both as a user and as an administrator. All of our deployment scenarios will have the dashboard as a component.

Foundation Scenario

Now that you have a basic environment set up, we want to set up your foundation, which is the basic Puppet module we've created to deploy a simple OpenStack controller. This foundation will be used in all subsequent chapters.

Controller Node

In order to configure the controller node, you will first want to get familiar with the default Hiera common.yaml file. Hiera is a tool that stores a key/value combination that can then be referenced by Puppet. In these deployment scenarios, all modifications we're making to default OpenStack Puppet modules are stored in this common.yaml file.

The Hiera common.yaml file you will be working with was placed on your filesystem with the setup.sh script that was run earlier. You will find this file at /etc/puppet/hiera/ common.yaml. Open with your preferred text editor using sudo and follow the instructions in the file for adding your IP addresses, passwords, tokens and secrets that you should change. Save the file.

> #### Caution
>
> Don't skip editing hiera/common.yaml.
>
> The IP addresses for your controller and compute node *must* to be set to reflect your environment. Puppet will fail with errors if you don't set these variables, and using the defaults with 127.0.0.1 will not work with a multi-node installation.
>
> Pay attention to updating the passwords, too. Remember, these default authentication credentials live on a fully public git repository.

With these changes completed, we can finally run the commands to apply the Puppet manifest that will install the foundational components for you.

```
$ sudo puppet apply /etc/puppet/modules/deployments/manifests/role/foundations.pp
```

This command may take some time to run. As it runs, you'll see a lot of output that describes what Puppet is doing.

> #### Running puppet apply Again
>
> The puppet apply command can be run multiple times. You may want to run it again if you need to make changes to the Hiera common.yaml for a setting or if you had a problem like loss of Internet access during a run or ran into other errors.
>
> Though it shouldn't happen, if you do run into errors that cause your deployment scenario to fail, you can use the --debug flag to run the Puppet command in debug mode. This will provide more detailed output, which can help you determine what went wrong.
>
> With this flag, your command would then be:
>
> ```
> $ sudo puppet apply --debug /etc/puppet/modules/deployments/manifests/role/foundations.pp
> ```
>
> This will be a lot of output. You can use pipe and tee to direct output to a file as well as showing it to you in STDOUT:
>
> ```
> $ sudo puppet apply --debug \
> /etc/puppet/modules/deployments/manifests/role/ foundations.pp | \
> tee ~/puppet_apply_foundations.log
> ```
>
> This will create a puppet_apply_foundations.log in your home directory for you to go through later.

While it's running, take a look at what is included in the foundations.pp Puppet role:

```
$ cat /etc/puppet/modules/deployments/manifests/role/foundations.pp
class deployments::role::foundations {
  include deployments::profile::base
  include deployments::profile::glance
  include deployments::profile::horizon
  include deployments::profile::keystone
  include deployments::profile::nova
  include deployments::profile::neutron
  include deployments::profile::rabbitmq
  include ::mysql::server
}

include deployments::role::foundations
```

On the surface this is very simple, but we'll dig into it a bit more to explain how it works.

Puppet Roles, Profiles and Modules

The OpenStack Puppet community maintains a series of open source Puppet modules for deploying OpenStack, which are used by this book. Modules are shared configuration tools that are generic enough for all kinds of organizations and companies to share them. They are loaded up in your deployment as a series of building blocks to create the deployment scenario you want. We also use a high level "deployments" module hosted on GitHub, which contains our roles and profiles.

We are using Puppet roles and profiles in order to organize the Puppet configuration of the OpenStack Puppet modules. By using roles and profiles we can create a series of files that define specific servers (roles) that contain similar things as defined in profiles, essentially gluing together the modules. As you can see in foundations.pp, it includes profiles like "base" which we will use in all of our scenarios.

You can tell the difference between roles and profiles inside of our deployments module and other modules in the configuration by looking at how they are included. However, the difference between roles and profiles is more than just their names. Roles are the "business-logic" definitions that encapsulate profiles. Profiles are the implementation definitions that encapsulate modules.

A role declaration in our deployments module will look something like this:

```
include deployments::role::foundations
```

You'll see this role included in foundations.pp. The role's puppet file includes itself to make them easier to consume.

A profile declaration is similar, but uses the deployments::profile prefix:

```
include deployments::profile::uca
```

Finally, when calling a module (or a component of a module) outside of our deployments module, you'll see something like:

```
include ::openstacklib::openstackclient
```

> To learn more about roles, profiles and modules, visit the official Puppet documentation https://docs.puppet.com/. Several valuable articles and blog posts have also been written about them. Because they become dated quickly, use your favorite search engine to find the latest.

Profiles

Each of these profiles configure a different component of your OpenStack deployment and you can dig into each one to learn what it's configuring.

Base Profile

The base profile is shared among all of our deployments.

```
$ cat /etc/puppet/modules/deployments/manifests/profile/base.pp
class deployments::profile::base {
  include deployments::profile::openrcs
  include deployments::profile::uca
  include ::ntp
  include ::openstacklib::openstackclient
  # add an alias to /etc/hosts to ensure sudo works
  host { $::hostname:
    ip => $::ipaddress,
  }
}
```

It sets up the openrc files that we will use for credentials later in this chapter to run our OpenStack client commands. We're adding the Network Time Protocol (NTP) configuration so time is kept synced on our systems and are also including installation of the OpenStack Client. The uca profile configures Ubuntu Cloud Archive (UCA). As explained in Chapter 1, we're using the UCA in order to get the recent OpenStack release version, Mitaka, for the Ubuntu Long Term Support release we're running, 14.04. Drilling down into this profile will show you that there's a section where the $release is defined. This is gathered from the Hiera common.yaml file and where set it to mitaka.

```
$ cat /etc/puppet/modules/deployments/manifests/profile/uca.pp
# Ubuntu Cloud Archive
class deployments::profile::uca (
  $release,
  $repo,
) {
  include ::apt

  class { '::openstack_extras::repo::debian::ubuntu':
    release         => $release,
    repo            => $repo,
    package_require => true,
  }

  Apt::Source<||> -> Package <||>
}
```

The final included section is the OpenStack Client (OSC), which we put on all of the systems so you can run OSC commands on whatever system you're on, along with the openrc credentials. This is an outside module called openstacklib that is not part of our deployments module.

Glance Profile

The profile for Glance, the imaging service, is where you start getting very interesting configuration options:

```
$ cat /etc/puppet/modules/deployments/manifests/profile/glance.pp
class deployments::profile::glance(
  $cirros_version = '0.3.4',
) {
  include ::glance
  include ::glance::api
  include ::glance::registry
  include ::glance::keystone::auth
  include ::glance::backend::file
  include ::glance::db::mysql
  include ::glance::notify::rabbitmq

  glance_image { 'cirros':
    location      => "https://download.cirros-cloud.net/${cirros_version}/cirros-${cirros_version}-x86_64-disk.img",
    name          => "Cirros ${cirros_version}",
    is_public     => 'Yes',
    container_format => 'bare',
    disk_format   => 'qcow2',
  }
}
```

This calls out to the OpenStack Glance module to pull in various components. In our profile we're making a few decisions about how we want this basic configuration to work. We're pulling in the API and Registry for Glance. We're then making sure we have Keystone and MySQL for Glance set up to interact with our existing Keystone and MySQL services. Puppet makes this very easy, but you can see how it was done manually back in Chapter 4 if you'd like a refresher. Finally, we're also using the storage back end "file" which is the default type of back end for Glance and means it's storing images on a filesystem. By default, they are stored in /var/lib/glance/images/ which is where you will find images you upload to Glance. Glance has the option of using different back ends, like the OpenStack Object Storage service (Swift) or Amazon's S3. We have a single image configured in the installation, a very small and simple Linux-based operating system called CirrOS. As you can see, this profile defines which version of CirrOS will be used as our initial image in Glance as well as various details about it.

If you're interested in further details about the OpenStack Glance module for the Mitaka release, you can browse it on your node filesystem or online:

- **Filesystem**—/etc/puppet/modules/glance/

- **Online**—https://git.openstack.org/cgit/openstack/puppet-glance/tree/?h=stable%2Fmitaka

Horizon Profile

The Horizon dashboard profile is very simple since no special code outside of the upstream puppet module is required in order for the dashboard to run.

```
$ cat /etc/puppet/modules/deployments/manifests/profile/horizon.pp
class deployments::profile::horizon
{
  include ::apache
  include ::horizon
}
```

It runs Apache, so we're pulling in a generic Apache module and it also needs the OpenStack Horizon module.

If you're interested in further details about the OpenStack Horizon module for the Mitaka release, you can browse it on your node filesystem or online:

- Filesystem—/etc/puppet/modules/horizon/

- Online—https://git.openstack.org/cgit/openstack/puppet-horizon/tree/ ?h=stable%2Fmitaka

Keystone Profile

With the Keystone identity profile, we're getting complicated again.

```
$ cat /etc/puppet/modules/deployments/manifests/profile/keystone.pp
class deployments::profile::keystone {
  include ::apache
  include deployments::profile::users
  include ::keystone
  include ::keystone::cron::token_flush
  include ::keystone::roles::admin
  include ::keystone::endpoint
  include ::keystone::db::mysql
  include ::keystone::wsgi::apache
  }
}
```

Since Keystone uses WSGI to run the service, it also requires the Apache module and also a specific keystone::wsgi::apache class. In addition, it pulls in several other components of the Keystone Puppet module, including a cron job, administrative role information and configuration for the endpoint. Finally, when you edited the hiera/common.yaml to change the passwords for the admin and test users, that was defining what "deployments::profile::users" brings in.

> ### Note
>
> In Chapter 4 you may recall that we configured Keystone with Fernet tokens. This is where the community recommendations are trending and was easy to do in our manual deployment. However, support for Fernet tokens came out somewhat recently, in the Kilo release. It is not yet default in OpenStack. For our Puppet-driven deployment scenarios we're still using the current default—UUID tokens.

If you're interested in further details about the OpenStack Keystone module for the Mitaka release, you can browse it on your node filesystem or online:

- **Filesystem**—/etc/puppet/modules/keystone/
- **Online**—https://git.openstack.org/cgit/openstack/puppet-keystone/tree/ ?h=stable%2Fmitaka

Nova Profile

The Nova compute controller profile is long but fairly straight-forward.

```
$ cat /etc/puppet/modules/deployments/manifests/profile/nova.pp
class deployments::profile::nova
{
  include ::nova
  include ::nova::api
  include ::nova::db::mysql
  include ::nova::db::mysql_api
  include ::nova::conductor
  include ::nova::consoleauth
  include ::nova::keystone::auth
  include ::nova::network::neutron
  include ::nova::rabbitmq
  include ::nova::scheduler
  include ::nova::scheduler::filter
  include ::nova::vncproxy

  $nova_deps = ['websockify']
  package { $nova_deps:
    ensure => 'latest',
    before => Service['nova-novncproxy']
  }
}
```

It pulls in various controller-specific components required to run the back-end work of the services managing compute on the controller node. You will see later that this differs from what we install on the Compute node. It also handles a dependency issue with websockify which was not resolved at the time of publishing.

If you're interested in further details about the OpenStack Nova module for the Mitaka release, you can browse it on your node filesystem or online:

- **Filesystem**—/etc/puppet/modules/nova/
- **Online**—https://git.openstack.org/cgit/openstack/puppet-nova/tree/ ?h=stable%2Fmitaka

Neutron Profile

The Neutron networking profile has several basic components, but there are also several sections that require some inspection.

```
$ cat /etc/puppet/modules/deployments/manifests/profile/neutron.pp
class deployments::profile::neutron(
  $extnet_device  = hiera('extnet_device', 'eth1'),
  $bridge_uplinks = hiera('bridge_uplinks'),
  $bridge_mappings = hiera('bridge_mappings'),
)
```

```
{
  include ::neutron
  include ::neutron::client
  include ::neutron::server
  include ::neutron::db::mysql
  include ::neutron::keystone::auth
  include ::neutron::plugins::ml2
  include ::neutron::agents::metadata
  include ::neutron::agents::l3
  include ::neutron::agents::dhcp
  include ::neutron::server::notifications

  exec { "${extnet_device} up":
    command     => "ip link set ${extnet_device} up",
    path        => '/sbin',
    user        => 'root',
    refreshonly => true,
  }

  file { "/etc/network/interfaces.d/${extnet_device}.cfg":
    content => "auto ${extnet_device}\niface ${extnet_device} inet manual\n",
    mode    => '0644',
    owner   => 'root',
    group   => 'root',
  }

  $dnsmasq_conf_content = hiera('dnsmasq_conf_contents',undef)
  if $dnsmasq_conf_content != undef {
    file { '/etc/neutron/dnsmasq.conf':
      owner   => 'root',
      group   => 'neutron',
      mode    => '0644',
      content => $dnsmasq_conf_content,
      notify  => Service['neutron-server'],
      require => Package['neutron-server'],
    }
  }

  Neutron::Plugins::Ovs::Bridge<| |> ~> Exec["${extnet_device} up"]

  $network_hash = hiera_hash('neutron_network', false)
  if $network_hash {
    create_resources('neutron_network', $network_hash)
  }

  $subnet_hash = hiera_hash('neutron_subnet', false)
  if $subnet_hash {
    create_resources('neutron_subnet', $subnet_hash)
  }

  $router_hash = hiera_hash('neutron_router', false)
  if $router_hash {
    create_resources('neutron_router', $router_hash)
  }

  $router_interface_hash = hiera_hash('neutron_router_interface', false)
  if $router_interface_hash {
    create_resources('neutron_router_interface', $router_interface_hash)
  }
```

```
  class { '::neutron::agents::ml2::ovs':
    bridge_mappings => $bridge_mappings,
    bridge_uplinks  => $bridge_uplinks,
  }
}
```

You see some network-specific information regarding network and subnet hashes and routers, which you may have edited while updating the heira/common .yaml file. We're also bringing up the secondary Ethernet interface (eth1) on the controller and handling bridges..

If you're interested in further details about the OpenStack Neutron module for the Mitaka release, you can browse it on your node filesystem or online:

- **Filesystem**—/etc/puppet/modules/neutron/
- **Online**—https://git.openstack.org/cgit/openstack/puppet-neutron/tree/ ?h=stable%2Fmitaka

RabbitMQ Profile

Finally, the RabbitMQ queuing profile is the simplest of all. It could have been included elsewhere, but we have it as a separate profile in case there is a need to add or tune anything about the service.

```
$ cat /etc/puppet/modules/deployments/manifests/profile/rabbitmq.pp
class deployments::profile::rabbitmq
{
  include ::rabbitmq
}
```

This uses the RabbitMQ Puppet module installed by setup.sh to set up and install RabbitMQ. You will have set a rabbit_password in the hiera/common.yaml, and this file also handles several other configuration options defined by our RabbitMQ deployment.

Testing the Controller Node

When your puppet apply command from earlier is complete, you will want to run some test commands to make sure everything was created properly and running. Let's start with some basic functionality of MySQL. The default password and hostname are stored in the root user's ~/.my.cnf file, so you can just run the following to see that the databases for Glance, Keystone, Neutron and Nova were created. In these example commands, we've included some sample output, which won't match exactly but will give you some idea what to look for.

```
$ sudo -H mysql -e "show databases;"
+--------------------+
| Database           |
+--------------------+
| information_schema |
| glance             |
| keystone           |
| mysql              |
| neutron            |
| nova               |
| performance_schema |
+--------------------+
```

You may also want to inspect the tables that were created, say, for Glance:

```
$ sudo -H mysql "-e show tables;" glance
+--------------------------------+
| Tables_in_glance               |
+--------------------------------+
| artifact_blob_locations        |
| artifact_blobs                 |
| artifact_dependencies          |
| artifact_properties            |
| artifact_tags                  |
| artifacts                      |
| image_locations                |
| image_members                  |
| image_properties               |
| image_tags                     |
| images                         |
| metadef_namespace_resource_types |
| metadef_namespaces             |
| metadef_objects                |
| metadef_properties             |
| metadef_resource_types         |
| metadef_tags                   |
| migrate_version                |
| task_info                      |
| tasks                          |
+--------------------------------+
```

The preceding command can also be run against the Nova, Neutron and Keystone databases to see their tables.

Next, let's see that the OpenStack services are responding properly to the test user. To do this, we'll first want to pull in credentials from our test openrc file, then we can run each command.

> **Tip**
>
> As you explore OpenStack commands you'll quickly learn that they often provide a lot of detail. We've worked to format it legibly in this book, but if you're struggling to read it, the command output for many of these commands is included in a GitHub repository for scripts and configurations sorted by chapter at https://github.com/DeploymentsBook/scripts-and-configs.

```
$ source /etc/openrc.test
$ openstack flavor list
+----+-----------+-------+------+-----------+-------+-----------+
| ID | Name      |   RAM | Disk | Ephemeral | VCPUs | Is Public |
+----+-----------+-------+------+-----------+-------+-----------+
|  1 | m1.tiny   |   512 |    1 |         0 |     1 | True      |
|  2 | m1.small  |  2048 |   20 |         0 |     1 | True      |
|  3 | m1.medium |  4096 |   40 |         0 |     2 | True      |
|  4 | m1.large  |  8192 |   80 |         0 |     4 | True      |
|  5 | m1.xlarge | 16384 |  160 |         0 |     8 | True      |
+----+-----------+-------+------+-----------+-------+-----------+
```

```
$ openstack network list -c ID -c Name
+--------------------------------------+----------+
| ID                                   | Name     |
+--------------------------------------+----------+
| aacadd44-a9fd-4fa9-9ed2-984c547c1539 | ext-net  |
| cd293246-5f09-4232-8e96-d70091234c66 | Network1 |
+--------------------------------------+----------+

$ openstack image list
+--------------------------------------+-------------+
| ID                                   | Name        |
+--------------------------------------+-------------+
| cdf2c591-3b16-4bd1-9bde-a2568e738492 | Cirros 0.3.4 |
+--------------------------------------+-------------+
```

Now that you have confirmed that the test user is working properly, you can run a couple commands that only the administrator can run, first by sourcing the admin rc file so you are using the correct credentials.

```
$ source /etc/openrc.admin
$ openstack role list
+--------------------------------------+--------------+
| ID                                   | Name         |
+--------------------------------------+--------------+
| 38e23d9c84eb46049286976efb93bdee     | admin        |
| 9fe2ff9ee4384b1894a90878d3e92bab     | _member_     |
| cc9de53b69f648569e3d9e280efed4da     | SwiftOperator |
+--------------------------------------+--------------+
$ openstack user list
+--------------------------------------+---------+
| ID                                   | Name    |
+--------------------------------------+---------+
| 067124f883ac49c3882fa2d09b1a9504     | glance  |
| 33c4b093cf0a48dfbf631a89689d3577     | admin   |
| 84fb1b3cba484f40bf653c312f2a6277     | nova    |
| 88572a2961c6441d95bcb1fd79804f49     | neutron |
| f7faf7ea833c4ddf8c12fcf8875f3eec     | test    |
+--------------------------------------+---------+
```

Finally, let's confirm that Open vSwitch (OVS) is working properly. The output of the following command should look similar to this with stanzas for bridges br-int, br-ex and br-tun:

```
$ sudo ovs-vsctl show
f5b2d445-6c9d-42b7-88c6-1e9de1cbfdac
    Bridge br-int
        fail_mode: secure
        Port br-int
            Interface br-int
                type: internal
        Port int-br-ex
            Interface int-br-ex
                type: patch
                options: {peer=phy-br-ex}
```

```
        Port patch-tun
            Interface patch-tun
                type: patch
                options: {peer=patch-int}
        Port "tapb3517edc-72"
            tag: 1
            Interface "tapb3517edc-72"
                type: internal
        Port "qr-584feae2-79"
            tag: 1
            Interface "qr-584feae2-79"
                type: internal
    Bridge br-tun
        fail_mode: secure
        Port patch-int
            Interface patch-int
                type: patch
                options: {peer=patch-tun}
        Port "vxlan-c0a87abf"
            Interface "vxlan-c0a87abf"
                type: vxlan
                options: {df_default="true", in_key=flow, local_ip="192.168.122.9", out_
key=flow, remote_ip="192.168.122.191"}
        Port br-tun
            Interface br-tun
                type: internal
    Bridge br-ex
        Port phy-br-ex
            Interface phy-br-ex
                type: patch
                options: {peer=int-br-ex}
        Port "qg-576e3418-87"
            Interface "qg-576e3418-87"
                type: internal
        Port br-ex
            Interface br-ex
                type: internal
        Port "eth1"
            Interface "eth1"
    ovs_version: "2.5.0"
```

Sometimes OVS isn't properly running after it is either freshly installed or the node is rebooted. This is a known bug with OVS. Restarting the OVS service resolves it, though you wouldn't want to do this in production without planning.

```
$ sudo service openvswitch-switch restart
```

Now you will want to log into the Horizon dashboard, which is opened by using your web browser to navigate to the IP address of your controller. If you're using the reference deployment from Appendix A, accessing the dashboard can be done on your host machine where you run the controller and compute VMs from. Otherwise you'll just need to make sure the machine you run the browser from can access the IP address that the controller is running on.

Figure 5.1   Horizon dashboard login page

> **Tip**
>
> Which IP address? The controller has two NICs, but only one of them has an address you
> can navigate to. This is the one assigned to eth0 and would have been allocated when you
> installed the controller.

Once you have a login screen (see Figure 5.1), you want to log in with username "test" and the test password you created when editing the hiera/common.yaml file.

If all of these commands worked, congratulations! You now have a running controller node. If you have errors, first go back and check your configuration to make sure you didn't skip a step. If that doesn't help, see the troubleshooting section later in this chapter for some resources to help you debug.

You'll now want to set up the other server, the compute node.

Compute Node

You are now creating a Compute node. The compute node will be the host of all of the compute Instances that you create. As discussed, it is important for security and performance to keep these separate from all of the tooling used to run OpenStack itself. We will configure the compute node in much the same way as we did the controller. First edit several variables in the default hiera common.yaml at /etc/puppet/hiera/common.yaml. Open with your preferred text editor using sudo and make similar changes to what you did in the controller file. Save the file.

> **Reminder**
>
> Don't skip editing hiera/common.yaml. These values need to sync up with what you used on
> the controller. Plus, the defaults are easy to guess and are stored on a public git repository.

With these changes completed, we can finally run the following command on your compute node to apply the Puppet manifest that will install the foundational components for you.

```
$ sudo puppet apply /etc/puppet/modules/deployments/manifests/role/foundations_compute.pp
```

As with the controller, you may also consider using the puppet apply command with the --debug flag in order to see more of what is going on. Either way, this command will take some time to run, so while it's running we can take a look at what is included in this foundations_compute.pp Puppet role:

```
class deployments::role::foundations_compute {
  include deployments::profile::base
  include deployments::profile::compute
}
include deployments::role::foundations_compute
```

This is a much simpler role than the foundations role. It only includes the base profile, discussed earlier on the controller and the compute profile.

Compute Profile

The first thing you may recognize is that the controller had a "Nova" profile and this module has a "Compute profile." This naming was used to distinguish the tooling installed on the controller to operate the centralized, management of Nova compute, and the services required on a node. The compute node is simply running the virtual machines themselves and doing some limited networking, but accepts instructions from services running on a controller. Looking inside the compute profile, you can see how it differs from the Nova profile on the controller:

```
$ cat /etc/puppet/modules/deployments/manifests/profile/compute.pp
class deployments::profile::compute
{
  include ::nova
  include ::nova::compute
  include ::nova::compute::libvirt
  include ::nova::compute::neutron
  include ::nova::network::neutron
  include ::neutron

  class { '::neutron::agents::ml2::ovs':
    bridge_uplinks    => undef,
    bridge_mappings   => undef,
    enable_tunneling  => hiera('neutron::agents::ml2::ovs::enable_tunneling'),
    tunnel_types      => hiera('neutron::agents::ml2::ovs::tunnel_types'),
    local_ip          => hiera('neutron::agents::ml2::ovs::local_ip'),
  }
}
```

The profile pulls in a very limited subset of components that are required for running the compute nodes, specifically dealing with a single compute daemon (::nova::compute) using libvirt. The Neutron Modular Layer 2 (ML2) plug-in for Open vSwitch is configured for networking. It is used to configure the tunnels needed for instance traffic.

Testing the Compute Node

The following can be run either on the controller or the compute node. For authentication, it's using the OpenStack command line client with the openrc credentials to query the APIs endpoints that were defined. We will be working with the test user for these commands since this user account has the ability to create instances.

```
$ source /etc/openrc.test
$ openstack image list
+-------------------------------------+--------------+
| ID                                  | Name         |
+-------------------------------------+--------------+
| cdf2c591-3b16-4bd1-9bde-a2568e738492 | Cirros 0.3.4 |
+-------------------------------------+--------------+
$ openstack flavor list
+----+-----------+-------+------+-----------+-------+-----------+
| ID | Name      | RAM   | Disk | Ephemeral | VCPUs | Is Public |
+----+-----------+-------+------+-----------+-------+-----------+
| 1  | m1.tiny   | 512   | 1    | 0         | 1     | True      |
| 2  | m1.small  | 2048  | 20   | 0         | 1     | True      |
| 3  | m1.medium | 4096  | 40   | 0         | 2     | True      |
| 4  | m1.large  | 8192  | 80   | 0         | 4     | True      |
| 5  | m1.xlarge | 16384 | 160  | 0         | 8     | True      |
+----+-----------+-------+------+-----------+-------+-----------+
```

The CirrOS image listed will be the image used to boot the instance. CirrOS is a very basic, cloud-focused Linux image. It's designed to run a very basic filesystem, networking and only the most basic Linux services by default. The image itself is only 13M and can very easily run with the smallest default OpenStack flavor (m1.tiny, with 512M of RAM and 1 VCPU). We'll want to use the "m1.tiny" flavor and Network1. This can be done with the following:

```
$ openstack server create --image "Cirros 0.3.4" --flavor m1.tiny --nic net-id=Network1 ferret
+-------------------------------------+----------------------------------------------------------+
| Field                               | Value                                                    |
+-------------------------------------+----------------------------------------------------------+
| OS-DCF:diskConfig                   | MANUAL                                                   |
| OS-EXT-AZ:availability_zone         |                                                          |
| OS-EXT-STS:power_state              | 0                                                        |
| OS-EXT-STS:task_state               | scheduling                                               |
| OS-EXT-STS:vm_state                 | building                                                 |
| OS-SRV-USG:launched_at              | None                                                     |
| OS-SRV-USG:terminated_at            | None                                                     |
| accessIPv4                          |                                                          |
| accessIPv6                          |                                                          |
| addresses                           |                                                          |
| adminPass                           | p3dqssrBRKW8                                             |
| config_drive                        |                                                          |
| created                             | 2016-01-08T18:14:48Z                                     |
| flavor                              | m1.tiny (1)                                              |
| hostId                              |                                                          |
| id                                  | cad9a045-85c4-4ec0-9dc4-a1d5bf65e5e4                     |
| image                               | Cirros 0.3.4 (cdf2c591-3b16-4bd1-9bde-a2568e738492)      |
| key_name                            | None                                                     |
| name                                | ferret                                                   |
| os-extended-volumes:volumes_attached | []                                                      |
```

```
| progress                          | 0                                         |
| project_id                        | 995f2fb58e9541fba9fcdce515557ffc          |
| properties                        |                                           |
| security_groups                   | [{u'name': u'default'}]                   |
| status                            | BUILD                                     |
| updated                           | 2016-01-08T18:14:48Z                      |
| user_id                           | b1cfddd9f26e495dade526d025af28ad          |
+-----------------------------------+-------------------------------------------+
```

This output shows you that it is building an instance with the name "ferret" and you can view the progress of creation by running the following:

```
$ openstack server list
+--------------------------------------+--------+--------+------------------------+
| ID                                   | Name   | Status | Networks               |
+--------------------------------------+--------+--------+------------------------+
| cad9a045-85c4-4ec0-9dc4-a1d5bf65e5e4 | ferret | ACTIVE | Network1=10.190.0.16   |
+--------------------------------------+--------+--------+------------------------+
```

More details can be shown with `openstack server show ferret`.

If the status is ACTIVE, you can now delete this instance. New ones will be created with different specifications in subsequent chapters so you can work with them.

```
$ openstack server delete ferret
```

This command should return with no output. You can run the `openstack server list` command again to confirm it's been deleted.

Now that you have a working compute and controller node, you have the foundation for the deployment scenarios in later chapters.

Launching a Test Instance on the Dashboard

For a more visual test that you can log into, we want to launch a very simple instance using the CirrOS image. This is very similar to what you did in Chapter 2, but we'll be doing a slightly simplified process without key pairs.

Launching an instance will be done with your non-administrative user, which was defined by default in the hiera/common.yaml as "test" and with whatever password you selected.

Once logged in to the Horizon dashboard, select Instances on the left-hand side. This will take you to the list of instances currently running on your system, which should be an empty list if this is your first time logging in. On the top right of your screen, you should see a Launch Instance button. Click on this button to bring up the Launch Instance walkthrough, which will have several fields for you to fill out. To refresh your memory about what these field mean, refer back to Chapter 2.

- **Instance Name**—test-instance (or select your own)
- **Availability Zone**—nova
- **Instance count**—1

Once these are filled in, click Next to go to the Source screen, as seen in Figure 5.2 where you will click on the + button to the right of the Cirros 0.3.4 image in the list to move it up to Allocated.

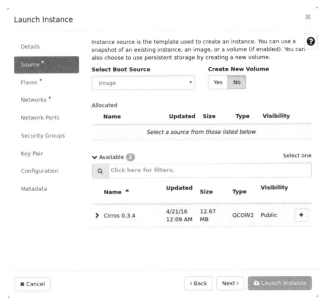

Figure 5.2   Horizon dashboard for selecting source image

Click Next again to get to the Flavor screen. Just like with the Source, you will want to click on the + to the right of a Flavor you wish to use to allocate it. For this instance, use m1.tiny. Click Next again to get to the final required screen, Networks.

As shown in Figure 5.3, we want to use Network1 for this instance. Again, click the + sign to the right of Network1 in the Available list to move it to Allocated.

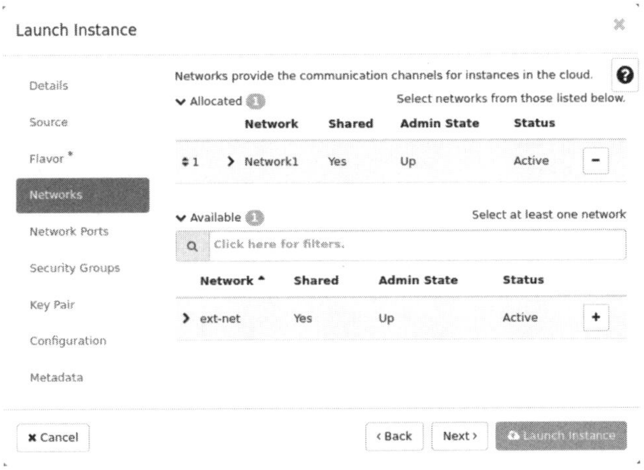

Figure 5.3   Network1 has been allocated to this instance

Remember, Network1 is for local traffic, and an ext-net is defined where you can add support for traffic outside of the local network. Only addresses from Network1 can be assigned directly to an instance.

With your network set, you can click Launch Instance button to create your instance. The Launch Instance window will close and you will see the Status of the instance in the list go from Building to Active. Once it's active, you want to look in the last column of the list of instances and select Console from the Actions column (see Figure 5.4).

This will bring up a Console in a separate window that you can log into. It's very common for the console to fail to respond to input, so at the top of the page you may need to choose the option to Click here to show only console in order to interact with the console. The console will have instructions for how to log in, which by default on the CirrOS image are:

```
"login as 'cirros' user. default password: 'cubswin:)'. use sudo for root."
```

Follow these instructions to log in. You then may want to confirm that your instance got an IP address. In the example in Figure 5.5 the command `ip addr` was run to show an eth0 with the IP address of 10.190.0.7. The next command run was `ping -c 4 10.190.0.1`, which pinged the gateway address that was configured four times to confirm local networking was working.

If this was all successful, congratulations, you're running an instance on OpenStack! With these foundations in place, you're now ready to move on to the first deployment scenario.

If you're having some trouble, the next section will help you with troubleshooting.

Figure 5.4   Select Console from the Actions column

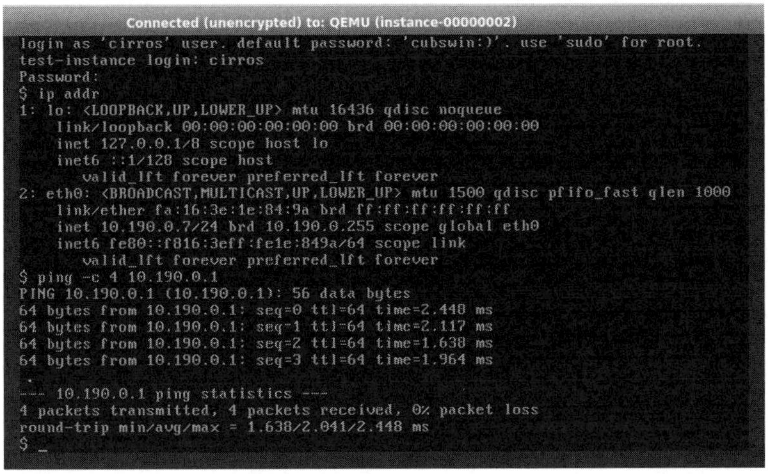

Figure 5.5   Initial CirrOS booted and connectivity checked

Troubleshooting

OpenStack has many moving parts, which unfortunately makes it so there are many things that can go wrong with a deployment. Although we have tested this with multiple configurations, there's always a chance that a missed step or something in the environment is causing you to see errors. The following are some tips we've collected to help you find your way.

- Go back through this chapter and check your configurations to make sure you didn't skip a step. It's easy to miss something. Also, check that your passwords are correct.

- Look for errors during the Puppet run. They may indicate specific issues like problems installing packages, starting services or communicating with OpenStack services.

- Browse the README.md file in the puppet-deployments repository on GitHub. We are maintaining a list of common issues at https://github.com/Deployments-Book/puppet-deployments/blob/master/README.md.

- Skip to Appendix F, "Finding Help with OpenStack" in order to ask for help from the OpenStack community.

- If you're using your own configuration and continue to struggle with it, you may want to see Appendix A for a working, virtualized example. You can either switch to that, or use it as a working reference to debug your current deployment.

Finally, Chapter 13, "Troubleshooting," covers common issues that operators run into when they are trying to deploy OpenStack. It may be valuable to look at some of these common issues in order to see if you're running into any of them now. That chapter also walks you through reviewing OpenStack logs to look for errors, which is a very valuable exercise when you're tracking down problems.

Summary

This chapter provided the foundation that will be referenced in subsequent chapters as you deploy various scenarios for OpenStack. You will be referring back to these instructions as you work through each of them. We also discussed how Keystone, Neutron, Nova, Horizon and Glance, along with message queuing and databases, are to be used for our deployment scenarios.

6

Private Compute Cloud

This village belongs to the Castle, and whoever lives here or passes
the night here does so in a manner of speaking in the Castle itself.
Nobody may do that without the Count's permission.

Franz Kafka

In the early days of OpenStack, one of the more common uses for the technology was getting server instances into the hands of developers quickly so they could rapidly prototype their ideas. Enter the private compute cloud, an Infrastructure as a Service (IaaS) OpenStack deployment that is used by a single organization. Today the private compute cloud remains a popular deployment type for many organizations, but it has grown to encompass full replacement of a company's virtualization solution across both their development and production infrastructure.

In this chapter, we focus on delivering raw compute power (processor and RAM) inside an organization through basic, ephemeral (temporary) virtual machines. We dive into the key components of a common private compute cloud, including how to use Nova, Keystone and Horizon.

Uses

Members of the OpenStack community meet for a summit every six months. Keynotes during this summit are frequently given by major players in the OpenStack community or by invited organizations who have used OpenStack in some capacity. While OpenStack was young, private deployments focusing on getting compute-focused power to their users were common examples.

Reasons for wanting a private compute cloud vary across types of organizations. Some are looking for a flexible infrastructure to manage an existing virtualized environment, and others are seeking to manage the administrative burden placed upon them.

Government Organization

At one summit, a major US government agency presented on how the use of OpenStack allowed them to provide on-demand access to a pool of virtual machines to their developers who were seeking to try out new ideas. On the IT side, provisioning of servers prior to using OpenStack was manually intensive. On the development side, a developer had to fill out a lot of paperwork and get several layers of approvals in order to get a server provisioned, which could take weeks or months. By the time the server was provisioned, they might not even remember the idea they had in the beginning or it may have become obsolete. In order to reduce the burden on IT, they sought out a solution that was self-service and on demand, elastic and had API access.

They selected OpenStack to suit their needs and within two weeks the team had a working prototype with several users. The next step brought them into a formal lab that had access to production data within the organization. The final step was bringing it into more formal production, where they took a closer look at automation, security and user creation and authentication through their existing Public Key Infrastructure. Ultimately, this resulted in the staff need and workload of IT being decreased, and users having a much better experience with the flexibility. Having a common, easily replicated infrastructure has also allowed increased ability for sharing between developers and departments.

Major Company

Another summit featured a major car manufacturer who spoke about their existing physical and virtualized infrastructure. They had written their own cloud software to manage their virtualized servers but were seeking to move to a more maintainable infrastructure as they began running into some problems. They needed to retain the benefits of automation, standardization and flexibility that the cloud-based environment in their data centers already used and have something they could fully understand and control.

OpenStack also provided them a stable API and, being open source, it avoided issues with licensing and increasing costs imposed by a vendor. Additionally, since they had the talent in house, having already written their own infrastructure, they chose to handle testing and deployment themselves rather than calling upon an outside company specializing in OpenStack. The option to decide whether to call upon internal talent or work with one of the many companies offering specialized OpenStack private clouds and support makes OpenStack really stand out as a leader in open source cloud technology.

With their private OpenStack deployment, they were able to write their applications on their internal cloud.

Requirements

For this exercise, reference the two nodes you created in Chapter 5, "Foundations for Deployments." You should have your series of two Virtual Machines or physical servers available with at least the minimum specifications defined in that chapter. If you wish to launch more than a couple of small Instances, you will want to have more resources on your Compute Node. Keep in mind that in the case of virtualization you will also need to leave some resources for the host system.

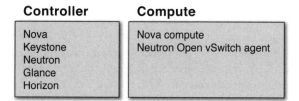

Figure 6.1   Components of a basic, two system OpenStack deployment

Select Components

In the following several chapters, you will be presented with a series of deployment options for OpenStack that will enable you to make an informed decision as to what components you wish to use in your environment.

For this deployment, we will be using a very basic OpenStack deployment (see Figure 6.1). We will install the following:

- Compute (Nova)
- Identity (Keystone)
- Networking (Neutron)
- Image service (Glance)
- Dashboard (Horizon)

Scenario

This is the simplest deployment scenario of OpenStack that we will explore. As explained, it is using only the services that we installed in Chapter 5, so there are no additional services to add. This simple deployment will enable you to do the following:

1. Add a new flavor to define resources (RAM, disk, etc.), which can be selected when you deploy instances.
2. Add a new disk image to the image service.
3. Create instances using your disk image and test on the private network.
4. Add a public, floating IP address to make an instance externally accessible.
5. Install and run a publicly accessible service on your instance.

We will walk through both using the dashboard (Horizon) and on the command line with OpenStack Client (OSC).

Launching an Instance: Dashboard

Using the OpenStack dashboard (Horizon) is the easiest way to start using OpenStack. It provides a graphical view of your OpenStack environment, and while it's not as feature complete as the command line clients, it does have all the features for basic administration and manipulation of your OpenStack environment and instances.

As we've seen in previous chapters, the dashboard is opened by using your web browser to navigate to the IP address of your controller. If you're using the reference deployment from Appendix A, "Reference Deployment," this can be done on your host machine where you run the controller and compute VMs from. Otherwise you'll just need to make sure the machine you run the browser from can access the IP address that the controller is running on.

Add a Flavor

A flavor defines the amount of RAM and disk (root, ephemeral and swap), as well as the number VCPUs to be allocated to an instance. By default, there are several flavors defined that are useful for most deployments (see Figure 6.2). These flavors are completely customizable. In order to add a flavor, you will need to log in as the admin user.

> **Note**
>
> Since the minimum requirements we defined for our deployment are so low, you will not be able to use all of the default flavors.

Most of the columns in this list are pretty straightforward if you're familiar with Linux filesystems: VCPUs are the number of processors for the guest, RAM is memory, Root Disk is the storage that the base image with root filesystem is copied to, and Swap Disk is the swap space on the system. Setting the flavor as public means that it's available to all the projects on the system. The less obvious columns include Ephemeral

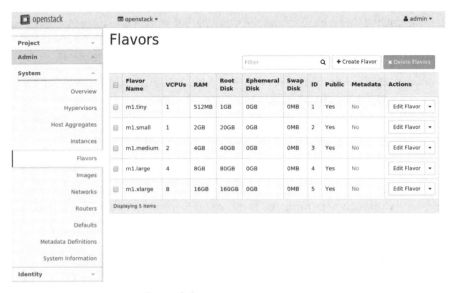

Figure 6.2   List of default flavors

Disk, which is additional ephemeral, or temporary, storage that effectively disappears when the instance is terminated. This may be the case if you're running a web front end, which connects to a separate back end or are doing data processing which gets data from an external database. The Metadata column is a link that brings you to a screen where you can specify more fine-tuned details for each resource, like specifying disk I/O preferences and preferences around the CPU and memory allocation and usage.

To create your custom flavor, you'll first want to come up with a name for your flavor. In this example, I'll use the name m1.smaller. Click Create Flavor on the top right of the table to bring up the screen for adding a flavor. The fields you want to fill out will be the following, also shown in Figure 6.3, and note that these fields accept integers only, no decimals:

- **Name:** m1.smaller
- **ID:** auto
- **VCPUs:** 1
- **RAM (MB):** 768
- **Root Disk (GB):** 5
- **Ephemeral Disk (GB):** 0
- **Swap Disk (MB):** 0

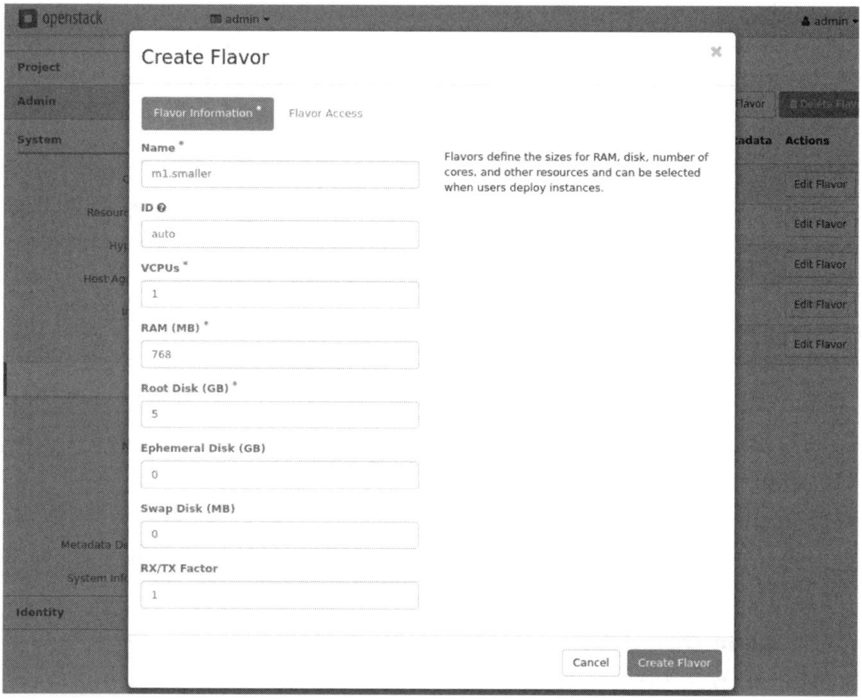

Figure 6.3   Add a flavor

Once these values are added, you can click the Flavor Access tab to see what projects will be given access to the flavor. If you make changes to the projects that have access, it will change your flavor from Public to Private. We want to keep this flavor public, so click Create Flavor and your new flavor will show up in the list with the others.

This flavor will be what we use in the next section with the image we upload. All further changes will be done with the test account, so you can now log out of the admin account.

Add an Image

Log in to the dashboard with the test user. This user will be used for the rest of the work we'll be doing to add an image and boot an instance.

Currently the only image you have loaded into OpenStack is the CirrOS image. This image is fine for testing functionality, but there's not a whole lot you can do with it. Instead of continuing to use this image, we're going to upload a new image to the image service (Glance) that can be used.

Since we're using Ubuntu for the base of our deployments, we can go ahead and use an Ubuntu 14.04 image for this as well. You want to download the Cloud image for 64-bit computers (QCOW2 disk image file for use with QEMU and KVM), which you can browse to from https://cloud-images.ubuntu.com/releases/.

At the time of writing, 14.04.4 was the most recent point release of the 14.04 release. Descend into that directory until you find a listing of 14.04 images. The file URL you want is to the file with this name: ubuntu-14.04-server-cloudimg-amd64-disk1.img. You can either download this image to the machine you're running your web browser on or use the URL and import the image into the image service directly from the URL. In our example, we'll be using the URL.

> **Tip**
>
> If you download the image yourself, get the md5sum of the .img file from the MD5SUMS file that resides in the same directory as you downloaded the image from. Run the md5sum command against the image you downloaded to confirm that the sums match.

In the dashboard, navigate to Images under the Compute section in the left-hand menu. On the top right, select Create Image to bring up the screen to add an image to the image service. In this screen, you'll want to fill in the following fields, as seen in Figure 6.4:

- **Name:** Ubuntu 14.04 Server
- **Image Source:** Image Location
- **Image Location:** the https URL from cloud-images.ubuntu.com
- **Format:** QCOW2—QEMU Emulator
- **Minimum Disk (GB):** 5
- **Minimum RAM (MB):** 768

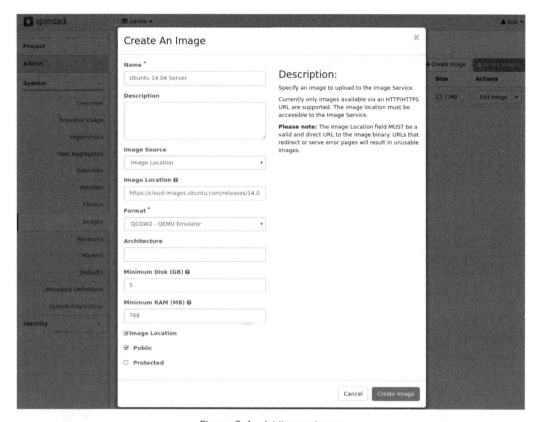

Figure 6.4   Adding an image

With these values filled in, you can now select Create Image to add this image into the image service. Because we used an Image Location, you may see the image Saving for several minutes as this is downloading the .img file that's about 220MB so it can import it into the service. Once the image has completed downloading you will see the Status column change to Active and it will now be available for use.

Pre-launch Access and Security

Before we launch our Ubuntu instance, we'll want to do some preliminary work to make sure the instance is accessible and usable when we bring it up. Once again in the left-hand menu under Compute, select Access & Security where we will want to edit two sections.

The first section to edit will be Security Groups which will have a default group that we want to edit. Security Groups are used to filter network traffic, and by default there are only a few rules and while they allow outgoing traffic, they block incoming. This means that with the current default rules, you won't be able to ping or SSH into your instances, which we will want. We'll also add a rule to allow TCP traffic over port 80 for when we set up a web server in a later step. We'll start with allowing ICMP ping to the systems, as illustrated in Figure 6.5. Rather than allowing all ICMP traffic, which is an option in the Rule dropdown, we can create a custom ICMP rule to only allow ping. To do this, use the following values:

- **Rule:** Custom ICMP Rule
- **Direction:** Ingress
- **Type:** 8
- **Code:** 0
- **Remote:** CIDR
- **CIDR:** 0.0.0.0/0

The Type and Code are not obvious, but these come from RFC 792 which define this information for ICMP. With the rest of the options set we're allowing traffic from anywhere to ping our instance. Click Add to add this to the list of rules.

The next two rules we want to add are easier, since they have default configurations already loaded. Click Add Rule again from the main screen and when the Add Rule screen shows up, go through the list in the Rule dropdown and select HTTP. Keep everything else as default and add this rule. Do the same for SSH. That is all you want to add to the Security Group at this time, but you now know how to adjust the rules for your

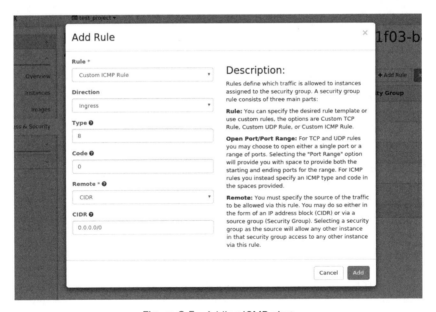

Figure 6.5   Adding ICMP ping

instances. Note that we edited the default security group, which is what instances will use unless you specify otherwise, but it's common to create multiple security groups for your instance types. A web server will want to grant access to HTTP, but you may want to close HTTP and only allow traffic to port 3306 if you're running a MySQL server.

> **Tip**
>
> You can modify Security Groups while instances using them are running. The new rules will be applied live to the running systems.

Moving on from Security Groups, you next want to go back to Access & Security in the menu on the left and this time select Key Pairs, which will upload your SSH key. With your SSH key added, you will be able to SSH into the servers (for images that support it, including CirrOS and Ubuntu). You may remember going through this process back in Chapter 2, "DevStack."

If you're familiar with SSH and already have your own SSH key (typically in your user home directory, with a default name of .ssh/id_rsa.pub) you can choose to import that key with the Import Key Pair option, as shown in Figure 6.6. This screen also explains how to generate your own key using ssh-keygen, which is what we recommend you do. When you've completed giving your key pair a name (I called mine elizabeth-desktop) and pasting your public key, you can click Import Key Pair to add the key to the list.

Alternatively, you can use the option to Create Key Pair if you wish to create a key to use through the interface. It will register your public key and have you download a .pem file. The .pem file is your private key that will then be used later when you log in.

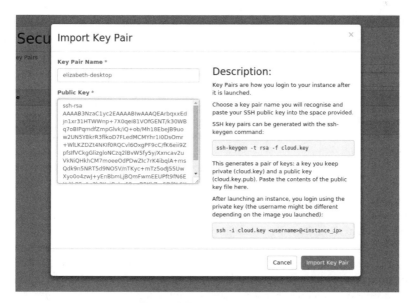

Figure 6.6   Import key pair

> **Caution**
>
> Don't lose this key! The key is only used while the system is being installed, so if you lose this key, you will not be able to get into your instance. This is non-recoverable, even for administrators.

Launch an Instance

Now that the background tasks are completed, we can get around to the business of launching an instance!

Much like how we launched a CirrOS instance in Chapter 5, we will be using a similar process to launch an Ubuntu instance, starting with navigating in the left panel under Compute to Instances and clicking Launch Instance to bring up the screen to walk you through configuring the options for your instance. Feel free to select your own Instance Name if you're not a fan of soft mountain rodents from the Andes, but otherwise you want to use the following and then click Next:

- **Instance name:** chinchilla
- **Availability Zone:** nova
- **Instance Count:** 1

The next screen will enable you to pick your image Source. This time select Ubuntu 14.04 Server by clicking on the + sign to the right of the instance name in the list of Available images. This will move it up to Allocated. Click Next to continue on to the Flavor screen.

On the Flavor screen, as seen in Figure 6.7, you will want to again select an option. Select the m1.smaller flavor you created earlier in this chapter by clicking on the + to the right of the Available flavor. On this screen you may notice some yellow warnings next to m1.tiny. These are warning you that the image you selected will not fit into that flavor. Click Next to go to the Networks screen where you will want Network1 to be the Allocated network. Remember, ext-net is only used for floating IP addresses and cannot be used here.

Before clicking Launch Instance, navigate to Security Groups. If you created a new one you wish to use rather than using the default as instructed switch to that one instead. Then click Key Pair and click the + next to your key pair to move it up to Allocated, as show in Figure 6.8.

You can also browse the Network Ports, Configuration and Metadata screens, which will likely come in handy later. It's common to use the Configuration screen to add a script to create some initial users or to bootstrap your configuration management environment if you're not using a custom image. For this instance, we won't be changing anything in these three screens though, and you can just click Launch to start your instance.

You can now watch as your instance goes through the Spawning phase and eventually has the State change to Active when the instance is available. If you wish to watch what has been going on with the instance as it boots, you go over to the Actions column and from the drop-down menu select View Log to see the log that has been created.

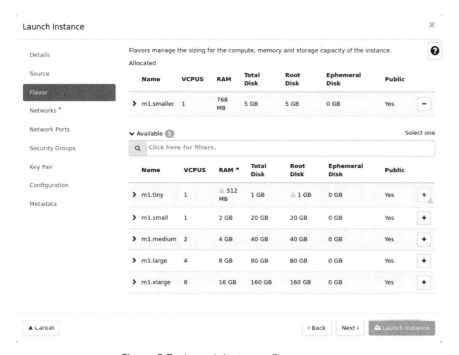

Figure 6.7   Launch instance, Flavor screen

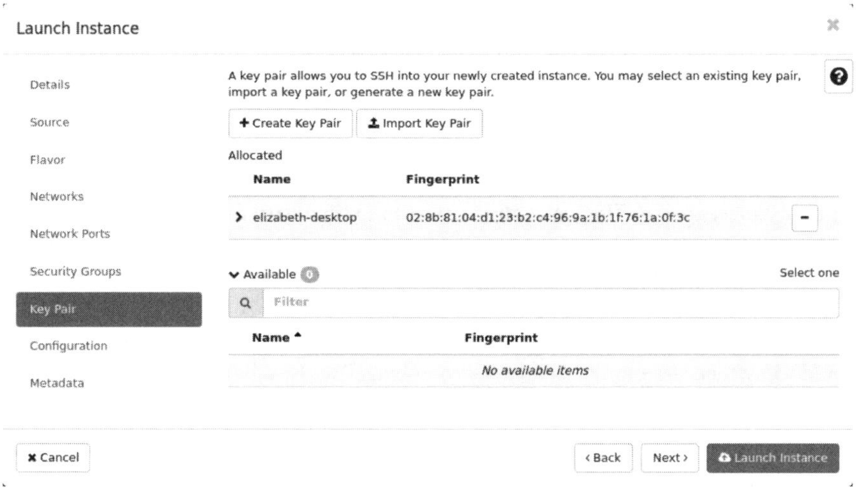

Figure 6.8   Launch instance, Key Pair screen

Depending on the speed of your systems, it may take a few minutes for the instance to fully boot and show you a login prompt. For reference, it took my systems about 10 minutes to boot and the process stopped for a while on a screen describing the network configuration. Once booted, the console will show you a screen which will look something like this:

```
Ubuntu 14.04.4 LTS chinchilla ttyS0

chinchilla login:
```

> **Tip**
>
> Where did the OpenStack instance get "chinchilla" from for the host name? When you defined the instance you created, you gave it a name. This name is used within OpenStack compute itself to reference the instance, but it is also used to set the hostname of the machine. It does this by using cloud-init.
>
> The cloud-init Python tooling is a powerful set of scripts and utilities. Learn more about other things it can do at: https://cloudinit.readthedocs.org/en/latest/.

From here, you can also navigate to the Console from the Log screen to interact with the system, but there is no default password for this image. You will need to use SSH to log in to the machine, which we'll talk about next.

Add a Floating IP Address

By default, in our configuration, your system will come with a private address that was assigned by the DHCP service (dnsmasq) running on your controller. If you're using the default configuration we provided, this will be an address in the 10.190.0.0/24 address block. This address is used for communication between the instances and is valuable if you're doing internal work where you only want the instances to be communicating with each other and not traversing a broader network.

In order to give your instance access to the outside world, we want to give it a floating IP address from the public provider network we defined. By its nature, a floating IP address is something that can be moved from instance to instance, as your needs change. When you destroy your instance, the floating IP address goes back to the pool and is available for other instances to use. Note that an instance has no control over or direct knowledge of its floating IP address; this is managed externally. It will not show up when you run the `ip addr` command inside an instance.

In our configuration the floating IP addresses come from the 203.0.113.0/24 address block. Note that this is not an actual public address block, it is the TEST-NET-3 defined in RFC 5735 which is designed to look like a public IP address block. As such, this address will only be accessible from the systems on your network that share an address in this address block.

Private versus Public Address Refresher

Can OpenStack give an instance a public address by default rather than assigning a private address?

Absolutely. Most of the documentation follows the same pattern that ours does to assign a private address and then assign a floating IP connected to a provider network as needed. However, it's common for operators to instead assign these addresses directly from a provider network if they know their services need to be on a specific network or on the Internet.

Refer back to Chapter 3, "Networking," for in-depth discussion about networking and the decisions made for this book.

We will now walk through how to add a floating IP to your instance so we can SSH into it and then run a web server on it. In the Actions menu for your instance you want to select Associate Floating IP to bring up the screen to work with your IPs. Under IP Address you can click on the plus sign to add a new IP, which will bring up the Allocate Floating IP screen. This will ask you what pool to get the addresses from and your only option should be ext-net. When you click Allocate IP it will select an address from the pool and make it available to assign to your VM, by default it will bring you back to the Manage Floating IP Associations screen with that new IP address filled in to the IP Address field, as seen in Figure 6.9.

You now click Associate to add it to your instance. This is done live and is typically available very quickly without rebooting your instance. You should get a green Success dialog and in the IP Address column for your instance you should have something like:

```
10.190.0.11
Floating IPs:
203.0.113.9
```

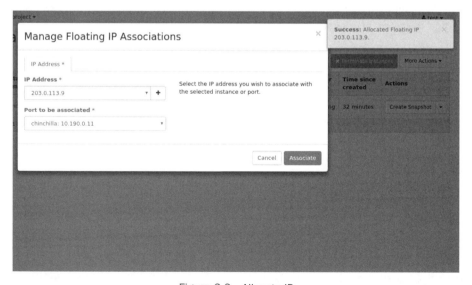

Figure 6.9   Allocate IP

This 203.0.113.0/24 address is what we'll use for SSH and to access any services on this machine. Using SSH to log into an instance and installing and using a public service on your instance are identical whether you used the OpenStack dashboard (Horizon) or the command line with OpenStack Client. Since these are identical, we'll explain how to do that at the end of the chapter. You can now learn how to do everything we've done above on the command line, or skip to the end of the chapter for the "Running a Service" section.

Launching an Instance: OpenStack Client

Using the OpenStack Dashboard can be a convenient way to interact with OpenStack if you're looking for a simple interface or are not comfortable with the command line. However, many operators prefer using the command line for interaction with OpenStack because it can be more convenient and faster, as well as offering more options and the capability to write scripts to complete actions. We'll now step you through the same work we did with the dashboard, but using the OpenStack Client instead.

In production, you will typically be running the client from a system external to your OpenStack deployment that has access to the OpenStack APIs that the client communicates with. To simplify things for these examples, we'll run all of these commands from the Controller node you created instead. When using the dashboard, you were logged in as a particular user to complete each task. With the OpenStack Client, you'll instead be sourcing an openrc credentials file that was created when you ran Puppet in Chapter 5. You may look at these files directly to see what they contain, but they issue a series of exports to your shell environment that will be your credentials when you run the subsequent commands.

Add a Flavor

First you'll want to add a new flavor to use. This will be similar to the flavor you created with the dashboard, but we'll give it another name. You'll be using the administrator account to create this flavor for all users.

Tip

OpenStack commands have a tendency to provide a lot of detail that doesn't always fit on these pages. Command output for many of these commands is included in a GitHub repository for scripts and configurations sorted by chapter at https://github.com/DeploymentsBook/scripts-and-configs.

```
$ source /etc/openrc.admin
$ openstack flavor list
+--------------------------------------+------------+-------+------+-----------+-------+-----------+
| ID                                   | Name       | RAM   | Disk | Ephemeral | VCPUs | Is Public |
+--------------------------------------+------------+-------+------+-----------+-------+-----------+
| 1                                    | m1.tiny    | 512   | 1    | 0         | 1     | True      |
| 2                                    | m1.small   | 2048  | 20   | 0         | 1     | True      |
| 3                                    | m1.medium  | 4096  | 40   | 0         | 2     | True      |
| 4                                    | m1.large   | 8192  | 80   | 0         | 4     | True      |
| 5                                    | m1.xlarge  | 16384 | 160  | 0         | 8     | True      |
| 74fa1799-055f-4411-a8d7-55826dba7d94 | m1.smaller | 768   | 5    | 0         | 1     | True      |
+--------------------------------------+------------+-------+------+-----------+-------+-----------+
```

```
$ openstack flavor create --ram 768 --disk 5 --ephemeral 0 --vcpus 1 --public m1.smaller2
+---------------------------+--------------------------------------+
| Field                     | Value                                |
+---------------------------+--------------------------------------+
| OS-FLV-DISABLED:disabled  | False                                |
| OS-FLV-EXT-DATA:ephemeral | 0                                    |
| disk                      | 5                                    |
| id                        | 874857cf-ca29-4dea-b121-aaf36517ac3e |
| name                      | m1.smaller2                          |
| os-flavor-access:is_public| True                                 |
| ram                       | 768                                  |
| rxtx_factor               | 1.0                                  |
| swap                      |                                      |
| vcpus                     | 1                                    |
+---------------------------+--------------------------------------+
```

You can run `openstack flavor list` again to see that your m1.smaller2 flavor was created and is almost identical to the earlier m1.smaller flavor created with the dashboard.

Add an Image

For this work onward, you'll be using the test user to run commands. In this step, you will add an image to your deployment for use. We'll once again use the Ubuntu server image, but we'll give it a different name.

```
$ source /etc/openrc.test
$ openstack image list
+--------------------------------------+--------------------+
| ID                                   | Name               |
+--------------------------------------+--------------------+
| 8b6b345c-1e08-426e-b24b-37df8e166ab0 | Ubuntu 14.04 Server|
| b592fbdf-cbb9-4159-bc22-f2a591b4c348 | Cirros 0.3.4       |
+--------------------------------------+--------------------+
$ wget https://cloud-images.ubuntu.com/releases/14.04.4/release/ubuntu-14.04-server-
cloudimg-amd64-disk1.img
$ openstack image create --container-format bare \
--disk-format qcow2 --min-disk 5 --min-ram 768 \
--file ubuntu-14.04-server-cloudimg-amd64-disk1.img "Ubuntu 14.04 Server 2"
+------------------+------------------------------------------------------+
| Field            | Value                                                |
+------------------+------------------------------------------------------+
| checksum         | 2a0bf21fb69d518d9c7a19dbc2d99eb7                     |
| container_format | bare                                                 |
| created_at       | 2016-05-02T20:12:45Z                                 |
| disk_format      | qcow2                                                |
| file             | /v2/images/cdeb610d-9064-4dc5-b63a-afa9a58c0f7c/file |
| id               | cdeb610d-9064-4dc5-b63a-afa9a58c0f7c                 |
| min_disk         | 5                                                    |
| min_ram          | 768                                                  |
| name             | Ubuntu 14.04 Server 2                                |
| owner            | d49446773bfb47bab30b3c4bca06d82d                     |
| protected        | False                                                |
| schema           | /v2/schemas/image                                    |
| size             | 259392000                                            |
| status           | active                                               |
| tags             |                                                      |
| updated_at       | 2016-05-02T20:12:47Z                                 |
| virtual_size     | None                                                 |
| visibility       | private                                              |
+------------------+------------------------------------------------------+
```

Since this is a local image file, the command may take a moment to return and then it will typically show up as active pretty quickly. If not, you can check the status as this image is loaded by using the `show` command. Once the status has changed to "active" you will be able to boot an instance with that image.

```
$ openstack image show "Ubuntu 14.04 Server 2"
+------------------+------------------------------------------------------+
| Field            | Value                                                |
+------------------+------------------------------------------------------+
| checksum         | 2a0bf21fb69d518d9c7a19dbc2d99eb7                     |
| container_format | bare                                                 |
| created_at       | 2016-05-02T20:12:45Z                                 |
| disk_format      | qcow2                                                |
| file             | /v2/images/cdeb610d-9064-4dc5-b63a-afa9a58c0f7c/file |
| id               | cdeb610d-9064-4dc5-b63a-afa9a58c0f7c                 |
| min_disk         | 5                                                    |
| min_ram          | 768                                                  |
| name             | Ubuntu 14.04 Server 2                                |
| owner            | d49446773bfb47bab30b3c4bca06d82d                     |
| protected        | False                                                |
| schema           | /v2/schemas/image                                    |
| size             | 259392000                                            |
| status           | active                                               |
| tags             |                                                      |
| updated_at       | 2016-05-02T20:12:47Z                                 |
| virtual_size     | None                                                 |
| visibility       | private                                              |
+------------------+------------------------------------------------------+
```

Pre-launch Access and Security

When using the Dashboard, at this stage you adjusted the settings adding an SSH key and to the default security group rules in order to add ping, SSH and HTTP access to your instances. We will first look to see how these currently look via the OpenStack Client.

```
$ source /etc/openrc.test
$ openstack keypair list
+-------------------+-------------------------------------------------+
| Name              | Fingerprint                                     |
+-------------------+-------------------------------------------------+
| elizabeth-desktop | 73:08:27:ee:8f:6d:07:0f:d3:d2:cb:2f:73:4e:38:ab |
+-------------------+-------------------------------------------------+
$ openstack security group rule list default
+--------------------------------------+-------------+------------+------------+
| ID                                   | IP Protocol | IP Range   | Port Range |
+--------------------------------------+-------------+------------+------------+
| 0743e044-5707-47fa-87a7-e6a5036e9d7c | tcp         | 0.0.0.0/0  | 80:80      |
| 3977d290-35cb-434a-8408-c886dd6e5887 | icmp        | 0.0.0.0/0  |            |
| 52d61ae0-6518-41de-831c-ebe9f0918cc0 |             |            |            |
| 742da90f-515a-47cc-b8c0-577ebb178ec8 | tcp         | 0.0.0.0/0  | 22:22      |
| 77d0bbfe-2fa1-4f7b-bc4a-57e09161e9c3 |             |            |            |
+--------------------------------------+-------------+------------+------------+
```

In this example, instead of directly replicating what we did with the dashboard, we'll create a key pair on the control node to use as a demonstration, and then add port 443 (HTTPS) access to our default group.

```
$ ssh-keygen -t rsa
Generating public/private rsa key pair.
Enter file in which to save the key (/home/elizabeth/.ssh/id_rsa):
Created directory '/home/elizabeth/.ssh'.
Enter passphrase (empty for no passphrase):
Enter same passphrase again:
Your identification has been saved in /home/elizabeth/.ssh/id_rsa.
Your public key has been saved in /home/elizabeth/.ssh/id_rsa.pub.
The key fingerprint is:
f6:9f:93:ab:ac:14:19:59:fc:72:6a:00:6f:71:31:cb elizabeth@control1
The key's randomart image is:
+--[ RSA 2048]----+
|         .+.     |
|     . .+oo      |
|      oooE.      |
|      +o. o      |
|      .S. +      |
|      . oo       |
|       ...  .    |
|       . . .o.   |
|        ..o.+o   |
+*----------------+
$ openstack keypair create --public-key .ssh/id_rsa.pub elizabeth-control
+-------------+-------------------------------------------------+
| Field       | Value                                           |
+-------------+-------------------------------------------------+
| fingerprint | f6:9f:93:ab:ac:14:19:59:fc:72:6a:00:6f:71:31:cb |
| name        | elizabeth-control                               |
| user_id     | e542c1e48d8d4373978f6ef272424b6d                |
+-------------+-------------------------------------------------+
$ openstack keypair list
+-------------------+-------------------------------------------------+
| Name              | Fingerprint                                     |
+-------------------+-------------------------------------------------+
| elizabeth-control | f6:9f:93:ab:ac:14:19:59:fc:72:6a:00:6f:71:31:cb |
| elizabeth-desktop | 73:08:27:ee:8f:6d:07:0f:d3:d2:cb:2f:73:4e:38:ab |
+-------------------+-------------------------------------------------+
```

You now have your old key pair as well as a new one that I named elizabeth-control to note that it's my key on the Controller node. If you wish to use your own key, you can adjust the --public-key to point to the key you want to load. If you make a mistake, you can use `openstack keypair delete` to delete an unwanted key pair.

Next we'll add port 443 to our default security group.

```
$ openstack security group rule create --proto tcp --src-ip 0.0.0.0/0 --dst-port 443:443 default
+-----------------+-----------------------------------------+
| Field           | Value                                   |
+-----------------+-----------------------------------------+
| group           | {}                                      |
| id              | c7a9c2d1-3f4c-4de5-999a-355db60f0ebc    |
```

```
| ip_protocol    | tcp                                    |
| ip_range       | 0.0.0.0/0                              |
| parent_group_id | 4e0a1f03-b869-49ec-9a06-2ff2b14db985 |
| port_range     | 443:443                                |
+----------------+----------------------------------------+
$ openstack security group rule list default
+--------------------------------------+-------------+-----------+------------+
| ID                                   | IP Protocol | IP Range  | Port Range |
+--------------------------------------+-------------+-----------+------------+
| 0743e044-5707-47fa-87a7-e6a5036e9d7c | tcp         | 0.0.0.0/0 | 80:80      |
| 3977d290-35cb-434a-8408-c886dd6e5887 | icmp        | 0.0.0.0/0 |            |
| 52d61ae0-6518-41de-831c-ebe9f0918cc0 |             |           |            |
| 742da90f-515a-47cc-b8c0-577ebb178ec8 | tcp         | 0.0.0.0/0 | 22:22      |
| 77d0bbfe-2fa1-4f7b-bc4a-57e09161e9c3 |             |           |            |
| c7a9c2d1-3f4c-4de5-999a-355db60f0ebc | tcp         | 0.0.0.0/0 | 443:443    |
+--------------------------------------+-------------+-----------+------------+
```

If you look closely at this final output, you will now see a TCP port 443 included here with the same details as you previously created in the dashboard ports 22 and 80 rules. Instances you create now with the default security group will allow 443 as well.

Launch an Instance

Having laid the ground work, launching an instance using the OpenStack Client takes just a single command, but you will have to manually define several options.

> **Caution**
>
> If you're still running the instance you created in the dashboard, you may want to shut that down before launching this instance in order to save resources. This can be done by logging into the dashboard, navigating to Instances and either selecting Shut Off Instance or Terminate Instance from the drop-down menu on the right. Shutting off the instance will allow you to bring it back up later. Terminating will delete the instance entirely.

You'll be using the new image and flavor you created to launch this instance. In this example I'm not using the SSH key I created in this stage, so I can instead log into it the same way I did with the instance I created in the dashboard. Just like in the dashboard, the availability zone will be "nova" and we're using the default security group that we've been adding rules to. Finally, the network we're using is Network1 so that by default this instance will get an address from the 10.190.0.0/24 network.

```
$ source /etc/openrc.test
$ openstack server create --image "Ubuntu 14.04 Server 2" \
--flavor m1.smaller2 --security-group default --key-name elizabeth-desktop \
--availability-zone nova --nic net-id=Network1 ferret
+-----------------------------+----------------------------------------------------------+
| Field                       | Value                                                    |
+-----------------------------+----------------------------------------------------------+
| OS-DCF:diskConfig           | MANUAL                                                   |
| OS-EXT-AZ:availability_zone | nova                                                     |
| OS-EXT-STS:power_state      | 0                                                        |
| OS-EXT-STS:task_state       | scheduling                                               |
| OS-EXT-STS:vm_state         | building                                                 |
| OS-SRV-USG:launched_at      | None                                                     |
| OS-SRV-USG:terminated_at    | None                                                     |
```

```
| accessIPv4                         |                                                            |
| accessIPv6                         |                                                            |
| addresses                          |                                                            |
| adminPass                          | Hq69dynxZeBD                                               |
| config_drive                       |                                                            |
| created                            | 2016-03-28T18:12:56Z                                       |
| flavor                             | m1.smaller2 (874857cf-ca29-4dea-b121-aaf36517ac3e)         |
| hostId                             |                                                            |
| id                                 | 41887a02-1efa-4b4d-8f64-d31c68da066e                       |
| image                              | Ubuntu 14.04 Server 2 (dd05b2e4-afa2-4c33-a99c-2f68b7312951) |
| key_name                           | elizabeth-desktop                                          |
| name                               | ferret                                                     |
| os-extended-volumes:volumes_attached | []                                                       |
| progress                           | 0                                                          |
| project_id                         | 44f0be93c3524ad59aab0e8f7a154aff                           |
| properties                         |                                                            |
| security_groups                    | [{u'name': u'default'}]                                    |
| status                             | BUILD                                                      |
| updated                            | 2016-03-28T18:12:57Z                                       |
| user_id                            | e542c1e48d8d4373978f6ef272424b6d                           |
+------------------------------------+------------------------------------------------------------+
```

As you can see from this output, the status is BUILD, which means the instance is being launched. You can check status of your instance building either by using openstack server list for the basic list of whether the system is up.

```
$ openstack server list
+--------------------------------------+--------+--------+---------------------+
| ID                                   | Name   | Status | Networks            |
+--------------------------------------+--------+--------+---------------------+
| 41887a02-1efa-4b4d-8f64-d31c68da066e | ferret | ACTIVE | Network1=10.190.0.13 |
+--------------------------------------+--------+--------+---------------------+
```

If there are any problems, you may want more detail by using the show command against the instance with openstack server show ferret, which will even provide a basic error message that can help you determine why it failed. For more on debugging see Chapter 13, "Troubleshooting."

Add a Floating IP Address

The final step we'll complete here with the OpenStack client is assigning a Floating IP Address to the instance so that it's externally accessible on the 203.0.113.0/24 address block. As explained earlier, this is not a real public address and will only be accessible from the systems on your network that share an address in this address block.

You may already have addresses available, so we'll start by doing a list.

```
$ openstack ip floating list
+--------------------------------------+---------+-------------+----------+-------------+
| ID                                   | Pool    | IP          | Fixed IP | Instance ID |
+--------------------------------------+---------+-------------+----------+-------------+
| 45744a5f-8cd4-4554-a6f1-4666353be00d | ext-net | 203.0.113.8 | None     | None        |
+--------------------------------------+---------+-------------+----------+-------------+
```

You may use this address, but you can also use the create command to add another address from the ext-net pool.

```
$ openstack ip floating create ext-net
+-------------+------------------------------------+
| Field       | Value                              |
+-------------+------------------------------------+
| fixed_ip    | None                               |
| id          | d8cc6592-efc2-450e-9726-ccf91d1a05c2 |
| instance_id | None                               |
| ip          | 203.0.113.10                       |
| pool        | ext-net                            |
+-------------+------------------------------------+
```

We can use this one we just created for this new instance by running the following, and then check to make sure the IP was assigned.

```
$ openstack ip floating add 203.0.113.10 ferret
$ openstack server list
+--------------------------------------+--------+--------+------------------------------------+
| ID                                   | Name   | Status | Networks                           |
+--------------------------------------+--------+--------+------------------------------------+
| 41887a02-1efa-4b4d-8f64-d31c68da066e | ferret | ACTIVE | Network1=10.190.0.13, 203.0.113.10 |
+--------------------------------------+--------+--------+------------------------------------+
```

Voila! The instance now has both a private address and the newly assigned 203.0.113.10 address. This address can be used to SSH into the system from another system on this network.

Running a Service

Whether you used the OpenStack dashboard (Horizon) or OpenStack Client (OSC) to bring up your first instance, you're now all set to start logging into your server and making changes.

Logging in with SSH

The Ubuntu cloud image that we're using does not have a default password to go with the default ubuntu user, so accessing it is done with an SSH key that you imported or created in an earlier step. Now you'll want to use this key and log in.

First, you will need to interface with the system that has the gateway address of 203.0.113.1 defined. If you're using instructions from Appendix A, this will be the host machine where your controller and compute VMs run. You can either SSH to this machine, or use a Terminal on the Ubuntu desktop on that machine directly to SSH into your instance. To see if your instance is accessible from the machine you're on, we can start out with a ping test. Look up what 203.0.113.0/24 address your machine has, and then use the ping command to test. For example if your address is 203.0.113.9 use the following command, which should get pings back from the server:

```
$ ping -c 5 203.0.113.9
PING 203.0.113.9 (203.0.113.9) 56(84) bytes of data.
64 bytes from 203.0.113.9: icmp_seq=1 ttl=63 time=3.56 ms
64 bytes from 203.0.113.9: icmp_seq=2 ttl=63 time=1.35 ms
64 bytes from 203.0.113.9: icmp_seq=3 ttl=63 time=1.50 ms
64 bytes from 203.0.113.9: icmp_seq=4 ttl=63 time=1.88 ms
64 bytes from 203.0.113.9: icmp_seq=5 ttl=63 time=1.58 ms
```

```
--- 203.0.113.9 ping statistics ---
5 packets transmitted, 5 received, 0% packet loss, time 4005ms
rtt min/avg/max/mdev = 1.354/1.979/3.566/0.812 ms
```

Now confirm that the SSH server is responding properly:

```
$ nc 203.0.113.9 22
SSH-2.0-OpenSSH_6.6.1p1 Ubuntu-2ubuntu2.6
```

If everything looks good, you can now log in with the ubuntu user and your private SSH key (which is called id_rsa, cloud.key, something.pem or whatever you named it):

```
$ ssh -i .ssh/id_rsa ubuntu@203.0.113.9
The authenticity of host '203.0.113.9 (203.0.113.9)' can't be established.
ECDSA key fingerprint is d3:b2:13:09:35:50:4b:01:86:0e:52:66:ff:5a:57:5d.
Are you sure you want to continue connecting (yes/no)? yes
Warning: Permanently added '203.0.113.9' (ECDSA) to the list of known hosts.
Welcome to Ubuntu 14.04.4 LTS (GNU/Linux 3.13.0-77-generic x86_64)
...
ubuntu@chinchilla:~$
```

Now that you're logged in, you can add a service.

A Simple HTTP Server

Since we're running a pretty restricted instance, we're going to forgo the popular Apache web server and instead use a very basic Python command that comes with Ubuntu to load up an HTTP server.

First run the following on your controller or wherever your SSH key for your Ubuntu instance is. Replace 10.190.0.8 with the address for the instance you've brought up:

```
$ git clone https://github.com/DeploymentsBook/http-files.git
$ scp -r http-files/nova/ ubuntu@10.190.0.8:
```

> **Tip**
>
> Since we don't assume you have Internet access on your instances, we are cloning this repository to your controller first. If you have taken the route of giving them access through a real floating IP on your network, you can clone this directly onto your instance or install something like Apache or another service you wish to test out.

A nova directory will now be in the home directory of your ubuntu user on the Ubuntu system. SSH into the Ubuntu system to launch the HTTP instance.

```
$ cd nova
$ python -m SimpleHTTPServer
Serving HTTP on 0.0.0.0 port 8000 ...
```

Now go back to the server you're SSHing in from and open up a browser and navigate to the instance address on port 8000. The address will be something like http://10.190.0.8:8000. You should see a page similar to what is show in Figure 6.10.

Congratulations, you're now running your first user-facing application on an OpenStack instance!

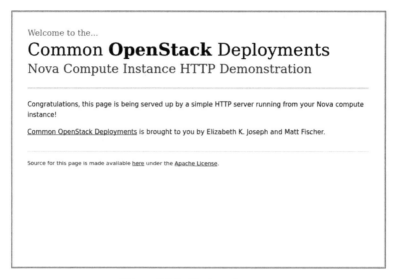

Figure 6.10   Basic web server

When you're done using your instance and are ready to get rid of it, you can log into the dashboard, navigate to Instances and either select Shut Off Instance or Terminate Instance from the drop-down menu on the right. If you simply shut off the instance you will be able to bring it back up later. Terminating the instance will delete the instance forever. You can also terminate an instance from OpenStack Client with the `openstack server delete <server>` command.

SDKs and the OpenStack API

We have explored using the OpenStack dashboard (Horizon) and the OpenStack Client (OSC) to interact with OpenStack.

But no chapter on interacting with your private cloud would be complete without discussing the Software Development Kits (SDKs) which speak to the OpenStack Application Programming Interface (API). With the rise of automation in operational environments, it's fair to say that most deployments use SDKs for the majority of their interactions with their OpenStack clouds. Software is written with the SDKs to manage your OpenStack instances and the resources they're using.

OpenStack SDKs are available for various languages, including Python, Java, Node.js, Ruby, .NET and PHP. If you can't find an API for your language of choice, the API can also be accessed by using cURL or via REST clients (both of which many languages have bindings for) or by simply calling the OpenStack Client (OSC) we used earlier in this chapter from within your program.

The latest documentation for the major SDKs and the OpenStack API can be found by going to http://developer.openstack.org/.

Summary

The ability to run a private compute cloud within your organization gives a significant amount of power to those using it. Whether you're a university with students who need access to server instances, or an organization with developers who need on-demand server resources, being able to offer these up to your users instantly is a powerful thing.

7

Public Compute Cloud

No house should ever be on any hill or on anything.
It should be of the hill, belonging to it, so hill and house could
live together each the happier for it.
Frank Lloyd Wright

Companies all over the world are deploying public compute clouds for customers looking to process data. The focus of these clouds is everything from on-demand compute power to storage systems, which we'll explore in later chapters. For compute-focused hosting, OpenStack provides a platform for dynamic applications that provide highly-available service to customers. Typically, these services are billed for based on resources used (RAM, CPU, disk, etc.) and the amount of time the instance is used for, often on an hourly increment.

This chapter will build upon what we've learned in Chapter 6, "Private Compute Cloud," and show you how you can track usage and ultimately bill for services on a public cloud run by your organization.

Uses

As the OpenStack Community has grown over the past several years, we've seen several companies spring up to offer services that compete with the current proprietary cloud solutions on the market. The OpenStack Foundation Marketplace has an entire section devoted to companies offering public clouds (http://www.openstack.org/marketplace/public-clouds/).

As a player in this market, companies can leverage the development of the open source platform of OpenStack and on top of it build in benefits to their customers such as geographic diversity, speed, high network speeds and even application integration to enable customers to build their products faster.

Traditional Technology Company

Traditional technology companies have the benefit of a long history and strong reputation for innovation and offering their customers solid products. In today's cloud-driven world, some traditional technology companies have taken to building public clouds. These typically are offered alongside their other offerings or in concert with their private cloud offerings.

During one OpenStack summit keynote, a company talked about how their customers are now using hybrid clouds, which blend a deployed series of private clouds alongside a public cloud. This company will go on-site to assist with the deployment of a private cloud, and then offer a public cloud for the public-facing components of their infrastructure.

Web Hosting Company

Companies that have specialized in web hosting have also begun offering public compute options. Many of these companies began by offering the purchase of a Virtual Private Server (VPS) to customers and also offer specific hosted services such as blogs or forum installations. With the move to cloud, these hosting companies have empowered their users to build their own applications using a framework similar to that which many of these traditional web hosting services have run off of.

Additionally, some companies are leveraging *portions* of OpenStack for their customers by offering object storage for individual files, which you'll learn about in Chapter 9, "Object Storage Cloud."

Requirements

In this deployment scenario you'll be using the controller and compute nodes you created in Chapter 5, "Foundations for Deployments." For this installation, you can use the same systems you used in Chapter 6, since we did not make any additions to that deployment beyond the foundation.

You may also want to set aside some time to let this deployment sit running. Since the metering collected by OpenStack is tracked over time, having a couple instances running over night will collect data so you can explore the next day or the next week.

Select Components

On top of the foundational tooling, we'll be adding the Ceilometer telemetry service to your deployment in this scenario. This will extend the basic installation to have to include following services, placement of which is demonstrated in Figure 7.1:

- Compute (Nova)
- Identity (Keystone)
- Networking (Neutron)
- Image service (Glance)
- Dashboard (Horizon)
- Ceilometer (Telemetry)

Controller

```
Nova
Keystone
Neutron
Glance
Horizon
Ceilometer
```

Compute

```
Nova compute
Neutron Open vSwitch agent
Ceilometer polling agent
```

Figure 7.1   Components of a two system OpenStack deployment
with the Ceilometer telemetry service

Architecture Overview

At the most basic, Ceilometer polls OpenStack services you have running. We'll be using Nova compute and Glance image store in our demonstration. It can also collect notifications from the notification bus. A collector gathers this information and puts it into a database. MySQL is configured for this purpose in our deployment to keep things simple, but MongoDB was the original and remains the recommended database.

From this data store, you interact with the API to query the data. This is accomplished through viewing the output in the Horizon dashboard, using OpenStack Client or the Ceilometer command line interface or through an external billing system that we'll briefly talk about later in this chapter. This basic overview is sketched out in Figure 7.2.

The data collected by the collector is tracked in the form of meters. A meter is what is actually being measured, such as CPU load, disk I/O, or the amount of space Glance

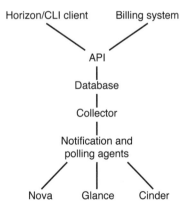

Figure 7.2   Ceilometer overview

images are taking up. Each of these meters is tracked as a type. Ceilometer understands the following meter types:

- **Cumulative**—Increasing over time, like how long an instance has been running
- **Gauge**—Discrete items such as the number of image uploads or floating IPs used and fluctuating values like disk I/O
- **Delta**—Change over time range, like bandwidth

In addition to this basic overview, Ceilometer has the concepts of transformers and publishers. A transformer enables you to manipulate original data and extend it to form new measurements or change dimensions, making it possible for different types of data to be presented to a client or other external system. A publisher enables you to redirect specified data to one or more targets, rather than requiring those targets to make requests for it.

Scenario

As mentioned, we'll be adding Ceilometer to our basic installation of OpenStack defined in Chapter 5 and used again in Chapter 6. Since we're adding another service, we'll need to use Puppet to pull in the additional components.

In this scenario you will be making changes to both the controller node and the compute node.

Controller Node Setup

On the controller you'll be using another puppet `apply` command, which will process our foundational public cloud role in Puppet:

```
$ sudo puppet apply /etc/puppet/modules/deployments/manifests/role/foundations_public_cloud.pp
```

While this is running, let's take a look at what we're running.

```
class deployments::role::foundations_public_cloud {
  include deployments::role::foundations
  include deployments::profile::ceilometer
}

include deployments::role::foundations_public_cloud
```

As you can see, this pulls in our foundations manifest, which should have run earlier if you're starting from a node you set up previously. It's then pulling in the Ceilometer profile that we've defined in the deployments composition module. That Ceilometer profile is where things get interesting. On your filesystem this will be located at /etc/puppet/modules/deployments/manifests/profile/ceilometer.pp and contains the following:

```
class deployments::profile::ceilometer
{
  include ::ceilometer
  include ::ceilometer::client
```

```
  include ::ceilometer::collector
  include ::ceilometer::agent::auth
  include ::ceilometer::agent::central
  include ::ceilometer::agent::notification
  include ::ceilometer::agent::polling
  include ::ceilometer::api
  include ::ceilometer::config
  include ::ceilometer::db
  include ::ceilometer::db::mysql
  include ::ceilometer::keystone::auth
}
```

We're installing the Ceilometer client so we can query against the data later in this chapter. Beyond that, you have components which go through the process in Figure 7.2:

1. The polling agent gathers measurements and puts them in queue.
2. OpenStack services send notifications on the standard notification bus.
3. The notification agent processes data from both the polling agent and notification bus and sends it to the target, which is the collector in our case.
4. The collector, or other target, stores the data in persistent storage, like a database, a file or in Gnocchi, a time series database storage system developed under the umbrella of the OpenStack Telemetry project. Again, we're using MySQL as a data store.

Authentication is handled with Keystone, so we're pulling in the components required for setting up authentication.

Compute Node Setup

Just like with the controller, we'll be using a puppet apply command to add another foundational role to our compute node so that data can be gathered from the nodes running on it.

```
$ sudo puppet apply /etc/puppet/modules/deployments/manifests/role/foundations_compute_
public_cloud.pp
```

This will take several minutes to run as it installs and configures the required components, which we can take to look at what's being pulled in:

```
class deployments::role::foundations_compute_public_cloud {
  include deployments::profile::base
  include deployments::profile::compute
  include ::ceilometer::agent::polling
  include ::ceilometer::agent::auth
}

include deployments::role::foundations_compute_public_cloud
```

This class is pretty much identical to the earlier foundations compute role we applied, but it now includes the polling and auth agents so that data can be collected from the hypervisor to get statistics about things like CPU and network usage.

Polling Hypervisors

The agent used for polling the hypervisor needs pretty significant view into what these systems are doing. This means it also needs support for how these hypervisors are being queried. In Mitaka, the following hypervisors are supported:

- KVM and QEMU, used in our reference deployment (via libvirt)
- LXC (via libvirt)
- UML (via libvirt)
- Hyper-V
- Xen
- VMware vSphere

There is also an Intelligent Platform Management Interface (IPMI) agent for queries against bare metal. We have specifically excluded support for IPMI in our deployment scenarios because we aren't supporting it.

Viewing Statistics: Dashboard

The Horizon dashboard support for Ceilometer is limited and will likely be considerably different in the future. For now, a quick view into the display of statistics can be seen by logging in as the admin user and navigating to the Admin, System, Resource Usage.

The first screen will give you a listing of some of the meters and data they have collected, as shown in Figure 7.3.

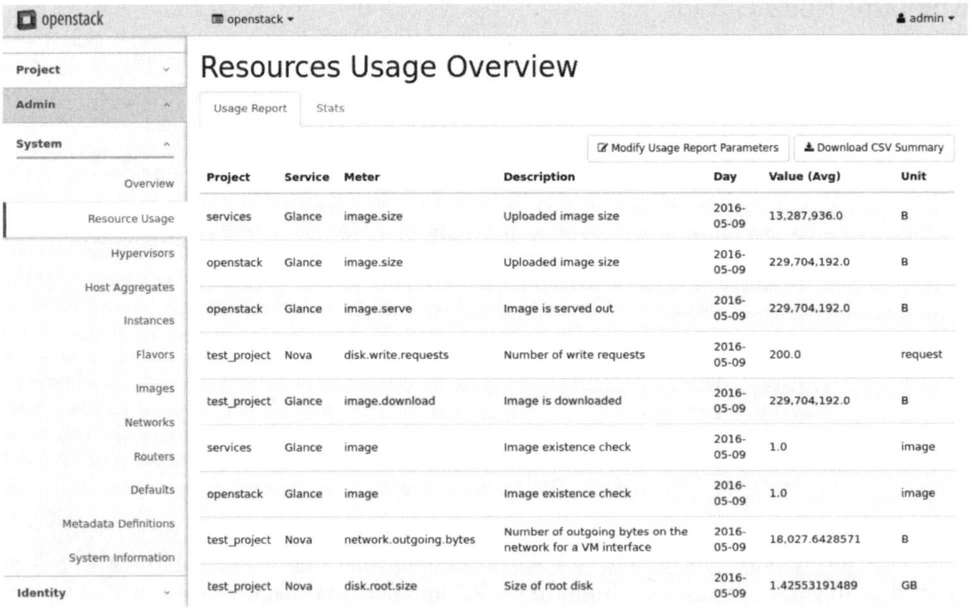

Figure 7.3   Ceilometer Usage Overview

As you can see, we're pulling data from both Nova and Glance, which are running on our current deployment. In this example, the system has been running for several days, collecting metrics about these services. During this time, instances have been created and destroyed, had varying workloads, and I have changed the number of images uploaded to and used by the Glance image store.

A graph view of the resources is attempted in the Stats tab of this screen, but it is not very advanced and will be redesigned in the near future. As we'll learn next, viewing and handling detailed data directly from Ceilometer comes from using the command line client, which queries the API.

Viewing Statistics: Command Line Client

The real power of Ceilometer, and where most interaction is done, is by using the command line client, which communicates with the API to gather statistics.

We'll first take a look at the meters we have available to browse through.

> **Note**
>
> Since there is not yet formal support in OpenStack Client for Ceilometer, we'll be using the Ceilometer client instead for these commands.
>
> Like the OpenStack client commands, Ceilometer client commands also tend to have verbose output that may wrap poorly on the page. Command output for commands in this chapter is included in a GitHub repository for scripts and configurations sorted by chapter at https://github.com/DeploymentsBook/scripts-and-configs.

To get a listing of meters, we can issue the `meter-list` command as the admin user (note that the output is truncated; actual output will be much longer and contain full Resource, User and Project IDs):

```
$ source /etc/openrc.admin
$ ceilometer meter-list
+----------------------+------------+----------+--------------+----------+------------+
| Name                 | Type       | Unit     | Resource ID  | User ID  | Project ID |
+----------------------+------------+----------+--------------+----------+------------+
| cpu                  | cumulative | ns       | f410c10b...  | 19ec...  | 983508f... |
| disk.allocation      | gauge      | B        | 0bcf0c0d...  | 19ecf..  | 983508f... |
| image.download       | delta      | B        | 6235a6cb...  | 19ecf..  | 983508f... |
| instance             | gauge      | instance | 0bcf0c0d...  | 19ecf..  | 983508f... |
| network.incoming.bytes | cumulative | B      | instance...  | 19ecf..  | 983508f... |
...
```

If you have more than one compute instance running, you will see multiple copies of your meters. You can restrict them by passing only the Resource ID on the command line, like the following:

```
$ ceilometer meter-list --query resource=29779773-64f4-4b0f-93db-e6041bf68b95
```

This will return the meters for only that instance. To get a full list of Resource IDs, you can also issue the `ceilometer resource-list` command, though it's difficult to parse these without the related meters. Note that since some of the resources may be for services like Glance, compute resources are not the only ones that exist. If you're not sure about what a resource is, you can get data about it by using `ceilometer resource-show <resource-id>`. For a resource like a compute instance, you'll see metadata about the host, flavor and disk size. For a Glance resource, you will see the image name, format and more, like the following:

```
$ ceilometer resource-show 6235a6cb-fa11-4cd9-9273-f83574d465ac
+-------------+----------------------------------------------------------------------+
| Property    | Value                                                                |
+-------------+----------------------------------------------------------------------+
| metadata    | {"status": "active", "name": "Ubuntu 14.04 Server", "deleted": "False", |
|             | "checksum": "742ec3c3d8a6b4f8caa7f14569d58eef", "created_at":        |
|             | "2016-05-09T19:14:15.000000", "disk_format": "qcow2", "updated_at":  |
|             | "2016-05-09T19:14:18.000000", "properties.description": "None",      |
|             | "protected": "False", "container_format": "bare", "min_disk": "5",   |
|             | "is_public": "True", "deleted_at": "None", "min_ram": "768", "size":  |
|             | "229704192"}                                                         |
| project_id  | c30a06988bc247c296cb4553d9a1473a                                     |
| resource_id | 6235a6cb-fa11-4cd9-9273-f83574d465ac                                 |
| source      | openstack                                                            |
| user_id     | None                                                                 |
+-------------+----------------------------------------------------------------------+
```

With these meters and resources in mind we'll now dive into a bit more about these. There are a couple queries you can do against the data: sample and statistics. Samples are individual raw data points associated with a particular meter. Statistics are a collection of aggregated data points over a time period, which you can define when querying.

Let's take a look at the disk usage sample for a single instance (output truncated):

```
$ ceilometer sample-list --meter disk.usage \
--query resource=89883a18-fc0a-4319-9f9c-e48ddbddf8c2
+-------------+------------+-------+-----------+------+----------------------------+
| Resource ID | Name       | Type  | Volume    | Unit | Timestamp                  |
+-------------+------------+-------+-----------+------+----------------------------+
| 89883a18... | disk.usage | gauge | 2564096.0 | B    | 2016-05-09T18:46:50.467369 |
| 89883a18... | disk.usage | gauge | 2564096.0 | B    | 2016-05-09T18:36:50.877118 |
| 89883a18... | disk.usage | gauge | 2170880.0 | B    | 2016-05-09T18:26:52.808036 |
...
```

Sample output contrasts with a statistic for the same resource and meter, which returns data demonstrating the aggregation of datapoints over time (output truncated) (Listing 7.1).

In this case, it looks like a few files have been added or changed this particular instance over time, so these differences are being measured.

Now let's do this same query again, but restrict it based on timestamps. We'll restrict it to a 60-minute period (Listing 7.2).

Nothing changed during this time, so the values are all very similar.

With this start, you can move on to do more advanced queries and track other variables. I'm sure you're already thinking of ways you can use this to track usage of your users and customers.

Listing 7.1

```
$ ceilometer statistics --meter disk.usage --query resource=89883a18-fc0a-4319-9f9c-e48ddbddf8c2
+--------+----------------+--------------+-----------+--------------+-------+--------------+-----------------+----------------+
| Period | Period Start   | Period End   | Max       | Min          | Avg   | Sum          | Count | Duration | Duration Start | Duration End   |
+--------+----------------+--------------+-----------+--------------+-------+--------------+-------+----------+----------------+----------------+
| 0      | 2016-05-0...   | 2016-05-...  | 2564096.0 | 2170880.0    | 2542250.66667 | 45760512.0 | 18 | 10197.317932 | 2016-05-09T... | 2016-05-0...   |
+--------+----------------+--------------+-----------+--------------+-------+--------------+-------+----------+----------------+----------------+
```

Listing 7.2

```
$ ceilometer statistics --meter disk.usage --query
'resource=89883a18-fc0a-4319-9f9c-e48ddbddf8c2;timestamp>2016-05-09T20:06:50.454570;timestamp<2016-05-09T21:06:50.125968'
+--------+----------------+--------------+-----------+--------------+-------+--------------+-------+----------+----------------+----------------+
| Period | Period Start   | Period End   | Max       | Min          | Avg   | Sum          | Count | Duration | Duration Start | Duration End   |
+--------+----------------+--------------+-----------+--------------+-------+--------------+-------+----------+----------------+----------------+
| 0      | 2016-05-0...   | 2016-05-...  | 2564096.0 | 2564096.0    | 2564096.0 | -2820480.0 | 5 | 2400.279797 | 2016-05-09T... | 2016-05-0...   |
+--------+----------------+--------------+-----------+--------------+-------+--------------+-------+----------+----------------+----------------+
```

Handling Metrics and Alerts

Now that you have a working cloud and some metrics, you will want to pass along this data to some kind of service to handle tracking and possibly billing. These services are external to OpenStack, with multiple companies and a couple open source projects, like CloudKitty, developed in the OpenStack ecosystem, offering support for the telemetry data coming from Ceilometer. Based on your needs, you'll want to research the appropriate solution for your environment. If none of the current vendors or projects meet your needs, you can write your own service that queries the API.

Once part of Ceilometer, alerts are now handled by the Telemetry Alarming service, Aodh. Like other OpenStack services, you configure alarms through the Aodh API. The alarm evaluator periodically communicates with the Ceilometer API and processes alerts through the alarm notifier, which then contacts the external systems to notify an alarm rule has been broken. This external system will be something you or your vendor creates to process the Aodh notification output.

Finally, given this data, it probably comes as no surprise that people are finding innovative ways to use this data. Utilization tracking can help a cloud operator script when they should automatically be adding resources. Problem in your infrastructure like a runaway log file or high loads? Statistics pulled from Ceilometer data can help pinpoint the instances that are struggling with disk space, CPU usage and more.

Summary

With the details from this chapter, you now have the framework to start tracking metrics on a hosted compute service. With a view into it from both the Horizon dashboard and the command line and API, you can track what your system is doing through regular polling and track usage and provide information to a billing system. You can even use it for debugging using the metrics provided through Ceilometer.

8

Block Storage Cloud

The road to the City of Emeralds is paved with yellow brick.
L. Frank Baum, *The Wonderful Wizard of Oz*

OpenStack provides two popular mechanisms for storage: object and block storage. Block storage is traditionally what you'd mount as a filesystem on your server. Object storage instead hosts individual files that are then referenced from within your application. In Chapter 9, "Object Storage Cloud," you learn about why you may want to use object storage with Swift to host files. This chapter covers block storage with Cinder.

Integrated with the rest of OpenStack, Cinder volumes can be created within an OpenStack cloud and then live mounted to a specified instance at the whim of a user. Additionally, you can unmount that volume from one instance and mount it on another with just a few commands.

Uses

One of the strengths of OpenStack is to avoid vendor lock-in, particularly when used in combination with versatile solutions like Cinder. Cinder provides an abstraction layer through the volume manager that hooks in to over 70 different proprietary and open source storage solutions. Additionally, it can be an interface to multiple back ends at once, enabling you to not only diversify your back ends across vendors but also change them out and do a planned migration as your organization sees fit.

Cloud Provider

Whether you're running a public cloud accessible to customers or a private cloud for use within your organization, offering the capability to extend the given filesystem requirements in place for the flavors can be a huge benefit.

With the capability to add block storage volumes on the fly, the storage requirements for default compute nodes can be kept small to preserve space for users who want to focus on compute power and give others the flexibility to add the storage they need on the fly. The flexibility to extend storage as needed helps scaling out resources without over-committing beforehand and makes migrations easier if data is kept on a single volume that can be moved to a new compute instance.

Another major benefit is that the compute nodes can be run on throw-away commodity hardware. The data needing to be stored can be either kept on expensive redundant enterprise hardware or on something that has built-in redundancy like Swift. As a result, compute nodes themselves could become independent, throw-away components of your infrastructure, spun up as needed and replaced with identical servers that attach to your storage back ends. Finally, upgrades are also simplified for your customers. If you have a new copy of your system you are testing, you can snapshot the production data from a Cinder volume and then attach it to your test system to see if it works.

Pets versus Cattle

If you're unfamiliar with the pets versus cattle metaphor in cloud computing, it's time to get you up to speed.

Prior to the recent rise in cloud computing, systems administrators would work with our managers to spec out hardware for servers and work out a budget to purchase it. A new server would be delivered to the facility where we'd install the operating system and put it into a rack in our data center. A nice label would go on the server designating a name, and over time we'd work to maintain and update this server. The server would be upgraded for years through operating systems and hardware failures and upgrades. We'd start noticing specific quirks about the hardware: one server may have a flaky onboard NIC so our notes explained that we added an additional card, another machine may take a while to boot up. We became familiar with these servers we grew and nurtured over time, like pets.

When workloads and businesses began moving to the cloud for their workloads, everything changed. Individual servers no longer had quirks and were easy to move around. A complete replacement of a server became more common than an in-place upgrade, and tools were written to manage fleets of servers operating in a larger infrastructure rather than working with individual servers. Instead of pets, servers became a lot more like cattle.

As a systems engineer and an animal lover, I retain a love for both pets and cattle, metaphorically or not. But this metaphor does effectively demonstrate the differences in how servers are treated today in a cloud environment.

Data Processing

Whether you're a film production company or a research institution, using compute nodes to do data processing and analysis is a common use for cloud-based infrastructures. But where is this data stored and how is it shared in your organization? What do you do when the compute nodes you're working on run out of space? With Cinder block storage, users are able to extend volumes after creation or simply create new volumes as they are needed and attach them to their running instances and mount them in a matter of minutes. Running out of hard drive space on an instance because you have too much data is no longer a problem.

Additionally, if you realize you need more processors or memory, it's simple to create a new compute instance and move the volume over to the new instance. All your data moves with you to your new server.

Keeping Backups

Making sure your data is backed up and replicated is a common concern, and Cinder offers several options for this. As mentioned earlier, it provides an abstraction layer for dozens of back ends, so you have a lot of options in your environment and on top of that, the different types of backups that Cinder offers.

Many virtualization technologies supported by OpenStack have built-in snapshot capabilities, but OpenStack's block storage also has one. This enables volumes to be backed up as snapshots to other block storage volumes and can be used on its own, using the existing configuration. Whether offered as a backup service by a cloud provider or as an automatic service for users on an OpenStack cloud, this is a valuable service.

You can also clone volumes. Many back ends are smart enough to do a copy-on-write in where zero copying actually happens. The new volume references an existing volume it was cloned from and writes data on top of that. This makes it very fast. Some snapshot features also just do this in the back end, but every vendor solution is implemented differently.

Moving beyond snapshots, Cinder also offers a backup service that enables you to back up your block data to an object store. This helps with the scenario of your entire block storage back end going completely off-line. Differential and incremental backups can be performed and, unlike a snapshot, it is only backing up data that was actually used, not the entire volume and unused bits.

We won't spend a lot of time on backup scenarios in this chapter. Instead we'll be focusing on adding volumes in a more instance-focused environment where you're adding volumes to instances, but they are great options to keep in mind.

Requirements

In this deployment scenario you'll once again be using the controller and compute nodes you created in Chapter 5, "Foundations for Deployments." We will be creating a 10GB volume group for use by Cinder on the controller and the minimum specifications defined in that chapter will easily support this.

Select Components

In addition to the foundational tooling, we'll be adding Cinder block storage to your deployment in this scenario. This will extend our very basic installation to have the following services. Their placement is demonstrated in Figure 8.1.

- Compute (Nova)
- Identity (Keystone)
- Networking (Neutron)
- Image service (Glance)
- Dashboard (Horizon)
- Block Storage (Cinder)

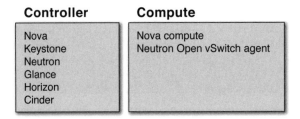

Figure 8.1   Components of a two-system OpenStack deployment with Cinder block storage

Architecture Overview

In Chapter 1, "What is OpenStack?" you were briefly introduced to the components that make up the block storage (Cinder) service: cinder-api, cinder-scheduler, cinder-volume and also cinder-backup. A user will likely only be exposed to the API. As operators though, understanding the architecture for the service is important as we seek to make decisions about how we build the system and debug problems.

When a user request comes in, either from the OpenStack dashboard (Horizon), the OpenStack Client (OSC) or through a Software Developer Kit (SDK), it interfaces with the API for Cinder. This API will talk to a database, for initially storing the request, and then set the status to creating and reserving quota usage. The API will also interact with a messaging queue. The messaging queue will pass requests on to the scheduler for Cinder, which makes decisions about where the change will be made. For example, if a user is requesting that a volume be created, the scheduler will determine which storage device meets the criteria the user is asking for, for the volume (size, disk type), and then send it to the appropriate volume manager. The volume manager for Cinder is what works directly with drivers to interface with the storage back ends. A storage back end may be a datacenter full of Ceph nodes or a proprietary Network-attached Storage (NAS) device that has a driver for Cinder. The volume manager will also be talking to the database to commit to the reserved quota once we know the volume is created successfully. The status of the volume is also set to "available" so the user knows the volume may be used. See Figure 8.2 for a view into how the individual services work together.

All official drivers that are available for Cinder go through verified testing by the upstream Cinder team in the OpenStack project. To accomplish this, every vendor is required to run continuous integration (CI) tests on all changes that report to the public OpenStack review system. To learn about the latest supported drivers, you can visit the OpenStack Marketplace Drivers page for an official listing: https://www.openstack.org/marketplace/drivers/.

Paying attention to the drivers and learning what is supported will be essential when you build out your production OpenStack deployment. When considering a solution, be sure to research the support for your storage back end of choice and look into factors like how long a solution or vendor has been supported in OpenStack and what they support when it comes to interacting with the Cinder volume manager.

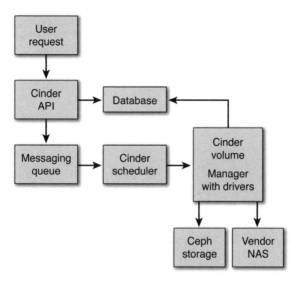

Figure 8.2   Cinder overview

Scenario

Extending beyond compute-focused deployments, like we saw in Chapter 6, "Private Compute Cloud," and Chapter 7, "Public Compute Cloud," with Cinder block storage means you can now offer real persistent storage to your users. Since we're adding an additional component, a bit of setup needs to be done with Puppet again to configure this storage.

Controller Node Setup

If you have your Controller and Compute nodes available from Chapter 5 you will only need to run a single command to add the support for Cinder block storage. In this scenario you will only need to make changes to the controller node. No modifications need to be made to the compute node.

> **Tip**
>
> Did you go through Chapter 7 before this chapter? You should create a new environment. Even though OpenStack is modular, we haven't designed our foundations modules to function together until you get to Chapter 12, "A Whole Cloud."

The command is another Puppet apply command, which will process our foundational block storage role in Puppet:

```
$ sudo puppet apply /etc/puppet/modules/deployments/manifests/role/foundations_block_storage.pp
```

This will take some time as it downloads everything required for Cinder and sets up configurations. If anything goes wrong and this command fails, remember that Puppet can also be run with the --debug flag in order to show more detail.

While this is running, we can take a look at what this file contains:

```
class deployments::role::foundations_block_storage {
  include deployments::role::foundations
  include deployments::profile::cinder
}

include deployments::role::foundations_block_storage
```

This is calling out to our foundations role, which means if you didn't set up a foundations role yet for your controller, it will do it now. This is mostly a safety measure; we would still recommend that you run it independently in case you need to do any troubleshooting.

It then calls our Cinder block storage profile, which you can view on the controller filesystem at /etc/puppet/modules/deployments/manifests/profile/cinder.pp, and it contains the following:

```
class deployments::profile::cinder
{
  include ::cinder
  include ::cinder::api
  include ::cinder::ceilometer
  include ::cinder::config
  include ::cinder::db::mysql
  include ::cinder::keystone::auth
  include ::cinder::scheduler
  include ::cinder::volume
  include ::cinder::setup_test_volume

  file { '/etc/init/cinder-loopback.conf':
    owner   => 'root',
    group   => 'root',
    mode    => '0644',
    content => template('deployments/cinder-loopback.conf.erb'),
  }
```

The profile pulls in various components to Cinder that we will need. Just like other services in OpenStack, Cinder requires an API, database and Keystone authentication. In case you wish to track usage with Ceilometer's telemetry service, we also include that. The config is pulled in to help manage arbitrary Cinder configurations you may wish to have. A scheduler in block storage is used in much the same way other OpenStack services use schedulers, to view the requirements the user is requesting for the volume, and then randomly pick a storage device back end that the volume can be created on that meets that criteria. As you may expect, pulling in cinder::volume is for the Cinder volume manager. As explained earlier in the chapter, this is what interacts with the drivers actually controlling the storage back end, whether it's a simple loopback device with LVM (Linux Volume Manager) like we will be using or a proprietary NAS device.

The final lines of this file use the Puppet module's capability to configure a test volume. For simplicity's sake we use this setup_test_volume, which creates a simple 10GB file mounted to a loopback (by default, /dev/loop2) device and added to LVM as a single logical group. An init file is also created in our cinder.pp profile to make sure the file is mounted and the volume group is activated if your controller reboots.

> **Note**
>
> What Is LVM? The official page for LVM is at: http://www.sourceware.org/lvm2/ and there are various resources and how-tos available for free online, particularly for basic control.

Once your `puppet apply` command completes, you're ready to start creating volumes and attaching them to instances!

Creating and Attaching a Volume: Dashboard

We will begin with the process for creating and attaching a volume using the OpenStack dashboard (Horizon). With the block storage (Cinder) component now installed, when you log into the dashboard with your test user you will see a section for Volumes in the left under Project in Compute, as show in Figure 8.3.

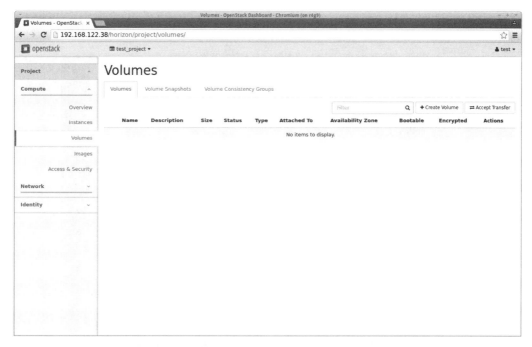

Figure 8.3   Empty, default Volumes page in the dashboard

Creating a Volume

On this page you'll want to click on the Create Volume button, which will bring up a dialog like the one in Figure 8.4 where you will put in information about the volume you wish to create. Some fields will be automatically filled out, but the rest will be up to you.

The volume name is what you will be using to refer to the volume. A description is optional and can be used for whatever you want, maybe as a reminder to yourself about what the volume is intended for. The volume source enables you to pre-populate the volume with a source of defined data. By default, it queries the Image Storage (Glance) service and enables you, as one of the options, to put an Image on your newly created volume. You may also want to create a volume source that has a basic filesystem and partition table for your new volume so it doesn't need to be created later after you mount it on an instance. For this scenario, we will just use No source, empty volume and will explain how to partition and format it after it is added to an instance.

The type of volume will inform the scheduler as to which type of storage back end you need to use. From the customer point of view, you want to define a type as tiered and varied storage with different properties, like how fast the storage device is, Quality of Service (QoS) requirements or whether a tier has replication. Prices may vary for the customer based on which options they select. From your perspective, this means one of these tiers may be using Ceph and another a proprietary NAS device that has the desired qualities for the tier being offered. We have not set a volume type, so it will remain as "No volume type" for this example. Our device only has 10GB, so we'll start out in

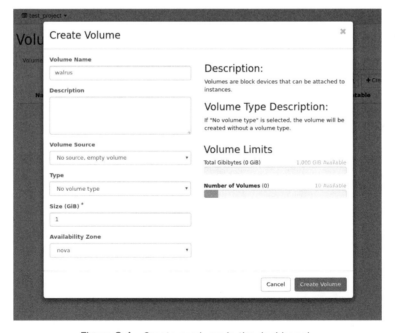

Figure 8.4   Create a volume in the dashboard.

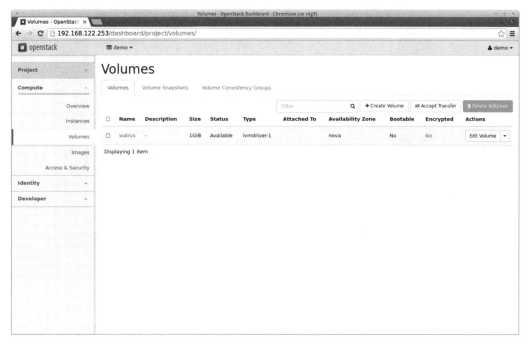

Figure 8.5   A volume called "walrus" has been created.

this test by creating a 1GB volume to attach to our instance. The availability zone is identical to the one in compute (Nova) and currently must match the zone where the instance you wish to attach it to resides. In our deployment scenario we only have a single availability zone, so the default of nova should remain selected.

When you have finished, you can click on Create Volume in order to begin volume creation. You will be returned to the Volumes page of the dashboard, which will show your new volume as you can see in Figure 8.5.

Attaching a Volume

A volume on its own is not of much value, so we'll now want to attach it to a compute instance. If you do not have an instance running, you can create a basic one with a CirrOS image now in the Instances dashboard. Refer back to Chapter 6 if you need a refresher on the steps to create an instance.

Attaching a volume in the dashboard is done by going to the drop-down menu on the right side of where your volume is listed. From that menu, select Manage Attachments to bring up the screen, where you can attach the volume to an instance (Figure 8.6).

In this example we have an instance running called "giraffe" and the UUID is also included, since names can be reused in compute (Nova). There is also an optional Device Name section where you can define what you want the device to be named when it's attached to the instance. This can safely be left blank and a name will be assigned automatically. When you're done selecting the instance to attach to, click on Attach Volume.

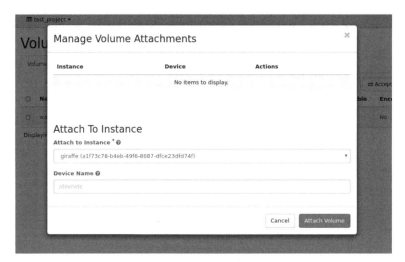

Figure 8.6   Managing volume attachments

When the volume completes attaching, you will be able to see it in the dashboard as "Attached to" with the instance name and the device it has shown up as (see Figure 8.7).

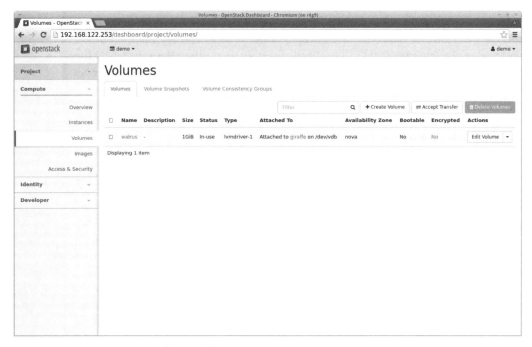

Figure 8.7   A volume has been attached.

You'll next want to log into the instance to see that the device has been attached success-fully, but this process is the same whether you're completing this process with the dashboard or through the command line. You can continue to learn the process for attaching a volume using the OpenStack Client on the command line, or skip to the "Using the Volume" section later in this chapter to see what you can do to use your new volume.

Creating and Attaching a Volume: OpenStack Client

As we've discussed previously, the dashboard can be a convenient way to interact with OpenStack to complete most of the simple operations you may need to do. You will find, however, that most operators prefer using the command line clients or SDKs to interface with the tooling. As such, we'll now walk through the same process we did with the dashboard but instead using the OpenStack Client (OSC).

The OSC is small and can easily be run from any system that has access to the API endpoints for the services. In our deployment scenarios, this means it must be on the same network as your controller node. You must also have access to the /etc/openrc.test file that was created on your controller and compute nodes, so for these commands we will assume you're running everything on your controller.

Creating a Volume

We will be using the test user in order to create this volume, since it will also be attach-ing to a compute instance owned by the test user. To begin, we'll bring the environment variables for the test user in from the openrc file. Then we can issue the command to create a 1GB instance using that storage back end. Aside from the name, we will be using the same specifications for creation of the volume as was used with the OpenStack dashboard (Horizon), which means creating a 1GB volume that is empty (no partition table, filesystem or data) and is in our default availability zone, called nova.

> **Tip**
>
> You'll notice that OpenStack commands often output a lot of detail that doesn't fit well on the pages of a book. A GitHub repository of much of this command output sorted by chapter is available at https://github.com/DeploymentsBook/scripts-and-configs.

```
$ source /etc/openrc.test
$ openstack volume create --size 1 --availability-zone nova seaotter
+--------------------+--------------------------------------+
| Field              | Value                                |
+--------------------+--------------------------------------+
| attachments        | []                                   |
| availability_zone  | nova                                 |
| bootable           | false                                |
| consistencygroup_id | None                                |
| created_at         | 2016-04-15T04:19:46.086611           |
| description        | None                                 |
| encrypted          | False                                |
| id                 | 53372cc5-087a-4342-a67b-397477e1a4f2 |
| multiattach        | False                                |
| name               | seaotter                             |
```

```
| properties        |                                          |
| replication_status | disabled                                |
| size              | 1                                        |
| snapshot_id       | None                                     |
| source_volid      | None                                     |
| status            | creating                                 |
| type              | None                                     |
| updated_at        | None                                     |
| user_id           | aa347b98f1734f66b1331784241fa15a         |
+-------------------+------------------------------------------+
```

To confirm this volume has been created, you can run a command to list the volumes (Listing 8.1).

As you can see, both the walrus and the seaotter volumes are listed here since they were both created in this chapter. The walrus volume is showing that it is attached to the giraffe instance.

If you need to make changes to a volume, use the `openstack volume set` command. Running that command alone will give you help output to assist you with making changes to all the parameters before the volume is attached.

Attaching a Volume

As mentioned earlier, you can't do much with a volume if it's not attached to an instance. You'll now want to add your new volume to an instance. First you'll want to see what instances are available:

```
$ openstack server list
+--------------------------------------+---------+--------+-----------------+
| ID                                   | Name    | Status | Networks        |
+--------------------------------------+---------+--------+-----------------+
| 823f2d7a-f186-4453-874d-4021ff2b22e4 | giraffe | ACTIVE | private=10.0.0.3 |
+--------------------------------------+---------+--------+-----------------+
```

With confirmation that you have an instance running, you can now run the command to attach the seaotter volume to the giraffe instance:

```
$ openstack server add volume giraffe seaotter
```

This command will have no output, but the next time you run `volume list` you will see that the volume has been attached (Listing 8.2).

Since the giraffe instance already had the walrus volume attached as /dev/vdb, you will notice that it has attached the seaotter volume as /dev/vdc.

Congratulations, you have successfully added a Cinder block storage volume to an instance on the command line!

Using the Volume

Whether you used the OpenStack dashboard or the command line to create and attach your volume, we will now want to actually confirm the volume was attached and then go ahead and use it with our instance. It may be easiest to use the console in dashboard in order to run the following commands, but if you followed instructions in an earlier chapter so that your CirrOS instance has been set up for SSH (Secure Shell), feel free to use SSH instead.

Listing 8.1

```
$ openstack volume list
+--------------------------------------+--------------+-----------+------+------------------------------+
| ID                                   | Display Name | Status    | Size | Attached to                  |
+--------------------------------------+--------------+-----------+------+------------------------------+
| 53372cc5-087a-4342-a67b-397477e1a4f2 | seaotter     | available |    1 |                              |
| 54447e7a-d39d-4186-a5b4-3a5fc1e773aa | walrus       | in-use    |    1 | Attached to giraffe on /dev/vdb |
+--------------------------------------+--------------+-----------+------+------------------------------+
```

Listing 8.2

```
$ openstack volume list
+--------------------------------------+--------------+--------+------+------------------------------+
| ID                                   | Display Name | Status | Size | Attached to                  |
+--------------------------------------+--------------+--------+------+------------------------------+
| 53372cc5-087a-4342-a67b-397477e1a4f2 | seaotter     | in-use |    1 | Attached to giraffe on /dev/vdc |
| 54447e7a-d39d-4186-a5b4-3a5fc1e773aa | walrus       | in-use |    1 | Attached to giraffe on /dev/vdb |
+--------------------------------------+--------------+--------+------+------------------------------+
```

Assuming you're using the dashboard, navigate to the Instances screen in the OpenStack dashboard and in the drop-down menu to the right of the instance you attached it to, select Console to bring you to a console for your instance. Once you're on the console page, if you're unable to type in the console, click Click here to show only console and you will be brought to a page that only has the console.

Follow the instructions to log into the instance, and run the following command:

```
$ dmesg
```

There will likely be a lot of output, but the last thing you are likely to see should be something like the following:

```
[  648.143431]  vdb: unknown partition table
```

This vdb device is your new block storage (Cinder) volume! At this phase it has no partition table or filesystem, so this will need to be set up using fdisk. Assuming the device is vdb in this example, partitioning can be done with `fdisk`:

```
$ sudo fdisk /dev/vdb
Device contains neither a valid DOS partition table, nor Sun, SGI or OSF disklabel
Building a new DOS disklabel with disk identifier 0xcf80b0a5.
Changes will remain in memory only, until you decide to write them.
After that, of course, the previous content won't be recoverable.

Warning: invalid flag 0x0000 of partition table 4 will be corrected by w(rite)

Command (m for help): n
Partition type:
   p   primary (0 primary, 0 extended, 4 free)
   e   extended
Select (default p): p
Partition number (1-4, default 1): 1
First sector (2048-2097151, default 2048): 2048
Last sector, +sectors or +size{K,M,G} (2048-2097151, default 2097151): 2097151

Command (m for help): p

Disk /dev/vdb: 1073 MB, 1073741824 bytes
16 heads, 63 sectors/track, 2080 cylinders, total 2097152 sectors
Units = sectors of 1 * 512 = 512 bytes
Sector size (logical/physical): 512 bytes / 512 bytes
I/O size (minimum/optimal): 512 bytes / 512 bytes
Disk identifier: 0xcf80b0a5

   Device Boot      Start         End      Blocks   Id  System
/dev/vdb1            2048     2097151     1047552   83  Linux
Command (m for help): w
The partition table has been altered!

Calling ioctl() to re-read partition table.
Syncing disks.
```

Now you'll want to create a basic filesystem on the new disk. It's only a 1GB volume, and this is a demonstration, so we'll use the ext2 filesystem:

```
$ sudo mkfs.ext2 /dev/vdb1
mke2fs 1.42.2 (27-Mar-2012)
Filesystem label=
OS type: Linux
Block size=4096 (log=2)
Fragment size=4096 (log=2)
Stride=0 blocks, Stripe width=0 blocks
65536 inodes, 261888 blocks
13094 blocks (5.00%) reserved for the super user
First data block=0
Maximum filesystem blocks=268435456
8 block groups
32768 blocks per group, 32768 fragments per group
8192 inodes per group
Superblock backups stored on blocks:
         32768, 98304, 163840, 229376

Allocating group tables: done
Writing inode tables: done
Writing superblocks and filesystem accounting information: done
```

The last step is creating a mount point and mounting your new volume. Let's say that you want to use this volume for photos and create a directory for that. Then we'll check to confirm it's the size we expect it to be.

```
$ mkdir photos
$ sudo mount /dev/vdb1 photos/
$ df -h | grep vdb1
/dev/vdb1            1006.9M     1.3M    954.5M   0% /home/cirros/photos
$ df -h /dev/vdb1
Filesystem             Size     Used Available Use% Mounted on
/dev/vdb1            1006.9M     1.3M    954.5M   0% /home/cirros/photos
```

Congratulations! A 1GB volume from the block storage service Cinder is now mounted on your system. Note that this was mounted using the root user, so you will need to either change the ownership to your user or use root to place files on it.

Tip

File permissions with block storage in Cinder can be a tricky thing to master. When using a Linux filesystem, files are referenced by user and group ID (UID and GID). Unless you are very diligent about keeping things consistent across your instances through something like custom images with default users and group or configuration management where IDs are specifically defined, these IDs can easily be different between machines.

As a result of these potential differences in IDs, mounting a volume from the block storage device on one instance and then detaching it to add it to another instance may land you in a situation where the ownership of files looks all wrong. Keep this in mind as you begin experimenting with moving volumes and always make checking permissions a step in your plans to move a volume to another instance.

Automation

As we explained in our chapters about private and public clouds, you don't only need to interact with OpenStack through the OpenStack dashboard or OpenStack client. Instead you may interact with the APIs through various SDKs, which you can learn about at http://developer.openstack.org/.

Summary

The need for expanding and moving storage of data is growing in modern environments, and Cinder block storage fits that need. It offers a variety of storage back-end drivers to support everything from open source tooling like LVM and Ceph to a host of tested proprietary storage solutions from an array of vendors. The deployment scenario using Puppet walked you through creating a volume and then attaching it to an instance where you could use it.

9

Object Storage Cloud

I paint objects as I think them, not as I see them.
Pablo Picasso

As explained in Chapter 8, "Block Storage Cloud," OpenStack provides two core ways for handling storage: object and block storage. Block storage is typically where you mount a storage device as an actual filesystem on your server. Object storage instead hosts individual files that are then referenced from within your application and accessed using a REST API. This means that instead of hosting files on a flat filesystem as in block storage, object storage enables storing of individual files, or objects, in a highly redundant and available storage system. Using an object store also enables you to tune access to these files through access control and make them selectively available across your platform.

This chapter walks you through the key concepts of using OpenStack Swift. From there, you create a very basic object storage configuration on your controller that you can then access and interact with via the Horizon dashboard and from your compute node.

Uses

Swift object storage was one of the two original OpenStack projects, the other being Nova. The fact that it was one of the original projects demonstrates how important object storage is to the vision of many cloud deployments.

As soon as object storage is made available to an organization, uses for it start cropping up. From building a system of shared documents around an object store or giving flexibility to developers to include files in their applications without having to worry about data access or integrity, being able to store files on a trusted, redundant storage system is valuable throughout an organization.

Web Hosting Company

There have been many strategies that web hosting companies have employed over the years to make their platforms highly available and make the most efficient use of resources. One of the latest is storing images and other binary objects in a managed object store rather than hosting them on individual filesystems.

By leveraging an object store, these companies and organizations have been able to benefit from the built-in redundancy and access to these resources should certain hardware components fail. They are also able to employ broad back-up strategies that are no longer completed on a per customer or per server basis, but instead back up all of the objects used by customers at once. They're also able to collectively use space allocated to all customers rather than leaving extra space available on flat filesystems that may never be used, thus reducing the amount of storage that is required overall.

File Sync and Sharing

There are several companies today that seek to make the sharing of files between individuals and companies easier by offering services that provide a link to a shared file that has been uploaded.

By using object storage with Swift in your organization, this can be done in-house with full control over your data. In this model, Swift is the storage and organization mechanism with an API for accessing the files. A user interface is built up around it so users can manually upload, share and access files. Going one step further, desktop and smartphone interfaces may also be developed to sync files between devices, such as photos taken on your phone or a music collection that is primarily managed on a desktop.

Log Storage

Log storage is a problem that's common across many industries, whether you're storing logs from servers or report logs from a space station. The OpenStack project infrastructure team doesn't yet have logs from any space stations, but the infrastructure for testing OpenStack does produce several gigabytes of storage per day in logs. For a long time, these were stored on a flat filesystem on a block volume and served by a basic web server. At some point, the team reached the maximum amount of storage available from the cloud providers and needed a solution to store more without the additional systems administration overhead of managing multiple log storage servers.

The team decided to use Swift for object storage. In this system, logs that come out of the build system are named using their build numbers then uploaded to Swift. From there they can be presented as a web listing index with their build numbers and made available to developers through a link in the code review system. All maintenance of storage has been off-loaded to the cloud provider running the Swift cluster, and the members of the infrastructure team no longer have to worry about the log server filesystem filling up or not having enough space in the long term. The infrastructure team can now focus on solving more interesting and complex problems rather than being troubled by the more mundane systems administration tasks. This holds true for developers and other contributors who produce files in an organization as well. You want them to focus on working with things they were hired to do, not worrying about things like file storage.

Requirements

As with the past chapters, in this deployment scenario you'll be using the controller and compute nodes you created in Chapter 5, "Foundations for Deployments." We will be uploading a series of small, simple files to the controller and the minimum specifications defined in that chapter will easily support this.

Select Components

In this scenario, we will be adding the components required for Swift Object storage. These will be in addition to the components we already have so we can offer a satisfying deployment scenario, but be aware that Swift can run independently of many of these components. As an example, you don't need a separate compute instance to take advantage of referencing objects stored in Swift. You can access Swift objects from any platform.

Using our Puppet configurations, your two node deployment scenario will have the following, placement of which is shown in Figure 9.1:

- Compute (Nova)
- Identity (Keystone)
- Networking (Neutron)
- Image service (Glance)
- Dashboard (Horizon)
- Swift (Object Storage)

Key Concepts

Before diving into using Swift, there are some key concepts that should be covered, but we will only do a simple overview of concepts you are likely to encounter. Advanced configuration will vary considerably based on your storage environment and a considerable amount has already been written about how things like the Ring and storage clusters actually work.

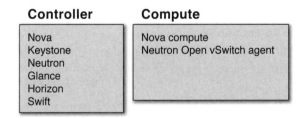

Figure 9.1   Components of a two-system OpenStack deployment with Swift object storage

Storage and Clusters

Swift operates as a cluster. A production cluster will span storage devices and zones where data is stored. As we'll discuss, you will be using Rings to map where data is located on your cluster so Swift components like the proxy-server and object-replicator find the actual device to store, retrieve or replicate your data.

> **Tip**
>
> Swift is built to distribute the files over a large number of commodity servers and directly attached disk drives to provide inexpensive, redundant and fast storage.
>
> As such, using Network-Attached Storage (NAS) for Swift is unnecessary because it introduces the potential for higher latency and possible overlap of redundancy that Swift already attempts to provide.
>
> However if it's more convenient in your environment, you may use NAS storage with Swift.

As we'll review later when we pull the components together, there are four different types of daemons in Swift: Proxy, Account, Container and Object. These are often deployed together, and a production cluster is made up of multiple physical proxy and storage nodes. In Figure 9.2 later in this chapter, you should imagine the Swift API ultimately connecting to any of these servers in the cluster with your containers and back ends, depending on the actions performed and objects you're requesting.

Rings

As you configure Swift you'll quickly become familiar with the concept of the Ring. It can be considered part database and part configuration file. Rings are used to determine where your data should reside on the Swift object storage cluster and describe options like the number of times data is replicated across the cluster. Rings exist for various layers of your cluster, with Rings existing for account and container databases, as well as handling individual object storage policies. They are built and managed with a Swift utility called ring-builder.

While you're getting started with the Ring, you'll also become familiar with the concepts of devices, partitions, replicas and zones which the Ring uses for its mapping of objects onto the physical location.

- **Zones**—Distinct, physically and operationally separated locations for data. A zone may be a rack or groups of racks of hardware that has its own power and connectivity separate from other zones. Beyond Zones you may also have Regions, which isolate the data further.
- **Devices**—The physical storage location for data, typically a disk. Devices can be weighted so that, for instance, bigger drives are assigned a higher weight and smaller drives a smaller weight. Throughout the standard life cycle of hard drives, you will add and remove devices from a Swift cluster.
- **Partitions**—Objects are located on Swift partitions. Partitions are what are replicated. The administrative documentation for Swift recommends a minimum of 100 partitions per drive to make sure there is even distribution across the drives and provides advice about calculating the number of partitions per drive. Be cautious not

to make it too high, since it increases replication time. Also note that these partitions are different than the disk partitions you are already familiar with.

- **Replicas**—These control how many times you want Swift to store your data across the cluster to ensure redundancy. The default is three.

This is a very basic introduction to Rings. The Swift Developer documentation located at http://docs.openstack.org/developer/swift/ contains a considerable amount of documentation that dives deep into storage decisions, Ring preparation and management and more. Of particular interest with regard to Rings are the "Swift Architectural Overview," which provides more detail about where the Rings play a role in a high level and "The Rings" section of the manual, which provides an in-depth description of the Rings. Finally, you will want to reference the "Deployment Guide" section of the Administrator Documentation, which provides an overview of service distribution and steps for manual Ring creation, manipulation and distribution.

Objects and Containers

As we've discussed, Swift is an object storage system. An object is a file of any type that you wish to store somewhere. This may be an image, a log, an mp3 or anything else. These objects are stored in what Swift calls a container, which is a collection of objects.

A container has specific attributes to define who has access to it and whether it is publicly available. These containers are stored in what Swift calls an account, which is a collection of containers. Accounts are the root storage location for data.

Container: An Overloaded Term

In Chapter 11, "Controlling Containers," we discuss using containers in OpenStack, but these are different containers than we talk about here.

As you can see from the architecture diagram, Swift has a concept of containers, referring to where you will place objects. However, broadly speaking, in OpenStack and in our later chapter, containers instead refer to technologies like Docker and Kubernetes, which provide an isolated operating system environment for running applications.

As you'll see later in this chapter, the container term in OpenStack Client (OSC) refers to the usage in Swift.

While we're on the topic of overloaded terms, there are a couple more. Regions in Swift are different than regions in Keystone. As briefly mentioned earlier, partitions in Swift are also not the same thing as your standard disk partitions.

Connecting to Swift

Interaction with Swift, like other components of OpenStack, is done through the API. The API communicates with a Swift proxy, which looks up the location of the account, container, or object in the ring and will complete the action accordingly. A basic demonstration of how this works is shown in Figure 9.2. While not shown in the figure, note that a cluster is made up of multiple servers all containing objects which are replicated across the cluster.

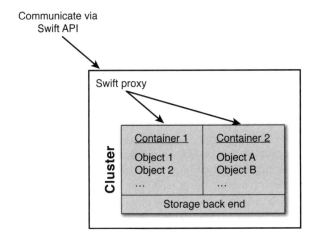

Figure 9.2   Overview of connecting to Swift.

A storage back end is typically multiple servers with disks, but it's flexible enough to be anything from a loopback filesystem for demonstration to NAS devices. In our deployment scenario we will use a simple trio of XFS filesystems mounted on our controller as a loopback device. This is only done for demonstration purposes so we can stay within our two-system and limited-resources constraints. A series of loopback devices like this would never be used in production because there is no fault tolerance.

Fault Tolerance

Discussed briefly when we talked about The Ring, engineers working on Swift have put a lot of work into redundancy and fault tolerance. We're not covering it in depth here and our deployment scenario does not address it, but the following is a quick primer.

Swift stores replicas of data across as many unique failure domains as possible. A failure domain is an area of the network impacted when a device or service experiences problems. This is handled by placing each series of devices in separate Swift zones.

Consider the simple scenario of using three isolated racks of servers, represented as three zones, with the default of three as the replica setting for the Swift cluster. Swift will store a replica (copy) of the object in each zone. If one of your isolated racks goes down, you are guaranteed that Swift still has two copies of the object in the other zones, so you can still access the object.

When the devices in your deployment are loopback devices in a single disk—as in our deployment scenario—if the disk has gone, all replicas go missing at once. But at this point, most of OpenStack is also gone as well, since everything but compute is running on your single controller.

Scenario

Just like we showed in Chapter 8, you can now offer real persistent storage to your users. This time we're providing storage in the form of objects rather than a filesystem, so this is particularly valuable for a series of individual files that you wish to access externally. Since we're adding an additional component, a bit of setup needs to be done with Puppet again to configure this storage.

> **Warning**
>
> Don't re-use your systems from Chapter 7, "Public Compute Cloud," or Chapter 8 without reinstalling since this example will remove the Ceilometer or Cinder components from your install.
>
> If you're looking to run all of these services together, see Chapter 12, "A Whole Cloud."

Controller Node Setup

Using your Controller and Compute nodes available from Chapter 5, you will only need to run a single command to add the support for Swift object storage. Additionally, in this scenario you will only need to make changes to the controller node. No modifications need to be made to the compute node.

The following is the puppet apply command that will process your foundational object storage role in Puppet:

```
$ sudo puppet apply /etc/puppet/modules/deployments/manifests/role/foundations_object_storage.pp
```

Depending on the speed of your systems and network, this will take some time as it downloads everything required for Swift and sets up configurations. If anything goes wrong and this command fails, Puppet can also be run with the --debug flag to show more detail.

While this is running, we can explore what this foundations_object_storage.pp file contains:

```
class deployments::role::foundations_object_storage {
  include deployments::role::foundations
  include deployments::profile::swift
}

include deployments::role::foundations_object_storage
```

As you have seen before, this is calling our foundations role to make sure all the basic components are installed. This is primarily for safety, and it is still recommended you follow the steps in Chapter 5 in order to make sure it has run without errors. It then includes the profile for Swift itself, which you can view on the controller filesystem at /etc/puppet/modules/deployments/manifests/profile/swift.pp and contains the following:

```
cat

class deployments::profile::swift
{
  include ::memcached
  include ::swift
```

```
include ::swift::keystone::auth
include ::swift::proxy
include ::swift::proxy::account_quotas
include ::swift::proxy::authtoken
include ::swift::proxy::cache
include ::swift::proxy::catch_errors
include ::swift::proxy::container_quotas
include ::swift::proxy::formpost
include ::swift::proxy::healthcheck
include ::swift::proxy::keystone
include ::swift::proxy::proxy_logging
include ::swift::proxy::ratelimit
include ::swift::proxy::staticweb
include ::swift::proxy::tempurl
include ::swift::proxy::tempauth
include ::swift::ringbuilder
include ::swift::storage::all

$swift_components = ['account', 'container', 'object']
swift::storage::filter::recon { $swift_components : }
swift::storage::filter::healthcheck { $swift_components : }

file { '/srv/node':
  ensure  => directory,
  owner   => 'swift',
  group   => 'swift',
  require => Package['swift'],
}

$loopback_devices = hiera('swift_loopback_devices', {})
if ! empty($loopback_devices) {
  create_resources('swift::storage::loopback', $loopback_devices)
}

$object_devices = hiera('swift_ring_object_devices', {})
if ! empty($object_devices) {
  create_resources('ring_object_device', $object_devices)
}
$container_devices = hiera('swift_ring_container_devices', {})
if ! empty($container_devices) {
  create_resources('ring_container_device', $container_devices)
}
$account_devices = hiera('swift_ring_account_devices', {})
if ! empty($account_devices) {
  create_resources('ring_account_device', $account_devices)
}

}
```

As you can see, we're pulling in quite a lot and then doing some configuration required for Swift to use a local storage point for the objects we'll be adding to it. We pull in memcached, which is used for caching specific types of lookups, such as auth tokens and whether a container or account you're referencing exists. It is not used for caching objects themselves. Just like other services, we'll be using Keystone for authentication, so we need to make sure Keystone support is included. In our deployment we're also pulling in all the storage mechanisms (`storage::all`) so you can work with them, but note we are using a series of three XFS loopback devices in this deployment example.

We're also pulling in various proxy manifests. Going through them one by one, you have:

- `account_quotas`—Provides the ability to set quotas on accounts (a Swift "account" corresponds to a Keystone "project," aka "tenant"). Note that the accounts themselves are part of Keystone.
- `authtoken`—The standard token support for authentication.
- `cache`—Support for caching, using memcached, for specific types of lookups.
- `catch_errors`—Catches errors occurring in proxy pipeline and translates it to corresponding error reporting.
- `container_quotas`—Provides the ability to set quotas on specific containers.
- `formpost`—Support for uploading objects using an HTML form POST.
- `healthcheck`—A simple tool to monitor whether the Swift proxy server is alive, and also used when adding multiple proxies to a load balancer.
- `keystoneauth`—Used to manage keystone middleware for the Swift proxy.
- `proxy_logging`—Provides custom logging for all external API requests made to the proxy server.
- `ratelimit`—Support for ratelimiting for both account and container so it can prevent a single account from using up too much resources in the cluster.
- `staticweb`—Support for the Swift static web middleware for creating static web sites.
- `tempurl`—Support for temporary access to objects.
- `tempauth`—Reference middleware to create custom authentication component. This should never be used in production but is useful for development and testing.

The final section of the Puppet profile for Swift sets up the XFS loopback devices (1-3) that will be used to store the objects we create for the containers.

Finally, Rings were discussed earlier in the chapter, and by calling the Swift ring-builder manifest we can manage these Rings.

> **Warning**
>
> Our deployment scenario is only an example and does not have the characteristics to make it production-ready. As such, our configuration of Rings using this module is also not production-ready, so be cautious here when you work to configure this for a real deployment. If the Puppet Swift module is not used correctly, the rings will be different on each host, and there is a high chance that the durability of the data is at risk.

> There are architecture changes being proposed to the Puppet module by members of the Swift team at the time of writing. These will make using the module easier and more accurate, as well as help protect operators from misconfiguration. The Puppet configuration may change considerably in the future.
>
> Rather than using the Puppet module, in many deployments the Rings are instead built somewhat manually and then copied to all nodes. This requires a deeper dive into using the ring-builder rather than the Puppet module than we're able to provide in this chapter, but it may be a better option for your deployment.
>
> As you prepare for your own deployment, also be sure to refer back to the "Key Concepts" section earlier in the chapter, and do your own more in-depth research about storage decisions you need to make.

Now let's get back to the Puppet command you ran. Once this command completes, you'll be ready to add files to your object storage and start sharing them.

Creating a Container and Object: Dashboard

In order to use Swift object storage, you'll first want to create a container to hold your objects. This is done in the Horizon dashboard by logging in with your test user and navigating to Object Store in the menu on the left.

From this screen, click the button labeled Container with a plus sign next to it, which will get you to the Create Container screen show in Figure 9.3.

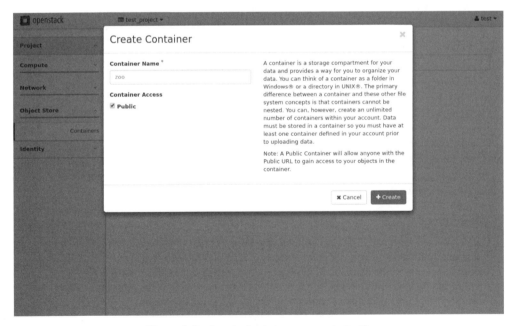

Figure 9.3   Create Container screen in Swift

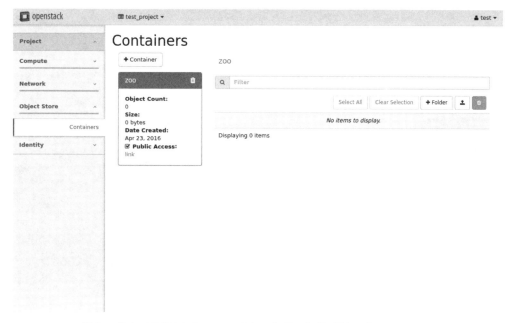

Figure 9.4   Looking at your container in the Swift Object Store screen.

Since a container is a collection of objects, let's call this one "zoo" and fill it with a bunch of animal-themed files. Also check the box that says "public" so that the container will be available outside of OpenStack via http. We'll be using this later in the chapter to display an object on a web page.

Once you click Create you will be sent back to the Object Store page where you can click the name of your container and see details about it as seen in Figure 9.4.

Now we actually want to add objects to your container. Remember, an object is just a file so you can upload all kinds of things as objects. As a simple test, we'll start with a simple text file. On the same machine you're running your web browser on to access the Horizon dashboard, open up a terminal and create a simple text file:

```
$ echo "Black and white striped African equid" > zebra.txt
```

Click the icon with the up arrow on it to the left of the red trash icon to upload this object. The Upload File To: zoo screen in Figure 9.5 will pop up to enable you to select the file from your filesystem and upload it. Click Upload File to complete this action.

You can do this a few times to upload several different types of files. Add an image file into the mix to use later in the chapter for a real world example of including an image on a web site. Since the Swift logo is a bird, we have uploaded eagle.jpg. A listing of files in the zoo container can be seen in Figure 9.6.

To learn more about a specific object, like size and content type, look to the right of the object and click the down arrow next to Download. Select the option that says View Details.

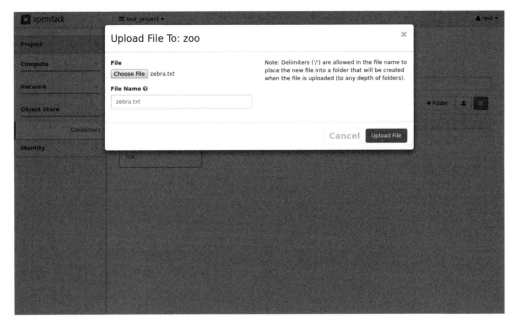

Figure 9.5   Create Container screen

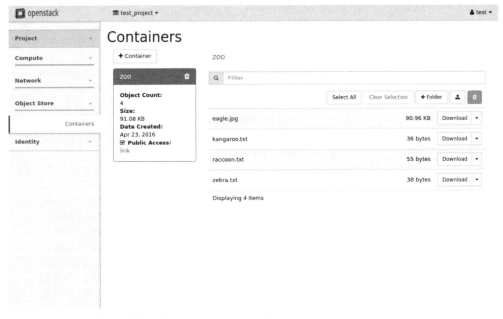

Figure 9.6   Object Store screen with zoo container and contents

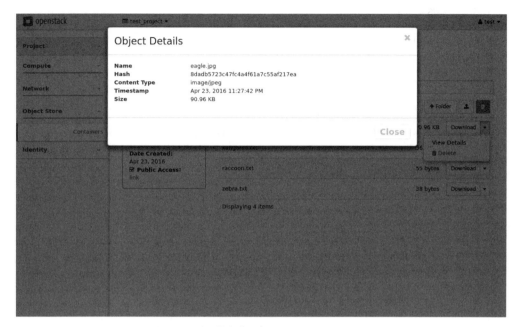

Figure 9.7   Details about an object in Swift

As shown in Figure 9.7, this will bring up a screen giving you basic information about the object.

Now that you have successfully created a container and added an object, you may continue to learn the process for creating a container and object using the OpenStack Client on the command line or skip to the "Using an Object" section later in this chapter to see how to use the objects you've created in a real-world example.

Creating a Container and Object: OpenStack Client

The Dashboard is a convenient way to interact with OpenStack, but the OpenStack client and the language-specific APIs enable you to effectively script these actions and do so on deployments that don't include the Horizon dashboard. This is particularly valuable when you're running Swift in a standalone deployment that does not include many of the other OpenStack components. For the sake of simplicity, log into the controller node in order to complete these actions.

Reminder

As with previous chapters, output from our OpenStack commands in this chapter is made available for copying and easier readability online in a GitHub repository sorted by chapter at https://github.com/DeploymentsBook/scripts-and-configs.

The first thing we'll want to do is use our test user to create a container where our objects will live. The test user will also be used to add objects to this container:

```
$ source /etc/openrc.test
$ openstack container create aquarium
+------------------------------------+-----------+----------------------------------+
| account                            | container | x-trans-id                       |
+------------------------------------+-----------+----------------------------------+
| KEY_33a65b0402b047c097d21864b72c06be | aquarium  | tx8d138f08d743482a88735-00571c050f |
+------------------------------------+-----------+----------------------------------+
```

Now we'll create a couple of simple text file objects to add to the container:

```
$ echo "An eight-legged cephalopod mollusc" > octopus.txt
$ echo "Common member of the sub-grouping of the mackerel family" > tuna.txt
```

Now add these objects to the container called aquarium:

```
$ openstack object create aquarium octopus.txt
+-------------+-----------+----------------------------------+
| object      | container | etag                             |
+-------------+-----------+----------------------------------+
| octopus.txt | aquarium  | 22d8654098afd1eeb1d22c5801c5466d |
+-------------+-----------+----------------------------------+
$ openstack object create aquarium tuna.txt
+----------+-----------+----------------------------------+
| object   | container | etag                             |
+----------+-----------+----------------------------------+
| tuna.txt | aquarium  | 1bef3811c46128a7b5d48d46ff04d9de |
+----------+-----------+----------------------------------+
```

To show these objects in the container, use the list command:

```
$ openstack object list aquarium
+-------------+
| Name        |
+-------------+
| octopus.txt |
| tuna.txt    |
+-------------+
```

> **Tip**
>
> Use the --long flag with the openstack object list command to get basic details about the files in the container.

You can also show details about the container itself, including how much storage is being used on it and the number of objects:

```
$ openstack container show aquarium
+--------------+----------------------------------------+
| Field        | Value                                  |
+--------------+----------------------------------------+
| account      | KEY_33a65b0402b047c097d21864b72c06be   |
| bytes_used   | 92                                     |
| container    | aquarium                               |
| object_count | 2                                      |
+--------------+----------------------------------------+
```

Let's say you've also added an image of an animal to your container, Swift will show you the attributes of that object with `object show`:

```
$ openstack object show aquarium dolphin.jpg
+----------------+------------------------------------+
| Field          | Value                              |
+----------------+------------------------------------+
| account        | KEY_33a65b0402b047c097d21864b72c06be |
| container      | aquarium                           |
| content-length | 172154                             |
| content-type   | image/jpeg                         |
| etag           | 3b67f3cdf756bc0e3df05820398251bb   |
| last-modified  | Sat, 23 Apr 2016 23:43:15 GMT      |
| object         | dolphin.jpg                        |
| properties     | Orig-Filename='dolphin.jpg'        |
+----------------+------------------------------------+
```

As you can see, this will show you the type of file (image/jpeg), size, date it was modified and more.

Using an Object

Whether you used the Horizon dashboard or OSC to create your objects, you'll now want to actually use that object. The first step will be making sure your container is public, and then you'll want to figure out the address for a particular file in it. In the dashboard, navigate to Object Store, Containers to view the zoo container you created earlier. Click zoo and make sure there is a check mark next to Public Access as shown in Figure 9.8.

Now click the Public Access link, which should bring you to a URL that looks something like the following:

```
http://10.190.0.8:8080/v1/KEY_33a65b0402b047c097d21864b72c06be/zoo
```

The 10.190.0.8 is the address of the server where your Swift proxy server daemon is running. Since both the dashboard and Swift (specifically, the Swift proxy server) are running on the controller in our scenario, this is the same address as your dashboard.

Figure 9.8   A container with Public Access enabled

Now, append the object name you wish to reference to it to load up your object in your browser. For instance, I have uploaded eagle.jpg image so I will use the following address to get to that object:

```
http://10.190.0.8:8080/v1/KEY_33a65b0402b047c097d21864b72c06be/zoo/eagle.jpg
```

If you'd rather use the OpenStack Client (OSC) for this, you can look to see if there is a read-acl set using the `container show` command:

```
$ source /etc/openrc.test
$ openstack container show zoo
+--------------+------------------------------------+
| Field        | Value                              |
+--------------+------------------------------------+
| account      | KEY_33a65b0402b047c097d21864b72c06be |
| bytes_used   | 93268                              |
| container    | zoo                                |
| object_count | 4                                  |
| read_acl     | .r:*,.rlistings                    |
+--------------+------------------------------------+
```

If the output does not contain the read_acl line, you can set it with the following Swift client command:

```
$ swift post -r .r:*,.rlistings zoo
```

If you run the show command again, it should have this line.

Now you'll want to craft the URL to access your object. This is in the following format, replacing the IP address with the correct one for your environment, and "account" and "container" with the values from the show command. The "object_name" will be the object you wish to reference (like eagle.jpg):

```
http://10.190.0.8:8080/v1/account/container/object_name
```

The result will look something like this:

```
http://10.190.0.8:8080/v1/KEY_33a65b0402b047c097d21864b72c06be/zoo/eagle.jpg
```

This can be loaded into your browser, where you should see the image, but it can also be included in a web page, like we'll demonstrate next.

Object in a Web Page

To do a more real-world demonstration, we've created a repository that includes a simple HTML file that you can use on an Ubuntu instance. Using your preferred method, follow the instructions outlined in Chapter 6, "Private Compute Cloud," for launching an Ubuntu 14.04 compute node. You may also want to add a floating IP address to the instance to improve access.

Once that node is running, you can run the following on your controller or wherever your SSH key is for your Ubuntu instance. Replace 10.190.0.8 with the correct address for the instance you've brought up:

```
$ git clone https://github.com/DeploymentsBook/http-files.git
$ scp -r http-files/swift/ ubuntu@10.190.0.8:
```

> **Tip**
>
> If you have configured your instances to be online via a real public floating IP address, you
> can clone the repository directly on the instance and have no need to scp the files over.
> We haven't made the assumption in these deployment scenarios that your instances have
> Internet access, so this is how we've configured things.

You will now have a swift directory in the ubuntu user home directory of your instance.
You will want to edit the swift/index.html file to include the URL for your object in
Swift, so take the URL you created earlier with your image and add it to the img src
line like so:

```
<img src="http://10.190.0.8:8080/v1/KEY_d49446773bfb47bab30b3c4bca06d82d/zoo/eagle.jpg"
alt="Image loaded from Swift">
```

To launch a simple http server, run the following on your instance:

```
$ cd swift
$ python -m SimpleHTTPServer
Serving HTTP on 0.0.0.0 port 8000 ...
```

As you can see, by default, this will load a simple HTTP server using Python on
port 8000. You can navigate to this on a system that has access to your instance by navigating to http://10.190.0.8:8000 in your browser, where 10.190.0.8 is the IP of your instance,
or your floating IP. The resulting page will look something like what you see in Figure 9.9.

Congratulations! You have now used an image object served up by Swift on a web page.

Welcome to the...

Common **OpenStack** Deployments

Swift Demonstration

Congratulations, this image is being served up by Swift:

If you followed the instructions in Chapter 9, "Object Storage Cloud" this will also be running on your Nova compute instance using a
simple Python HTTP server.

Common OpenStack Deployments is brought to you by Elizabeth K. Joseph and Matt Fischer.

Source for this page is made available here under the Apache License

Figure 9.9   A simple web site referencing an object from Swift

Beyond Swift

In this chapter we've focused heavily on OpenStack Swift object storage, but like much of the OpenStack ecosystem, this is not your only option. The popular distributed object store and filesystem Ceph is also frequently used with OpenStack deployments.

Summary

The capability to offer object storage to your users greatly extends the storage flexibility of your OpenStack deployment. You are now more informed about the rationale behind usage of object storage and understand the key components of Swift. Finally, we have demonstrated how to set up and add to a basic deployment scenario with Puppet and use the resulting objects stored in a real-world example.

10

Bare Metal Provisioning

If we want things to stay as they are, things will have to change
Giuseppe di Lampedusa, *The Leopard*

As OpenStack made inroads into more data centers, the next logical step for the OpenStack project was to better support that environment, and so began a bare metal provisioning project, Ironic. Ironic began as a plug-in for Nova compute but quickly spun into its own project as the scope increased, with the need for drivers for various hardware on which the service would be provisioned. With the first official release in OpenStack Kilo in the spring of 2015, today bare metal provisioning is used in production in several data centers and can actually be run independently from a broader OpenStack deployment.

Uses

The most obvious use for bare metal provisioning is in a data center where automated control of machines is valuable. Ironic makes handling the booting and day-to-day management of physical hardware just as easy as working with virtual machines. It enables physical hardware to use software images commonly used in a virtualized environment and provides a familiar environment and framework for users of OpenStack. Ironic has been used to deploy images of OpenStack nodes themselves, effectively enabling an operator to help install and provision pre-built, tested, qualified images to actual hardware.

Cloud Hosting Company

If a company is already using OpenStack in their infrastructure to provide cloud hosting services, Ironic is a natural fit. The bare metal service has a driver for Nova that offers Ironic hosts a sort of hypervisor which allows for variations to the underlying hardware to be presented to the user, such as super high memory, or GPU compute capabilities. By using this driver, instead of offering support for a virtualization technology, you get control over hardware that's being provisioned for customers. While you still need to provide basic information to Ironic to inventory your hardware, and it doesn't actually act as a formal configuration management database (CMDB), it vastly simplifies the management of the hardware.

Internal Cloud

An organization running an internal cloud deployment in a data center may find incredible value in management of their servers using Ironic. One of the most challenging parts of running an internal cloud for systems administrators can be handling the inventory of hardware, which Ironic makes easier by taking care of it once the initial enrollment is completed. With a few OpenStack commands, you can see the state of systems enrolled with Ironic, whether they are running or have failed in some way. For those failures, you can dig into the error messages to determine how to handle them further. An internal cloud doesn't have to be running on OpenStack to take advantage of Ironic, since Ironic can be run independently and manage hardware regardless of what software is ultimately deployed on it.

Database Hosting

Many of the concerns surrounding the hosting of databases on virtualized systems have been addressed with solutions like specifically tuned virtual machines that have hardware supporting high I/O and memory. However, this is still a hardware solution, and there are many instances where organizations continue to want to host databases directly on bare metal. Ironic can assist in these organizations by providing a provisioning mechanism for installation of database servers on demand. From there an organization can either leverage tooling such as OpenStack Trove, which provides an interface for databases as a service, or an internal solution for provisioning.

> **Tip**
>
> Interested in learning more about OpenStack Trove for databases as a service? Currently the developer documentation is your best source of overview, installation and usage information—http://docs.openstack.org/developer/trove/.

High-Performance Computing

In the realm of High-Performance Computing (HPC), where users are doing analytics processing or using their systems as render farms, Ironic has been used as a provisioning service. In these environments the full computing power of the system is being used, and so virtualization is not desired in most cases since the hypervisor introduces overhead that is unnecessary. Ironic deployed without the other components of OpenStack in this environment provides an effective way to manage the hardware in the HPC cluster, though there are many HPC users who are deploying Ironic with the Nova computing components and the Glance image service.

Architecture Overview

As a high-level overview, administration of Ironic is done through an API that calls out to a series of bare metal drivers that use common solutions like PXE (Preboot eXecution

Environment) and IPMI (Intelligent Platform Management Interface) to interact with the bare metal servers. These may also use one of the growing number of vendor-supported drivers for specific hardware. As briefly explained in Chapter 1, "What is OpenStack?" Ironic is comprised of several different services that work together to accomplish provisioning and hardware interaction.

The ironic-conductor, of which there are typically several instances of in a production deployment, is what truly drives Ironic. The conductor uses the messaging queue, typically RabbitMQ just like the other services use, to communicate with the API and vice-versa. When the conductor receives a message from the API it can then act upon it. The database also interacts with the API, but in a much more minimal way: to request status and complete the creation of new database entries, such as nodes and ports. The appropriate drivers for your environment running from the conductor, in turn, interact with the hardware.

The Ironic RESTful API is used by both the user enrolling hardware, which we will cover later, and the ironic-python-agent that will call the API to enable the conductor to know where the machine is located so the conductor can connect to the node being deployed. A database (MySQL by default) is used to store information about the servers and is updated by the RESTful API and by the ironic-conductor.

The vendor-contributed drivers may be open source or proprietary, but typically they provide the specific hooks into the existing management interfaces on the devices. For instance, the iLO drivers are built to work against specific versions of the iLO management engine on HPE ProLiant servers. These drivers use the existing HPE proliantutils Python utility libraries to assist with this interaction. The Cisco UCS driver is designed to be used with certain versions of the UCS Manager on managed Cisco UCS B/C series servers. The existing Python SDK developed for this management interface (UcsSdk) is

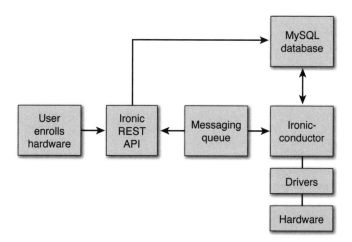

Figure 10.1   Ironic overview

leveraged to help with this interaction. Drivers may either have Ironic use built-in tooling, if it exists, or use standard tools like IPMI for the management of hardware. As the bare metal service has matured, a requirement for all included (otherwise known as "in-tree") drivers is that the vendors are doing continuous integration testing to ensure quality.

A developer-level overview of the various in-tree drivers is available at http://docs.openstack.org/developer/ironic/deploy/drivers.html.

Installation

We have used Puppet to orchestrate the deployments in this book. Due to the strong hardware nature of Ironic, it was determined there is not an example deployment that would be both valuable and versatile enough for inclusion in this book.

However, Puppet modules for Ironic do exist and are available with the rest of the Puppet modules. For Mitaka, see the branch at https://git.openstack.org/cgit/openstack/puppet-ironic/tree/?h=stable%2Fmitaka.

An example ironic.pp is included with that module to get you started. Configuration of your specific environment will depend heavily upon the hardware you have available, which again is why it's difficult for us to show a reference deployment. You can search through the available drivers to match up your hardware, or you can look at the SSH driver if you're really interested in doing a virtualized test.

Aside from Puppet, Ansible playbooks and Chef cookbooks are also available. See more about where to find these modules in Appendix B, "Other Deployment Mechanisms." A manual installation guide is provided in the Ironic developer documentation at http://docs.openstack.org/developer/ironic/deploy/install-guide.html.

Finally, if you just want to try it out, you can use Ironic with DevStack. Refer back to Chapter 2, "DevStack," for a refresher on how DevStack works, and then see the DevStack documentation for the current process for enabling the Ironic plug-in.

Bifrost

Bifrost is a set of Ansible-based configuration management scripts that are used to deploy Ironic independently from the rest of OpenStack. It strives to pull in as few OpenStack requirements as possible, to provide the closest thing to a standalone Ironic deployment as you're likely to find. Bifrost has developer documentation at http://docs.openstack.org/developer/bifrost/ that includes the location of the code repository and installation instructions.

Using Ironic

Once Ironic is installed, you'll likely want to enroll some hardware. Hardware enrollment is handled by a user who provides details about the hardware to the Ironic API. This is done by using the `ironic node-create` command and providing details about the system. The following example of enrollment will assume you're using hardware that has an IPMI interface.

> **Tip**
>
> As discussed earlier, there are various drivers for Ironic, from standards like IPMI to vendor-specific drivers, which can be proprietary or open source, and either live in the Ironic source code tree or not. The example being used here uses the abilities that IPMI has for Ironic. If you are using something like HPE iLO instead, you will want to look at the documentation for that driver to learn about the options required and supported, as well as the *versions* of hardware and firmware supported.

To get started, you will first want to load a Linux kernel executable (vmlinuz) into the Glance image service, as well as a Linux initial RAM disk (initrd). For example, consider the following:

```
$ openstack image create --public --disk-format aki --container-format aki \
my-vmlinuz < vmlinuz-custom
+------------------+------------------------------------------------------+
| Field            | Value                                                |
+------------------+------------------------------------------------------+
| checksum         | 79da4a6e81e2a8fd87d26620c45806c7                     |
| container_format | aki                                                  |
| created_at       | 2016-04-13T03:06:07Z                                 |
| disk_format      | aki                                                  |
| file             | /v2/images/ea003044-f792-408b-b6cd-46a701528c65/file |
| id               | ea003044-f792-408b-b6cd-46a701528c65                 |
| min_disk         | 0                                                    |
| min_ram          | 0                                                    |
| name             | my-vmlinuz                                           |
| owner            | 583e438e7fff4b33b3e52136f3a4b34d                     |
| protected        | False                                                |
| schema           | /v2/schemas/image                                    |
| size             | 6731856                                              |
| status           | active                                               |
| tags             |                                                      |
| updated_at       | 2016-04-13T03:06:08Z                                 |
| virtual_size     | None                                                 |
| visibility       | public                                               |
+------------------+------------------------------------------------------+
$ openstack image create --public --disk-format ari --container-format ari \
my-initrd < initrd.img-custom
+------------------+------------------------------------------------------+
| Field            | Value                                                |
+------------------+------------------------------------------------------+
| checksum         | 4c2022e27a9914c6718fd0d6f106314d                     |
| container_format | ari                                                  |
| created_at       | 2016-04-13T03:06:41Z                                 |
| disk_format      | ari                                                  |
| file             | /v2/images/34103a9b-b706-4ba9-a929-f7f5dc8f4b1e/file |
| id               | 34103a9b-b706-4ba9-a929-f7f5dc8f4b1e                 |
| min_disk         | 0                                                    |
| min_ram          | 0                                                    |
| name             | my-initrd                                            |
| owner            | 583e438e7fff4b33b3e52136f3a4b34d                     |
| protected        | False                                                |
| schema           | /v2/schemas/image                                    |
```

```
| size          | 27109374                                                |
| status        | active                                                  |
| tags          |                                                         |
| updated_at    | 2016-04-13T03:06:42Z                                    |
| virtual_size  | None                                                    |
| visibility    | public                                                  |
+---------------+---------------------------------------------------------+
$ openstack image list
+------------------------------------------+--------------------------+--------+
| ID                                       | Name                     | Status |
+------------------------------------------+--------------------------+--------+
| 34103a9b-b706-4ba9-a929-f7f5dc8f4b1e     | my-initrd                | active |
| ea003044-f792-408b-b6cd-46a701528c65     | my-vmlinuz               | active |
+------------------------------------------+--------------------------+--------+
```

With this in place, you'll then want to run the `ironic node-create` command that has the details for the bare metal server, including IPMI address and login information as well as number of CPUs, memory (in MB) and disk (in GB):

```
$ ironic node-create -d pxe_ipmitool -i ipmi_address=10.0.0.5 -i ipmi_username=ADMIN \
-i ipmi_password=ADMINPASS -i deploy_kernel=ea003044-f792-408b-b6cd-46a701528c65 \
-i deploy_ramdisk=34103a9b-b706-4ba9-a929-f7f5dc8f4b1e -p cpus=2 \
-p memory_mb=32000 -p local_gb=80
+--------------+--------------------------------------------------------------+
| Property     | Value                                                        |
+--------------+--------------------------------------------------------------+
| chassis_uuid |             Liberation Serif;Times New Roman                 |
| driver       | pxe_ipmitool                                                 |
| driver_info  | {u'deploy_kernel': u'ea003044-f792-408b-b6cd-46a701528c65',  |
|              | u'ipmi_address': u'10.0.0.5', u'ipmi_username': u'ADMIN',    |
|              | u'ipmi_password': u'******', u'deploy_ramdisk':              |
|              | u'34103a9b-b706-4ba9-a929-f7f5dc8f4b1e'}                     |
| extra        | {}                                                           |
| name         | None                                                         |
| properties   | {u'memory_mb': 32000, u'local_gb': 80, u'cpus': 2}           |
| uuid         | 5e9809ea-4f6a-4a3d-b7a4-d28fcd6fcb80                         |
+--------------+--------------------------------------------------------------+
```

Next, the user needs to create a port to register the MAC addresses of all the physical network interfaces that you intend to use on the bare metal node so that Ironic knows what MAC address to associate with the node you just created. The following continues using our example UUID:

```
$ ironic port-create -a 5a:ba:01:02:f0:a1 -n 5e9809ea-4f6a-4a3d-b7a4-d28fcd6fcb80
+-----------+--------------------------------------+
| Property  | Value                                |
+-----------+--------------------------------------+
| address   | 5a:ba:01:02:f0:a1                    |
| extra     | {}                                   |
| node_uuid | 5e9809ea-4f6a-4a3d-b7a4-d28fcd6fcb80 |
| uuid      | 652be9f9-221b-4368-8912-b93381464f88 |
+-----------+--------------------------------------+
```

Now you'll want a flavor to associate with this physical hardware definition, and others like it if you have an array of identical hardware. The flavor should match the specifications of the hardware you defined in your ironic node-create command exactly.

```
$ openstack flavor create --ram 32000 --disk 80 --vcpus 2 my-baremetal
+----------------------------+-------------------------------------+
| Field                      | Value                               |
+----------------------------+-------------------------------------+
| OS-FLV-DISABLED:disabled   | False                               |
| OS-FLV-EXT-DATA:ephemeral  | 0                                   |
| disk                       | 80                                  |
| id                         | dc8b4734-84f8-458c-86a0-c14573bb6b52 |
| name                       | my-baremetal                        |
| os-flavor-access:is_public | True                                |
| ram                        | 32000                               |
| rxtx_factor                | 1.0                                 |
| swap                       |                                     |
| vcpus                      | 2                                   |
+----------------------------+-------------------------------------+
```

With this step complete, you're ready to boot an image onto the hardware. Since this is the first time using this hardware, it's recommended that you issue a command to shut it off before deploying an image on it:

```
$ ironic node-set-power-state 5e9809ea-4f6a-4a3d-b7a4-d28fcd6fcb80 off
```

Then you can use the standard openstack server create command to boot a node, noting that you will need to specify the network the hardware is on so that Ironic can find it. The network can be found using the openstack network list command. The flavor you will want to boot will be a standard disk image that you wish to boot, like Ubuntu server. The image ID for that can be found with the openstack image list command:

```
$ openstack server create --nic net-id=00fdcb62-a708-40f0-876c-261b15fe6977 \
--image 73fc38f9-ee28-4b76-8b30-0d6f99296ed4 --flavor my-baremetal Ubuntu
```

> **Tip**
>
> Having trouble creating the server? Make sure the node has the status of available after it's been enrolled.

Ironic Inspector

Defining all your hardware can be a tedious task, even if you have a proper CMDB that has an inventory of all your hardware already. In order to fill this gap, a relatively new tool for Ironic has been created called Ironic Inspector. Heavily dependent upon the hardware in your infrastructure, the tool is designed to take information provided by the hardware driver about the hardware (CPU, memory, disk, etc.) to enable automatic characterization of node properties. This information is then used for matching up the hardware with the available flavors so that the servers are now made available. Note that since Inspector gets the information from a driver, you will still need to do some basic node creation work in order to supply the credentials, like if you're using iLO, the username, password and IP address where the interface can be accessed.

Managing Ironic

Beyond basic hardware enrollment and launching of images onto your new hardware nodes, you can also use Ironic to check the power state of machines, their availability and whether they've been placed in maintenance mode with the `ironic node-list` command.

Details about a specific machine can be viewed with `ironic node-show name` where name is the name of the node from output of the `ironic node-list` command.

> **Tip**
>
> The UUID of the physical node can also be used in place of the name in the `ironic node-show` command. We suggest name here because it's easier and unlike many other OpenStack services; node names *are* unique in Ironic.
>
> Also remember, the Ironic node names do not relate to instance UUIDs or the names of the instance that is using the node.

Ironic also supports *cleaning* of nodes, by which the data is removed in order to prepare the hardware for a new instance. This functionality depends upon the driver you are using and not all of them support it, though currently you can be confident that all of the agent_ drivers support it.

See the official documentation for Ironic at http://docs.openstack.org for the latest on how to manage your servers. It is constantly in development to add features and increase stability. As the project matures you will continue to see new drivers from hardware vendors and stronger support for automation of processes like is done with Ironic Inspector.

Community

The Ironic development community is largely made up of representatives from various hardware companies and parties interested in an automated hardware deployment for OpenStack itself. Known as a particularly friendly community, both getting support from developers and contributing your own changes to the project are straightforward exercises.

The Ironic team also has a sense of humor, using a play on the words "bare metal" to have a mascot named Pixie Boots, a metal band drummer bear.

Figure 10.2   Pixie Boots, the Ironic mascot

Summary

Ironic bare metal provisioning extends the OpenStack tooling from the world of virtualization and enables physical machines to be managed and used in a fashion similar to that of virtual machines. In this chapter, you learned the basic options for installation of Ironic and were walked through the enrollment of hardware and booting of your first bare metal-based instance. The basic maintenance of a bare metal deployment was also briefly explained, as well as a glimpse into the community building and supporting it.

11

Controlling Containers

You never change things by fighting the existing reality.
To change something, build a new model
that makes the existing model obsolete.
R. Buckminster Fuller

In systems administration today, containers such as Docker, Kubernetes and Linux Containers (LXC) are a popular topic. With the rise of containers happening alongside the maturity of OpenStack itself, OpenStack has worked to sync up with the latest technology for supporting the running and management of containers.

OpenStack began by supporting the most basic Virtual Machine-like manipulation of individual container instances, but has quickly moved into producing a whole project within OpenStack to support the container ecosystem, allowing for native tooling provided in the container ecosystem to control various container technologies.

What Is a Container?

Containers can be thought of as miniature, isolated operating systems for running individual applications. It provides some isolation from the host system for processes, while still sharing host resources like the kernel and generally avoiding hardware emulation that is common in Virtual Machine (VM) technologies.

The concept of containers likely sounds familiar. The new found popularity for containerization draws from a history of systems that includes BSD jails, zones in Solaris, Linux-VServer and more recent iterations such as cgroups and Linux Containers (LXC).

A few things have changed in recent years to strengthen popularity. First was the development of user-friendly tooling around creation of containers, largely driven by the introduction of Docker. There was also the growing popularity of container *images* that include all software dependencies to launch a specific service, running in a container. Finally, with Kubernetes, Docker Swarm and Apache Mesos, there was now orchestration available for managing these containers, which in some environments now measure in the thousands. Today individual containers can easily be treated as completely disposable, with the capability to tear down and replace containers on demand.

The capability to ship small, fully functioning container images has also been a boon to developers and systems administrators alike. Teams can now easily test, deploy and move around these isolated applications in containers from host to host. Given the existing capability of OpenStack to build and scale large platforms, support for containers was a natural fit.

Uses

There are many reasons why a company would want to use containers inside their infrastructure, from isolation to consolidation of services to the smaller images and quicker launch times. If an organization is already using OpenStack to provide management for other components of their infrastructure, using it for containers is typically valuable.

Public Cloud Company

A public cloud company that already leverages virtual machines in their infrastructure may choose to also offer Docker or Kubernetes. By using Magnum (discussed later in this chapter), they may use an existing OpenStack framework and can easily pull in their respective orchestration engines, such as Docker Swarm. With this framework in place, their customers have a way to configure and deploy their own grouping of containers and control it through OpenStack and the native tooling. Offering customers the option of containers can benefit the cloud company in other ways too—because they are sharing resources, more containers than VMs will fit on a server.

Online Gaming Company

A gaming company that is already using OpenStack for VMs and that may deliver their content over the web may be interested in using containers in order to quickly develop, test, deploy and iterate over changes they make to the games offered. The flexibility brought by deploying the games in containers enables developers to work on scale and high availability without necessarily being on the production environment. Using the much smaller, process-specific and portable containers can help replicate production environments locally. The added velocity of development will help deliver more features to gamers more quickly. The ability to run more containers than VMs also changes how deployments can be done. In addition to making sure you sustain high availability, what if you want to roll out a change to a game to only a subset of your users? You have much finer control of the percentage if you have more instances running.

> **Note**
>
> When researching containers and OpenStack, you may learn that there have been both casual and official efforts to run OpenStack itself inside of containers. However, this chapter focuses only on work done to support the management of containers for handling the processes that your infrastructure provides to your users.

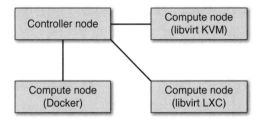

Figure 11.1   Controller and compute nodes with containers. A controller node with several compute nodes running: standard VM libvirt with KVM and container-focused libvirt with LXC and the Docker-Nova driver.

Container Drivers for Nova

The OpenStack story with containers began early with a series of drivers for compute that directly interacted with specific container technologies. First, there was the ability to use libvirt (already supported by OpenStack) with LXC. Then came the Nova-Docker driver, which allowed the user to use Docker like they would another virtualization technology and launch Docker instances via Nova compute. In this model, you would also have compute nodes for each of these. So you may have one node that runs your standard VMs with KVM driven by libvirt, another node that uses LXC with libvirt and a third that uses the Nova-Docker driver (see Figure 11.1).

Unfortunately, these have some very clear limitations. Since you're treating a container like a VM, your tooling reflects commands you'd run against a full VM—you lose out on the container-specific tooling. Since containers are process-focused rather than server-focused, this means a very different approach is needed to get the full value of using containers.

This is where the Magnum project comes in.

Magnum

The OpenStack Liberty release was the first production-ready release of Magnum. Magnum provides more complete support for containers. The project also sought to simultaneously provide consistency when deploying containers in OpenStack, while also preserving the capability to use features specific to each container technology supported. This meant having a common mechanism for orchestration using Heat (covered briefly in Chapter 1, "What is OpenStack?"), multi-tenancy of separate clusters using Keystone for identity and multi-host networking with Neutron. It also meant that every service is handled by Magnum in the same way, by using the Magnum API to create bays (defined in the next section and shown in Figure 11.2), within which each Container Orchestration Engine (COE) runs. By allowing OpenStack to manage things like networks and infrastructure beyond what you do in OpenStack itself, management of containers becomes considerably simpler.

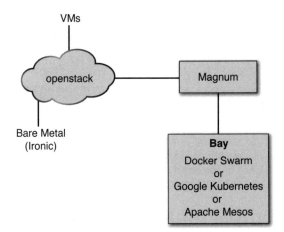

Figure 11.2   Basic Magnum structure

To provide control into each COE, the native API and tooling for each can be used, so if you wish to interface with the Docker API or use the native Kubernetes command line client, kubectl, against your containers, you're able to do so. The Mitaka release includes support for the Docker Swarm, Kubernetes and Apache Mesos COEs.

Magnum Concepts

As you can see from Figure 11.2, Magnum has a concept of "Bays" where a specific COE is run from. Beyond Bays, Magnum also has the concept of container and node for all of their containers, and additional ones for Kubernetes. Loosely speaking, you have the following concepts:

- **Container:** The container running your process.
- **Node:** A member of a bay, this is the bare metal or virtual machine where work actually executes.
- **Bay:** A collection of node objects where work is scheduled, this is where your COE lives.

Figure 11.3 illustrates the relationships among the three concepts.

More support is being added regularly. If you're using Kubernetes, for example, you will also have the concept of a Pod, which is a collection of containers running on one physical or virtual machine that, as a layer, sits between your containers and nodes and can also support a replication controller.

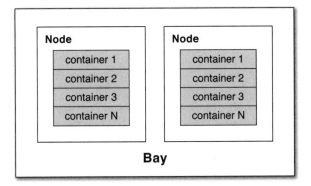

Figure 11.3   Containers, Nodes and Bays

Installing Magnum

The Magnum Puppet modules for Mitaka were still being developed and tested at the time of writing, so there will soon be a Puppet-driven way to configure Magnum for your infrastructure. As of writing, the best way to try out Magnum is to deploy our Foundations framework discussed in Chapter 5, "Foundations for Deployments," with a custom Compute node that will use Magnum.

Summary

Containers are a popular topic and OpenStack has met the challenge head-on. It started off by supporting container-specific Nova compute drivers from a very early date. The Magnum project, which we gave a quick tour of, then brought in more comprehensive support for the common container technologies out there today, including Docker, Kubernetes and Apache Mesos.

III

Scaling and Troubleshooting

Familiarity with various deployment types of OpenStack only gets you so far. Once you have a use case and have a basic cloud set up, you may wish to grow that cloud and will have a use for scaling your architecture, whether that means adding more storage nodes or increasing the power of your compute cluster. Troubleshooting is also a vital part of any OpenStack operator's toolkit. Deployments vary considerably, and every environment is likely to have nuances that you'll have to know how to deal with. Finally, various vendors in the OpenStack ecosystem exist to support your larger deployment and augment it with public cloud offerings.

A Whole Cloud

Two drifters
Off to see the world,
There's such a lot of world
To see.
Johnny Mercer, *Moon River*

This final scenario in this book brings all of the pieces together that we've presented in the earlier standalone scenarios. You'll be able to see how Cinder block storage and Swift object storage also feeds into Ceilometer telemetry and be able to use both Cinder block and Swift object storage in your instances. As we bring these pieces together, we'll also talk a bit about scaling beyond these scenarios.

Uses

We've explored a variety of uses for OpenStack already, from universities looking to give out instances to their researchers to car companies looking to handle their compute load and cloud storage to syncing companies offering automated data handling to their customers. Hopefully you've begun to see how components of OpenStack can fit into your own organization and have started making plans for how to use it.

Since this chapter brings together several of the pieces, you will finally get a view into what the manifests and configurations look like in a more complicated deployment.

Requirements

The requirements remain the same as we've used throughout the book, with the controller and compute nodes you created in Chapter 5, "Foundations for Deployments." The minimum requirements will still work for this scenario, but if you have additional resources to devote to a deployment, this one is the one to spend the resources on, since we'll be running all the services.

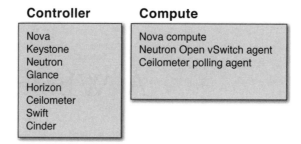

Figure 12.1   Components of a two-system OpenStack deployment
with telemetry, block storage and object storage

Select Components

In this scenario we'll be bringing in all the components.

- Compute (Nova)
- Identity (Keystone)
- Networking (Neutron)
- Image service (Glance)
- Dashboard (Horizon)
- Ceilometer (Telemetry)
- Cinder (Block Storage)
- Swift (Object Storage)

Figure 12.1 shows the service placement across our controller and compute node.

Scenario

We'll need to configure both the controller and compute nodes for this scenario. You can reuse one of your old scenarios if you'd like, or start fresh from the foundations configured in Chapter 5.

Controller Node Setup

A new manifest that contains all the manifests needed for your deployment will be used for this scenario.

```
$ sudo puppet apply /etc/puppet/modules/deployments/manifests/role/foundations_whole_cloud.pp
```

While this is running, we can open up the file to have a look at everything we're including in this role:

```
class deployments::role::foundations_whole_cloud {
  include deployments::role::foundations_block_storage
  include deployments::role::foundations_object_storage
  include deployments::role::foundations_public_cloud
}

include deployments::role::foundations_whole_cloud
```

As you can see, this is pulling in roles described in detail in previous chapters where each scenario was demonstrated. By pulling them in together, we're creating a controller that has all the characteristics of the public cloud, with telemetry, block storage and object storage chapters.

Compute Node Setup

In this scenario, we'll be reusing the compute public cloud manifest used back in Chapter 7, "Public Compute Cloud," since this is the only scenario for which we needed modifications to the compute node. This adds support for the Ceilometer polling agent so data can be gathered from compute instances.

```
$ sudo puppet apply /etc/puppet/modules/deployments/manifests/role/foundations_compute_
public_cloud.pp
```

Since this is the same role we used previously, there's no need to repeat what is included in this role. Refer back to Chapter 7 if you need to. Our previous install with Ceilometer telemetry did not include Cinder or Swift, so you'll see some new meters this time around.

Exploring the Deployment: Dashboard

Hopefully, you've started to become pretty familiar with Horizon, the OpenStack Dashboard. Log into the dashboard with your admin user to get an initial view into your system with all the components loaded, as shown in Figure 12.2.

In the Admin section you'll see Ceilometer telemetry options under Resource Usage as well as Cinder block storage in the Volumes section. If you click Project in the left-hand menu, you'll now see the Object Store section for Swift. Figure 12.2 shows the Volumes screen with a couple volumes created and one attached to an instance.

Now navigate to System Information to see the services running, as shown in Figure 12.3. You will see all your services and their statuses. In this example, my controller is running on 192.168.122.9, so that is the Host for all of my services.

Log out as the admin user and log back in with the test user so you can launch a couple CirrOS images. Running instances will give Ceilometer something to track. You can also create Cinder volumes. Attach them to running instances. Perhaps also take some time to create another object storage container and add some files to it. The goal here is to become even more familiar with this tooling while you have all these services running.

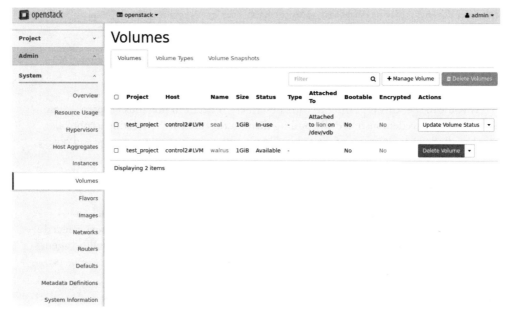

Figure 12.2 Horizon dashboard admin view with Volumes selected

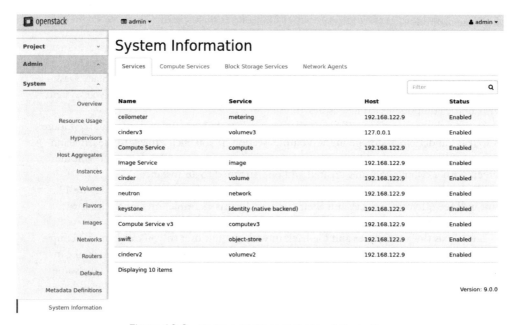

Figure 12.3 Horizon dashboard System Information

Exploring the Deployment: Command Line Client

As you've learned, the OpenStack Client (OSC) can do everything that the Horizon dashboard can and more. The System Information screen in the dashboard is very similar to what you see when listing services with OSC:

```
$ source /etc/openrc.admin
$ openstack service list
+----------------------------------+--------------------+--------------+
| ID                               | Name               | Type         |
+----------------------------------+--------------------+--------------+
| 29b6fa87b8a6482cbf31a60e0dac9c26 | keystone           | identity     |
| 3c1b214c8e3a4fc4b62dabe2f34dc963 | Compute Service v3 | computev3    |
| 3d5f4103620746e2bae3f5c43fc0e023 | Image Service      | image        |
| 88dcf889462f433ab9035f606402b78a | neutron            | network      |
| 9e8ac41f98dc483fb12a1f6f2605d2f2 | cinder             | volume       |
| ae28d29d3d904447a633641dc804de7b | cinderv3           | volumev3     |
| b44923e869f74cd4acf54ebb3517d8e0 | ceilometer         | metering     |
| b9bdc44e813f481981e33820745e369a | cinderv2           | volumev2     |
| f4a8ddc46eef47f59d8fc6610182292b | swift              | object-store |
| f73b98720cd54fb9ba7057a593d09911 | Compute Service    | compute      |
+----------------------------------+--------------------+--------------+
```

Run this command with `--long` to get even more information about each service running and a view that's even more similar to the dashboard.

You can also list the Ceilometer meters once you have an instance running with `ceilometer meter-list` and refer back to Chapter 7, "Public Compute Cloud," to refresh your memory on polling other statistics. In this chapter we added Cinder, so if you've created some volumes you'll see a new volume.size meter to work with. For Swift, if you've created a container and uploaded objects, you'll see new meters like storage.objects and storage.objects.size.

Being proficient with OSC is an important part of administrating a deployment. With this whole cloud deployment, do some similar instance launches and shutdowns of instances. Refer back to previous chapters to create a block storage volume and mount it on an instance, create a container and add some files to it to reference in your instances. Or come up with your own project to do or experiments for how far you can push this deployment scenario as you familiarize yourself with the tooling. See Appendix E, "OpenStack Client (OSC)," and the development documentation with a command listing for more OSC commands at http://docs.openstack.org/developer/python-openstackclient/command-list.html.

A Bigger Cloud

As you become more familiar with OpenStack and start planning your own deployment you'll grow your cloud well beyond the pair of servers we've been working with. You'll also need to make sure your services are reliable and secure, and eventually you'll likely want to add more services than we've covered.

High Availability and Scaling

High Availability (HA) is a major consideration for most production OpenStack deployments. You want to minimize the downtime of user-facing services so that users don't have failures when they try to launch an instance or find themselves unable to reach their compute instances or files in object storages. It's also important to minimize data loss. As covered in depth in Chapter 9, "Object Storage Cloud," a lot of work has been put into Swift to make sure data is protected. Services such as Cinder Block Storage also have backup and snapshot utilities to minimize data loss, and you can run additional protections on other back ends.

Entire books can be written and a whole upstream guide exists on how to specifically configure OpenStack to be highly available, but we'll touch the surface here on the high-level pieces to consider having redundancy for in your production deployment hardware-wise:

- Pieces of your physical network, including cables, switches and routers
- Storage back ends, whether they are a fleet of commodity hardware servers or an array of Network-Attached Storage (NAS) device
- On-premises services in your data center such as power, fire protection and air conditioning

A deep dive into further high availability concepts and configurations can be found in the OpenStack High Availability Guide at http://docs.openstack.org/ha-guide/.

In OpenStack itself, you'll want to horizontally scale your compute and storage nodes. Our scenarios only have one compute node and all of our storage is on the controller, but storage and compute are typically the first things that will be added in a deployment. You'll be adding more compute nodes as your number of instances grows. By always having more than are being used, you can fail over instances from one node to another. All the storage tooling includes ways to easily grow and re-balance the storage.

When you get to the point of moving beyond simple horizontal scaling of individual stateless services and storage, you'll want to dive deeper into the configuration of individual services. The OpenStack Administrator Guide is a great place to start (http://docs.openstack.org/admin-guide/), and the OpenStack Operations Guide covers further scaling, troubleshooting and more real-world operational tasks (http://docs.openstack.org/ops-guide/).

Additional Components

We have explored some of the early and basic components of OpenStack in our deployment scenarios. In Chapter 10, "Bare Metal Provisioning," and Chapter 11, "Controlling Containers," we introduced the concepts of control of bare metal and containers from within an OpenStack deployment in order to extend your deployment beyond launching of Virtual Machines.

As we talked about in Chapter 1, "What is OpenStack?" there are also projects beyond the ones we've covered and more projects being created every release. The current list of official projects that have placed themselves under OpenStack governance as managed by the Technical Committee is maintained at http://governance.openstack.org/reference/projects/. All projects being maintained within the OpenStack community, but may not be necessarily owned by an official team, can be found by navigating the OpenStack git repositories at https://git.openstack.org/cgit/openstack/.

In addition to the services mentioned in Chapter 1, there are a few services that have a deployment rate of 10% or more, based on user survey feedback, and are worth keeping an eye on for your own work:

- **Designate:** DNS as a service
- **Trove:** Databases as a service
- **Sahara:** Data processing (Hadoop, Spark)
- **Murano:** Application catalog

Most of these services have Puppet modules that you can find at the aforementioned OpenStack git repositories. All puppet modules are prefixed with puppet-, like puppet-trove and puppet-sahara.

Learn about what other organizations are doing and the services they're using by visiting the latest user survey at https://www.openstack.org/user-survey/.

A Project Navigator also exists on the OpenStack web site to learn about some of the more popular components at https://www.openstack.org/software/project-navigator.

Summary

Previous chapters gave you service-by-service deployment scenarios and covered basic navigation of each of those. This chapter brought them all together. You learned how to deploy a scenario that includes telemetry for metrics, block storage and object storage all at once and how to work with it through the dashboard and command line client. As you look into the future of your work with OpenStack, we also touched upon and provided resources for scaling, HA and additional components you may want to consider supporting in your production deployment.

13

Troubleshooting

Humpty Dumpty sat on a wall,
Humpty Dumpty had a great fall.
All the king's horses and all the king's men
Couldn't put Humpty together again.
English nursery rhyme

As we have learned, OpenStack is a complicated infrastructure project. Even if you followed the instructions in this book precisely and everything worked well, using OpenStack in production will not be the same. Troubleshooting your OpenStack deployment to find where failures are lurking is a vital skill.

Your toolbox for debugging may include sifting through log files or running specific commands manually. There are also services such as OpenStack's Identity (Keystone) and Networking (Neutron) that can cause failures throughout your infrastructure if there is a configuration problem. We talk about debugging those.

Reading Displayed Errors

Whether you're using the dashboard or the command line, an error may manifest immediately, which may start pointing you in the right direction.

When looking for an error, the first step will be determining which service is the problem. Are you having trouble launching an instance? If you're using the dashboard, your first indicator may be a pink box that pops up to tell you something is wrong. In Figure 13.1 it says "Error: Failed to perform requested operation on instance "zebra", the instance has an error status: Please try again later [Error: No valid host was found. There are not enough hosts available.]."

By clicking on the name of the instance that failed, in this case "zebra," you will see more details about the node itself. This will remind you of the settings you selected. It will also give you access to exposed log files and an Action Log that will show actions performed against the instance. The Console will not be available since that is only active when an instance is running. See Figure 13.2 for this detailed view.

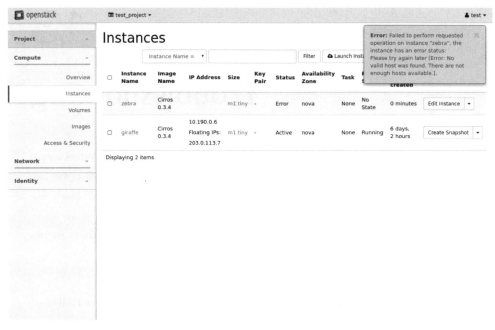

Figure 13.1   Instance launch error in the Horizon dashboard

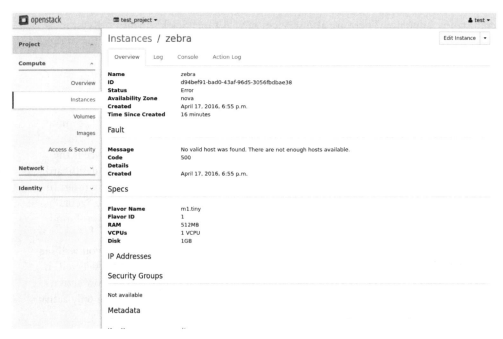

Figure 13.2   Instance details

If you have used the OpenStack Client (OSC) to create this instance, you would not get an immediate response, since the output only tells you that the instance is being created. Instead you may look at the listing of instances and then query that one specifically to read the error message. Note that we are using the ID of the instance to show details about the instance because the instance Name is not a unique identifier. You could have a whole herd of instances called zebra (Listing 13.1)!

As you can see, the listing showed that the instance was in an "ERROR" state. Full details will show you details about your instance, and "fault" will show the error message that is the same as what was shown in the dashboard.

Regardless of whether you're viewing this output at the command line or in the dashboard, the first thing this can help you do is see whether you've made a mistake. Given this error, it's easy to assume that the region you're trying to launch it in really doesn't have enough resources, but what if you're sure it does? Did you perhaps launch it in the wrong region? Did you use the wrong image or flavor? These are easy to identify and easy to correct without going any further with troubleshooting.

More often than not, things are more complex. Using the error above as an example, you'll want to keep in mind that it is given by a service that can only see part of the picture. A misconfiguration may signal to the service that the host does not satisfy the requirements, even if that host should be able to receive the instance request as specified. It does not necessarily mean that the service itself has a configuration problem.

To make matters worse, you may not even see an error message. You may discover that a block storage volume simply won't attach to an instance or your network isn't working as you expected it to.

These situations are when looking at the logs come in.

Logs

In a production deployment of OpenStack, especially a large one, you will likely have a centralized logging system where all servers send logs to—maybe it's even backed by the OpenStack Object Storage (Swift)! Having a centralized log system can also help with valuable older logs rotating out of existence, since having logs of a functioning services to compare to your failures can be valuable. However, in this chapter we make the assumption that logs are being stored locally on each OpenStack node and will be referencing them accordingly.

After looking for obvious errors in your interface, log files will be your next stop in most troubleshooting scenarios. Logs for OpenStack services are typically found in /var/log/service-code-name, so you'll find the logs for Compute (Nova) services in /var/log/nova.

> **Tip**
>
> Depending on the service and whether they contain sensitive data, such as hints about authentication, log files will vary in terms of permissions. You may need to use administrative access (using `sudo`) to view them.

Listing 13.1

```
$ source /etc/openrc.test
$ openstack server list
+--------------------------------------+---------+--------+------------------------------------+
| ID                                   | Name    | Status | Networks                           |
+--------------------------------------+---------+--------+------------------------------------+
| d94bef91-bad0-43af-96d5-3056fbdbae38 | zebra   | ERROR  |                                    |
| a1f73c78-b4eb-49f6-8687-dfce23dfd74f | giraffe | ACTIVE | Network1=10.190.0.6, 203.0.113.7   |
+--------------------------------------+---------+--------+------------------------------------+

$ openstack server show d94bef91-bad0-43af-96d5-3056fbdbae38
+-------------------------------------+-----------------------------------------------------------------------------------------------------------------------------+
| Field                               | Value                                                                                                                       |
+-------------------------------------+-----------------------------------------------------------------------------------------------------------------------------+
| OS-DCF:diskConfig                   | AUTO                                                                                                                         |
| OS-EXT-AZ:availability_zone         | nova                                                                                                                        |
| OS-EXT-STS:power_state              | 0                                                                                                                           |
| OS-EXT-STS:task_state               | None                                                                                                                        |
| OS-EXT-STS:vm_state                 | error                                                                                                                       |
| OS-SRV-USG:launched_at              | None                                                                                                                        |
| OS-SRV-USG:terminated_at            | None                                                                                                                        |
| accessIPv4                          |                                                                                                                             |
| accessIPv6                          |                                                                                                                             |
| addresses                           |                                                                                                                             |
| config_drive                        |                                                                                                                             |
| created                             | 2016-04-17T18:55:00Z                                                                                                        |
| fault                               | {u'message': u'No valid host was found. There are not enough hosts available.', u'code': 500, u'created': u'2016-04-17T18:55:03Z'} |
| flavor                              | m1.tiny (1)                                                                                                                 |
| hostId                              |                                                                                                                             |
| id                                  | d94bef91-bad0-43af-96d5-3056fbdbae38                                                                                        |
| image                               | Cirros 0.3.4 (c30caf80-5e19-4356-a33a-99af2f8612c9)                                                                         |
| key_name                            | None                                                                                                                        |
| name                                | zebra                                                                                                                       |
| os-extended-volumes:volumes_attached| []                                                                                                                          |
| project_id                          | 28e1c9a0502847ad994fa4f02286531b                                                                                            |
| properties                          |                                                                                                                             |
| status                              | ERROR                                                                                                                       |
| updated                             | 2016-04-17T18:55:04Z                                                                                                        |
| user_id                             | aa347b98f1734f66b1331178424lfa15a                                                                                           |
+-------------------------------------+-----------------------------------------------------------------------------------------------------------------------------+
```

Debug Mode

In our deployment examples, we made a decision to turn debugging off. A change can be made in your /etc/puppet/hiera/common.yaml file in order to adjust debug level for each service and then you run the appropriate `puppet apply` command for that deployment scenario. Having debugging enabled is rarely the default because it produces a considerable number of logs that are unnecessary when a deployment is functioning normally. If you're not using Puppet in your production deployment, you will want to refer to the documentation for each service to learn how to turn on debugging, but it will typically look something like this:

```
debug=True
```

As with any modification to a configuration file, we recommend that you make a backup of the configuration file you began with, even if you're using a configuration management system. Having a starting point can help when you forget where you began or are seeking to pass off debugging to another engineer. You will then need to restart the respective service or services that are logging to that file for the debug change to take effect.

> **Tip**
>
> There are cases when debugging is left on for particular services for auditing or long-term debugging. Be aware of the problem spots in your infrastructure so you can make informed decisions about whether a service should run with debugging on long term or not.

Understanding Log Messages

There are two main things you should keep in mind about OpenStack when reading log messages:

- It is written in Python, so you may encounter a lot of Python tracebacks, which provide stack trace information. As such, standard Python documentation on reading errors can be used if the errors are not obvious to you.
- OpenStack is modular—it depends on various different components. When you see an error in one service, it may actually be due to a problem in another. We'll dive into specifics of the likely candidates in the "Key Services" section of this chapter.

When debugging systems which are written in Python, a good general strategy is to first look at the last line in the traceback. This may give you a clear indicator of what went wrong. If the last line is not helpful, go to the top of the traceback and read through it for anything obvious.

If you don't find anything in the traceback itself just yet, look at the lines in the log file above it. If you have debug enabled, you may need to sift through some lines to find actual errors. A command that a service depends on may be failing to complete successfully, you may have an authentication problem or perhaps there is an error about running out of resources, like memory. Once you find the error, having the debug lines available can help you further track down exactly what the service was doing before and after the problem started.

Moving beyond tracebacks and debug lines, you may also be able to use an error message you received from an OpenStack service to start the search through your logs. Services like Nova may run several daemons on a node. Using `grep -i <error message> /var/log/nova/*.log` may narrow down not only where in a log file to look, but *which* log you need to look at.

> **Tip**
>
> Doing a lot of debugging? Logs can get very big, which can make them difficult to search and work with. Use `logrotate` to make rotate out logs that are older than what you're looking at, or manually make backups of older logs so you can focus on smaller log snippets and share them with your team.

Beyond this, I like to think of debugging OpenStack through log files as more of an art than a science. As you start exploring the log files, you will have to think about what behavior you're seeing and which service and server is responsible for it. Are you debugging a problem with launching a node? You may want to start on the compute node and look in /var/log/nova/nova-compute.log to see what the compute node itself is telling you. In most cases, the errors in this log will lead you to the real problem— perhaps it's with networking? You'll then need to determine wither it's a problem with the networking service (Neutron) server, which handles API requests and processes them on the control node, or with a specific agent or plug-in. Perhaps Open vSwitch is caus- ing a problem, in which case you'll want to view the logs for the openvswitch-agent on the compute node. Perhaps your problem is actually with the dhcp-agent running on the controller node. There are logs for that, too.

Being able to identify behavior and pinpoint the exact source of your problem often takes experience. Certain behavior and types of error messages will, over time, assist with your troubleshooting technique, and you'll find yourself improving over time.

Key Services

When you browse an OpenStack deployment environment, you may notice that there are three components that almost every other component relies on:

- Identity (Keystone)
- Queuing service (typically RabbitMQ)
- Networking (Neutron)

Misconfiguration or incorrect configuration assumptions in these services can cause problems for everything else. A service that can't reach the messaging queue will fail to be able to send along API requests. This is a very common problem and can be found in log files by searching for failures to connect to the AMQP server.

> **Tip**
>
> RabbitMQ has a GUI that runs on port 15672. Access can be gathered from the credentials you set up in the Puppet Hiera configuration. If you find yourself struggling with the queuing service it's worth looking into usage, but it's beyond scope here.

An identity service that does not have an authentication account for a service will not be able to verify the service has the correct rights to perform certain actions. A misconfigured network can cause services not to be able to reach each other at all, which we'll talk about in the "Networking" section.

It is incredibly common for a troubleshooting scenario to include several of these key services. Even though your problem may seem to be with compute, be sure to browse log files for these other services to make sure you're not encountering a broader problem.

Networking

Due to the complexity and importance, we made a decision to create an entire chapter devoted to networking early in the book. As explained in Chapter 3, "Networking," the environment you have for OpenStack and your use case will heavily influence the decisions you make with regard to your networking configuration. A fundamental understanding of how OpenStack tackles networking, in addition to advice and guidance from your own network administration staff, is incredibly helpful for having a successful deployment.

With that in mind, our first word of advice is to refer back to that chapter and the series of diagrams provided in order to make sure you understand how everything should be configured. Once you understand that, you will be able to more intelligently debug.

Once you get to the step of debugging, there are a few tools that are particularly helpful, which we'll give examples of here in order to get you started.

Network Debugging Tools

Many of these tools we'll cover will be familiar to Linux professionals and we won't do a full tutorial of them, there are plenty of guides on-line and in-print. Instead, we'll focus on how they can be used with and are particularly valuable in an OpenStack environment.

`ip` and Network Name Spaces

The `ip` command should be familiar to Linux professionals. It replaced a series of tools, including ifconfig, route and even some uses of netstat, for configuring, manipulating and viewing the networks on your system. At the simplest, you may run `ip addr` to see what addresses are directly assigned to your interfaces or `ip -d link` to see more specifics about the device configuration. The `-d` flag tells you roughly what kind of device each interface is, which can be very valuable when tracing your way through the network configuration.

Things get more complicated when you begin looking at tenant networking, which our deployments have. For the tenant network (our default is the 10.190.0.0/24 network), you will not see the IP addresses or devices by simply using the `ip` command on your controller node. Instead, these networks live in network name spaces that need to be accessed with the `ip netns` command. For example, in order to see the network where the DHCP server runs you'll need to use:

```
$ sudo ip netns
qrouter-1c1c7574-9114-438f-aa33-1eb969478f6a
qdhcp-961c7aa2-4c7b-452f-bc65-6b7cbb2b798a
```

The name space ID for the DHCP server begins with qdhcp-. In order to run commands in this name space to view details about and manipulate that network, you will use the `exec` command with the name space ID and the command you wish to run. The following runs `ip addr` on the qdhcp network name space:

```
$ sudo ip netns exec qdhcp-961c7aa2-4c7b-452f-bc65-6b7cbb2b798a ip addr
1: lo: <LOOPBACK,UP,LOWER_UP> mtu 65536 qdisc noqueue state UNKNOWN group default
    link/loopback 00:00:00:00:00:00 brd 00:00:00:00:00:00
    inet 127.0.0.1/8 scope host lo
       valid_lft forever preferred_lft forever
    inet6 ::1/128 scope host
       valid_lft forever preferred_lft forever
13: tap4c049b01-60: <BROADCAST,MULTICAST,UP,LOWER_UP> mtu 1400 qdisc noqueue state UNKNOWN
group default
    link/ether fa:16:3e:83:01:c6 brd ff:ff:ff:ff:ff:ff
    inet 10.190.0.5/24 brd 10.190.0.255 scope global tap4c049b01-60
       valid_lft forever preferred_lft forever
    inet6 fe80::f816:3eff:fe83:1c6/64 scope link
       valid_lft forever preferred_lft forever
```

As you learned in the networking chapter, the tap interface here is what has the address for your DHCP server. A test you can use to see if a new instance can effectively ping may be to ping this address from your instance, or to confirm you can ping the gateway for this network.

```
$ sudo ip netns exec qdhcp-961c7aa2-4c7b-452f-bc65-6b7cbb2b798a ping -c 2 10.190.0.1
PING 10.190.0.1 (10.190.0.1) 56(84) bytes of data.
64 bytes from 10.190.0.1: icmp_seq=1 ttl=64 time=0.322 ms
64 bytes from 10.190.0.1: icmp_seq=2 ttl=64 time=0.054 ms

--- 10.190.0.1 ping statistics ---
2 packets transmitted, 2 received, 0% packet loss, time 999ms
rtt min/avg/max/mdev = 0.054/0.188/0.322/0.134 ms10.255.202.6
```

As you can see, various commands can be run using this network, and so it's very valuable for testing connectivity on these network name spaces that may seem invisible otherwise.

You may have noticed there is also a name space ID that begins with qrouter-. This name space is used to provide routing at Network Address Translation (NAT) between the private instance tenant network and the external provider network. Go ahead and run similar exec commands on that interface and refer back to the networking chapter to learn more about what is happening.

tcpdump

The tried and trusted `tcpdump` (http://www.tcpdump.org/) command is essential in the toolkit of any OpenStack administrator. It may be used for tracing the tricky to isolate provider network traffic going to and from the instances and various other things. Whether it's your physical interfaces or ones in the network name spaces, once you determine that you are unable to ping an instance or traffic is behaving inconsistently, you'll need to learn why. It can help you answer questions like "Where is traffic stopping?" and "Are specific types of traffic being blocked?" From there you can isolate which part of the network you need to troubleshoot.

A useful `tcpdump` command on eth0 of your control interface may look like the following:

```
$ sudo tcpdump -i eth0 -vvv
```

While this is running, make sure you do something that should show output, like pinging the server you're running this on. Use Control-c to stop the capture. If traffic is running on the interface, you will likely see a great deal of traffic. Adjust this command as needed to listen on various interfaces. Remember, this can even be used in conjunction with the `ip netns exec` command to see traffic on the networks in name spaces.

> **Tip**
>
> Not a `tcpdump` guru yet? Learning how to read `tcpdump` output takes skill and experience. When you add in learning about how OpenStack uses networking, you may find yourself struggling.
>
> Do yourself a favor. Save the output from `tcpdump` into a file and load it up in the graphical tool Wireshark (https://www.wireshark.org/). This tool gives you a visualization of the packets that were captured and enables you to drill into them. An example of a `tcpdump` command you can use with Wireshark is as follows:
>
> ```
> $ sudo tcpdump -i eth0 -w packet_debug.pcap
> ```
>
> As before, the interface you wish to listen on follows the -i flag, which you may want to change. The -w flag goes on to define the filename you're saving it to. Use Ctrl-c to stop the capture when you believe you have enough data.
>
> You then load this packet_debug.pcap file into Wireshark for analysis. It's still not going to be easy until you get the hang of it, but it's easier than looking at the raw logs!

MTUs

There was a section about maximum transmission unit (MTU) size in the networking chapter. As a reminder, if you find inconsistent behavior in how network traffic is flowing, such as you can ping an instance but SSH starts and times out during a handshake, you may want to look at the MTU size. Remember the diagram of the packet, and spend some time thinking about how your network is configured and what kind of encapsulation is happening to figure out what your MTU size should be.

Both the `tcpdump` command and the `ip` command can be of assistance in looking into MTU size issues. The `tcpdump` command can help you figure out where the packets get stuck. If used early enough in the life of the packet, like at an originating tap interface, tcpdump can help you figure out how large the packet is early on. The ip link -s command can be used to show interface statistics, including packets dropped because they were too large.

Open vSwitch and Linux Bridges

In our deployment scenarios we use Open vSwitch (OVS, http://openvswitch.org/) as the core mechanism for handling bridges. Many operators have reported struggling with quirks related to current versions of OVS. You will want to make yourself familiar with the basic OVS details. That means commands like ovs-vsctl show as well as those to help with debugging to look at flow control and other details, but that level of debugging is beyond the scope of what typical operators should need starting out.

> **Tip**
>
> If you are in a development environment, don't be afraid to restart the OVS daemon (using sudo service openvswitch-switch restart). Once you've confirmed your configuration is correct and the output of ovs-vsctl show is inconsistent with what you have configured and understand to be accurate about how the deployment should be working, then go ahead and restart the OVS daemon.
>
> In production, this may still be the correct solution to certain OVS problems, but be aware that restarting this service will cause major network service disruption. It may take anywhere from a few minutes to an hour to fully come back if you have a very large scale deployment. Long term, if you struggle with OVS in production, you may consider moving to a Linux Bridge model instead but that configuration is beyond the scope of this book.

Now, while we do specify OVS in our configurations, Linux Bridge is actually also used for iptables, which we'll discuss next, for your instances. If problems arise here, the bridge-utils package, which includes brctrl to look into and manipulate bridges for instances is, installed on your compute node.

iptables

Another bit of debugging centers around another standard Linux tool—iptables (http://www.netfilter.org/projects/iptables/). Starting with the most basic of commands, you can run sudo iptables -L in order to get a listing of iptables rules. Just like the other commands, this can also be used in conjunction with the ip netns exec command to look at the qrouter network name space, which, as you may recall, runs iptables for the instances. That means you could run something like the following on the controller node to get a listing of rules from both iptables:

```
$ sudo iptables -nL
$ sudo ip netns exec qrouter-1c1c7574-9114-438f-aa33-1eb969478f6a iptables -L
```

Since iptables is used for OpenStack's firewalls, doing a mere listing only scratches the surface of what iptables can do. The `iptables` command is used for adding and removing rules to do various types of traffic manipulation. If you find yourself needing to dig further into your install with `iptables`, use the online documentation for it or a reference book (e.g., Steve Suehring. 2015. *Linux Firewalls.* Upper Saddle River, NJ: Addison-Wesley) to dive deeper.

Configuration Files

While building your own OpenStack deployment, you will find yourself looking at configuration files for services. In our sample deployments, Puppet creates these files, so you should not be editing them directly. However, understanding what you want Puppet to place in these files becomes important as you make decisions about your own deployment. If you do move on from Puppet entirely, or are doing a manual installation, you will be editing these configuration files by hand.

Most of the OpenStack config files are INI format files. The Puppet modules maintain the integrity of these files. If you are editing them manually, be sure to make a backup of the original file and then view and edit them with syntax highlighting for INI files enabled to help you spot problems. Some services, like Heat, also use templates that are in YAML, and you may even find some files in the OpenStack ecosystem that use JSON.

Whether your config file is INI, YAML, JSON or something else entirely, don't lose an afternoon to a missing or extra comma in a configuration file. Use a tool that highlights errors of these formats as effectively as possible. All modern text editors and software IDEs (integrated development environments) have support for these formats. There are also command line linter tools for YAML and JSON that can go into test jobs for configuration changes.

> **Tip**
>
> All these formats allow a considerable amount of leeway. You probably will not find a perfect solution or one that you can fully automate to confirm the files are correctly formatted. The best they can do is help, especially for simple syntax errors.

Puppet

We are using the official OpenStack Puppet modules in this book in order to craft our deployment scenarios, along with a deployments composition module that brings the pieces together specifically for this book. These have been tested and should work flawlessly. However, if you wish to make changes or find you're having problems, there are a few things you can do to figure out where your problem is.

The first tool you have is running `puppet apply` with the `--debug` flag, for example:

```
sudo puppet apply --debug /etc/puppet/modules/deployments/manifests/role/foundations.pp
```

This will provide considerably more output than the standard `apply` command, enabling you to track down exactly what Puppet is doing with every step and helping you find the problem. If there is a lot of output, you may want to pipe this output to a file so you can search through it and reference it later.

Exploring the Modules

As discussed in Chapter 5, "Foundations for Deployments," we're setting configuration variables specific to our deployment in a Puppet Hiera key/value store located in /etc/puppet/hiera/common.yaml. The source of this file is in our GitHub repository at: https://github.com/DeploymentsBook/puppet-data in the hiera directory. By default, we do have you make changes that impact this file in order to describe your environment. This file can also be edited and added to in order to change other things you expect.

The composition module we use is automatically pulled in by the setup.sh script you used in the foundations chapter, but you can find it directly at https://github.com/DeploymentsBook/puppet-deployments. As we went over in that chapter, this module describes the components of the official OpenStack Puppet modules we wish to pull in and makes some basic configuration changes to that are not defined in our Hiera store. These direct changes are things like bringing up an interface or making sure our example object storage (Cinder) loopback volume is mounted after the server is rebooted.

Finally, the official OpenStack Puppet modules reside on the Git server for the OpenStack project with all the other projects at https://git.openstack.org/cgit/.

Every project begins with "puppet-" and then has the specific service that it's created for, so you have puppet-nova, puppet-glance, and so on. Searching the web interface will find them all. By exploring these modules, you will learn which of the ever-growing number of options for each service the modules support as well as how they are implemented and end up in your configuration file. If you believe something is not being configured correctly, but your Puppet Hiera common.yaml has the right information, the Puppet module is the right place to look.

> **Tip**
>
> Are you sure your Puppet Hiera common.yaml file is correct?
>
> Syntax errors in this file are incredibly common and are almost non-detectable; you can put anything in that file and it's not going to throw an error. A missing colon or incorrect declaration of a variable can mean the difference between your service working or failing. Be sure to double-check.

More Puppet Help

Beyond these basic OpenStack-specific tips, you may want to reference the Puppet documentation at https://docs.puppet.com/ if you find yourself struggling with Puppet specifically. You can also see Appendix C, "Long-Lived Puppet" to learn more basics about how Puppet works and how you can run it on a more permanent basis in a deployment.

Mitigating Breakage

Wouldn't it be great if you didn't have to deal with OpenStack breaking at all? Like any infrastructure, between upgrades, scaling and unexpected hardware mishaps, we'll likely never get there, but there are things you can do to mitigate breakage in your deployments.

First, follow the best practice of most operations teams today: keep all configuration files in a revision control system (RCS). Whether you use Git, SVN or an internal system unique to your organization, make sure you're using something. Making a change that breaks your deployment and not remembering what you changed can be a huge waste of time. Keep a history of configuration files so it's easy to roll back if something goes wrong.

Secondly, have a way to test your changes. At the very least, have tooling that checks for the most basic things: configuration file syntax and unit tests for your custom code. The next step may be having a smaller scale development environment where you deploy changes to first and then run a script to check for various tasks, such as accessibility of API endpoints and the capability to complete basic tasks. When you finally go into production, many operators also segregate their production deployment, allowing certain regions of their deployment to have the new changes applied. This enables them to roll back just a subset of their deployment if unexpected problems occur and otherwise progress confidently if it goes well.

As a continuation to testing, you may also want to put together a full Continuous Integration (CI) system to test OpenStack. You can build your own with the help of an open source CI system like Jenkins (https://jenkins.io/) or look at what the OpenStack Infrastructure team has built for the OpenStack project. Before any change lands in the development version of OpenStack, it is tested with a complex series of tools put together or built by the OpenStack Infrastructure team. It includes code review (Gerrit: https:// www.gerritcodereview.com/), queue management of patches to make sure they are all tested against each other (Zuul: http://docs.openstack.org/infra/zuul/), management of a fleet of hundreds of test nodes running tests (Nodepool: http://docs.openstack.org/infra/ nodepool/) and finally the merging of patches into the project RCS, Git. Dozens of companies have now adopted this fully open source CI system for use inside their own organizations. Using it enables them to test OpenStack with the specifics of the deployment scenarios they have running and additions in the form of proprietary plug-ins and agents. Learn more about the CI system used in the OpenStack project by visiting http://docs.openstack.org/infra/system-config/.

In addition to standard testing of the components you change, be aware that upstream changes can impact your deployment as well. Ubuntu packages are updated for security and major bug fixes. In our deployment scenarios, we specify usage of the stable/mitaka branch of the Puppet modules, but even these upstream Puppet modules are also sometimes modified for security or bug fixes. Consider locking down any of these kinds of changes for your production deployment until you can test them.

While we have not devoted the resources to cover an upgrade scenario in this book, these final few tidbits of advice to help avoid breakage are specifically related to upgrades.

First, follow all the suggestions above and make sure you're testing everything before going into production. Next, always read release notes for the services you are using. OpenStack is a still a relatively young project, and it is developed in a space that is continually evolving. With each release you're bound to discover that the API version endpoint you should be using has changed, or there's a new database schema (or a new database!). Perhaps a feature you have been using has been deprecated in favor of a new one. These are all things to watch out for, and all should be covered in the release notes for each project.

Requesting Help

Sometimes you really get stuck. Perhaps you are still learning how all the components work together. Or the problem really requires a subject matter expert. Maybe an upgrade broke something you were depending on. There are countless reasons why you don't want or need to only depend upon your own knowledge or that inside your organization to find help with a problem.

When you get to this point, sanitize your configuration and log files as much as possible to remove usernames, passwords and keys, and then reach out to the OpenStack community. The OpenStack community has mailing lists for users and more advanced operators, a question and answer format web forum, various IRC (Internet Relay Chat) channels and in-person events around the world where you can get assistance. There are also dozens of companies offering professional assistance on a contract or ongoing basis. Learn more about the specifics around OpenStack help resources available in Appendix F, "Finding Help with OpenStack."

Summary

Any operator of an OpenStack deployment becomes quickly skilled in the art of troubleshooting a deployment. In this chapter we've covered key ideas and tools that can be used to get started including demonstrations of how to read error messages and the related logs, key services you should keep an eye out for and ways to tackle debugging of networking. To conclude, we explored how Puppet is used for the deployments in this book, reviewed some tactics for mitigating breakage in your deployment and covered a quick summary of how to request help.

Vendors and Hybrid Clouds

Never think you've seen the last of anything.
Eudora Welty

Much of what has been covered so far has sought to explain how to run OpenStack in a contained environment as something you run yourself, whether you're building an infrastructure for use within your organization or are building a compute cloud for customers. In this chapter we'll explore the ecosystem beyond this by talking about how vendors can help with deployments and how you can also leverage public clouds for what may become a hybrid cloud environment. Finally, we walk through how OpenStack enables you to avoid vendor lock-in with some examples of organizations that have successfully run their infrastructure across multiple clouds.

Vendor Ecosystem

No tour of OpenStack would be complete without mentioning the vast vendor ecosystem that has built up around OpenStack. There are various companies that have gotten involved with supporting OpenStack, including:

- Traditional customer hosting companies that have recently moved to offering cloud solutions
- Well-established technology companies that have now found their customers wanting a cloud solution
- Completely new companies that have sprung up to specifically offer cloud-centric solutions

These companies will offer a range of services from public to private. We'll cover public services in more depth later in the chapter. Private offerings can range anywhere from coming into your organization and building a full OpenStack deployment to more specific offerings that promise you a solution, like object storage for the sharing of files securely within your organization. As a technologist, understanding the fundamentals of what is going on in your environment is valuable, but these companies come in with the expertise needed to maintain and scale the deployment as your needs change.

If your organization is large enough that you can devote full-time staff to managing your OpenStack-driven environment, there are also vendors who specialize in training and consulting services. These services are valuable for when your team needs to learn more about a specific component of OpenStack or simply is seeking some solid expertise to get over some kind of hurdle you're facing.

The OpenStack Foundation maintains a Marketplace to find vendors at http://www.openstack.org/marketplace/. This marketplace also provides a tour of some of the distributions and appliances that are built around OpenStack and seek to make deployment and management easier. These distribution offerings almost always need vendor interaction for you to explore, but there are some that offer community editions or other simplified samples of their products if you wish to explore them on your own.

In earlier chapters we used Puppet to deploy OpenStack. Some vendors use these open source Puppet modules or others covered in Appendix B, "Other Deployment Mechanisms," but oftentimes they have built their own or added on top of the open source options. It's valuable to ask how they're doing a deployment, so you can become familiar with their tooling so you know how the pieces are coming together.

Beyond just deployment mechanisms, as you explore the vendor ecosystem you should keep in mind that you'll likely be moving into other proprietary software components. The base is still OpenStack, but the tooling around it will likely be something developed or licensed by the vendor to provide value to their customers over their competitors. It's important to understand this as you get into licensing agreements, so you can make the appropriate decisions along with your legal department.

Public and Hybrid Clouds

Beyond simply running OpenStack on your own, you can become a user of OpenStack clouds by exploring public clouds or leveraging a hybrid cloud environment in your organization.

Public Clouds

The OpenStack Marketplace mentioned earlier has a section completely devoted to public clouds. As discussed in depth in Chapter 7, "Public Compute Cloud," a public cloud is run by a third party, and you are able to interact with it to spin up instances (typically virtual machines), add block storage to your instances, interact with object storage or manage networking between your instances. It may even be somewhat transparent to you that you're using OpenStack, aside from your familiarity with the user-level tooling, as administration of OpenStack itself is handled by the vendor.

With the capability to simply hook in to a public cloud without handling maintenance and scaling, this is a very compelling option for many organizations. Public clouds can get you the ability to grow exponentially and leverage the services OpenStack provides without a large up-front investment or making it a core competency of your organization. As you evaluate the options, there are several points to keep in mind centered around location, cost and data sovereignty and security.

Location

One of the most common practical considerations an organization may have is the collection, processing and storage of data. If you're a web-based organization and all of your data is coming from customers who interact with your company over the Internet, it may make a lot of sense to manage this data in the cloud. You can leverage data centers around your country and the world provided by your public cloud vendor without having to build that out yourself, and the data is just as close to you and your customers as something you might serve up from your own data center.

On the other hand, if your organization is doing more in-house data processing, like collecting and passing data between machines that do work on-site or downloading it from a specially tuned device that only has access to a single location, you may need to evaluate whether a public cloud makes sense for you. There are certainly still the scaling and geographically distributed risk-mitigation benefits, but your organization becomes heavily dependent upon a fast and reliable Internet connection. This can be a costly investment and introduce more risk into your environment. A consideration here may be using public clouds as a backup location.

A big driver for other organizations may be established corporate IT policy or PCI Security Standards, so it's important to be aware of the specific requirements within your organization.

Cost

Running OpenStack in-house can be expensive in terms of the investment in hardware, data center space and staff. However, many organizations find that once they reach a certain scale, this price works out for them better than continuing to pay a vendor for use of their public cloud.

Some of the things to consider when evaluating cost and the benefits you gain from using a public cloud include the following:

- **Growth potential:** Will your infrastructure continue to grow as your organization succeeds?
- **Age, size and maturity of your organization:** Your organization may have leveraged public clouds early on, so an investment didn't need to be made in hardware, space and staff. As the organization continues to mature and succeed, it's vital to do regular re-evaluations to see whether that investment now makes sense.
- **Proprietary offerings that you need:** Does the public cloud you're using offer features you can't find either in open source or through strategic use of in-house development? Early stage vendor lock-in is common, and it's important to regularly evaluate what you depend upon and when or if it ever makes sense to bring this in-house.
- **Core competencies:** Your organization may make a decision that they don't want to be in the business of paying a team of engineers to manage a private infrastructure. Make sure this discussion happens so that use of the public cloud can continue to be justified and budgeted for.

As you can see, there is often a time when companies decide to stop using public clouds, but this is not universally true. In the name of core competencies for a company, many choose to use public clouds long term in order to focus their development efforts elsewhere.

Data Sovereignty and Security

Sometimes overlooked by companies when they start using public clouds, the topic of data sovereignty is not one that should be ignored. To quickly define it, data sovereignty is the concept in which data processed and stored is subject to the laws of the country in which it is located. On a day-to-day basis, users of the cloud are not familiar with where their photos are stored or where their streaming music comes from, but as the person working to place that data, it's important to keep your customers safe by being familiar with where that data is stored and the laws that govern that. When evaluating a public cloud platform, be aware of where the data centers are and your options for moving it. This potential risk can be weighed against things like latency when placing data far outside your customer range and cost that comes from hosting in less popular locations for data centers or countries.

It's also important to be familiar with data security laws in your country. In the United States there are federal laws around the storing of everything from medical data (HIPAA) to financial data (FACTA) to data about children (COPPA). This is in addition to any state and local regulations that may be in place. It's important to do an evaluation of the type of data you'll be storing and make sure your public cloud provider is able to meet your data security requirements on the infrastructure side.

Hybrid Clouds

Beyond the topic of simply leveraging public clouds, many organizations now take advantage of hybrid clouds, which are a mix of both public and private clouds, sometimes even spanning across multiple public clouds.

Uses

To begin with a series of real world examples like you've seen in earlier chapters, the following are a couple places where hybrid clouds are used today.

OpenStack Infrastructure Team

On a day-to-day basis, the development teams within the OpenStack project submit hundreds of patch proposals that all need tests to be run on them before their peers review the code for inclusion. The OpenStack Infrastructure team handles the thousands of tests kicked off per day from these proposals by running a fleet of OpenStack instances across multiple public clouds, multiple private clouds run by companies to support specific components of the project that need specialized testing and a private "infra-cloud" that the team manages itself to expand upon the donated resources provided by the public cloud companies.

The tooling for interaction with all these clouds is similar as they all use OpenStack. The team has discovered that there are small differences that crop up between how different companies structure their public and private clouds, but these typically can be overcome by testing and making changes before they are brought into production. If changes occur to a cloud the team interacts with, they also have a mechanism to specifically disable a single provider without disruption aside from decreased test capacity.

Government Research Organization

As discussed when talking about public clouds earlier in this chapter, there are many considerations when looking to leverage public clouds in an infrastructure. When you're a government agency focused on scientific research, many of these are especially important. One government research organization has been very public about their hybrid cloud deployments and has expanded outside the realm of OpenStack offerings by running a hybrid cloud that uses OpenStack as a private cloud and then reaching out to two entirely different types of public cloud offerings.

In their infrastructure, they've leveraged a cloud management platform offered by a vendor that enables them to use similar tools to manage OpenStack and various third-party cloud providers with the same tool set. The management platform vendor handles abstraction of the tools and APIs to make this possible and works closely with their customers to make sure they have access to the various features offered by each public cloud vendor, while still providing a uniform experience across several types of clouds.

This solution has enabled them to store data collected from their scientific instruments locally to their facility for sharing among researchers using their OpenStack private cloud. It has also given them a gateway for citizen scientists and enthusiasts to also interact with subsets of data through web and API-based platforms that run on public clouds.

Vendor Lock-in

With the sharp rise of open source software in the past decade, many companies have become more aware of the risks involved with proprietary vendor lock-in and how open source software helps them avoid this. Open infrastructure like that provided by OpenStack also plays a role here that is just now being discovered by organizations as they find their licenses and rates for proprietary software cloud solutions and public clouds increasing.

By using OpenStack, you are buying into a solid core of software that you can build the rest of your infrastructure around without worrying about that core rising in cost as you come to depend upon it. Even as you explore the realm of vendor-specific, and even proprietary, OpenStack distributions and appliances, the risk of lock-in is significantly lower because you're still working with the same core software deep down. You simply have more options when prices increase too much or your vendor becomes unavailable.

Finally, OpenStack runs on commodity hardware. You are not beholden to a hardware vendor who is selling you hardware specific to the software that needs to be purchased at a premium. Existing commodity hardware in a modern virtualized infrastructure should work fine for OpenStack, so you may not need to purchase any new hardware to try OpenStack.

Migrate to a New Cloud You Run

Consider the situation where the vendor you were using to handle your OpenStack stops offering those services. In addition to the consultants and ecosystem of other vendors that you find both in the OpenStack space and with proprietary cloud offerings, your organization can also choose to migrate to a cloud that's run in-house. The switch will likely not be pain-free, but, on the other hand, you'll likely be working with a familiar set of OpenStack tools and using the same open source components at a basic level, reducing the learning curve for the technology and giving your organization a place to start.

As you embark on this, you can either hire in-house talent to complete this work, hire another vendor or consultant to run your private cloud or even consider moving to a public cloud. If you choose to run it yourself, consultants and vendors are also available to complete initial stand up and staff training.

Migrate to a Cloud Run by a Vendor

Whether public or private, you have many options as you reach out to a new vendor. Again, with OpenStack at the core of your current infrastructure, you have the option of working with another OpenStack focused vendor who can quickly get up to speed with exactly what you need and want directly in OpenStack terms. If you're migrating to a public-run cloud, familiarity with the OpenStack components will save you a lot of time as you migrate your services.

Summary

The business community that has sprung up around OpenStack is one of its greatest assets. As you work to build an OpenStack-powered cloud, there will always be vendors available who specialize in various components and can offer varying levels of support and consultation, from full-stack support in-house to part-time services to help with scaling.

Beyond private clouds that are run within your organization, OpenStack opens the door for leveraging public clouds and even running a hybrid cloud. While they come with caveats that are important to consider, public clouds are a proven way to get an infrastructure running without a high up-front investment and enable companies to continue operating without running a physical environment themselves. With the hybrid cloud you can use both your private and various public clouds to give your organization a significant amount of flexibility.

A

Reference Deployment

The authors of this book have worked hard to make the demonstration Puppet deployments work on the user's preferred hardware or virtualization configuration. In Chapter 3, "Networking," there are diagrams which demonstrate the logical and physical diagrams for how a system should be set up.

If you are struggling with your own configuration or don't have a preference as to the tooling you use, the following is a reference deployment you can use that has been tested. We make all the decisions about the hardware, software and virtualization technology required.

Requirements

This reference deployment will use a single computer (server, desktop or laptop) running Ubuntu 14.04. The controller and compute host will be run virtually on KVM. The server must have at least the following specifications:

- 1 NIC
- 50G of hard drive space
- 8G of RAM
- Hardware virtualization in the CPU enabled

This reference deployment will be using the following software installed from the Ubuntu software archives: KVM and qemu for virtualization, libvirt to manage the controller and compute nodes, Virtual Machine Manager and OpenSSH to access the controller and compute nodes and Linux bridging on the host to manage the provider networks.

Installation

Follow these steps to create the reference deployment.

1. Install Ubuntu 14.04 Desktop. This will be the host machine for your controller and compute hosts and you can also run your graphical tooling from here.

2. Install packages to support the environment:

```
$ sudo apt-get install openssh-server libvirt-bin qemu-kvm qemu-system \
virt-manager bridge-utils
```

3. Your user should have been added to the libvirtd group, but if not you can add it with:

```
$ sudo adduser your_username libvirtd
```

4. Log out and log back in for this to take effect.

5 Set up your network bridges:

```
$ sudo brctl addbr virbr1
$ sudo ip addr add 203.0.113.1/24 dev virbr1
```

The 192.168.122.1/24 network will assign IP addresses directly to the KVM-based virtual machines you will launch. The 203.0.113.1/24 network will function as the external network, which we'll be able to use to assign fake public addresses to the OpenStack instances from this address pool.

> **Note**
>
> You should already have a virbr0 with 192.168.122.1/24, which was set up automatically when you installed libvirt. Confirm by browsing the output of:
>
> $ ip addr show
>
> If it was not, you will want to look into the virsh networking documentation for how to manipulate virsh-created networks. See: http://wiki.libvirt.org/page/Networking.

6. Now we'll create the disk images. Remember, you need 50G of hard drive space available for these two. If you don't have that much, you may be able to shrink these disks slightly, but it will reduce the space you have to work with on the controller and compute nodes:

```
$ sudo qemu-img create -f qcow2 -o preallocation=metadata \
/var/lib/libvirt/images/controller.qcow2 30G
$ sudo qemu-img create -f qcow2 -o preallocation=metadata \
/var/lib/libvirt/images/compute.qcow2 20G
```

7. Download the latest Ubuntu 14.04 64-bit PC (AMD64) server image from http://releases.ubuntu.com/trusty/ and place it in /var/lib/libvirt/images/. This location is important as it will be used in a command later. You need to use sudo to place the image in this directory.

8. With these images created and the Ubuntu disk image in place, use the libvirt command to create your controller node with 4G of RAM and 2 NICs:

```
$ sudo virt-install --connect qemu:///system -n controller --vcpus=2 -r 4096 \
--network=bridge:virbr0 --network=bridge:virbr1 \
-f /var/lib/libvirt/images/controller.qcow2 \
-c /var/lib/libvirt/images/ubuntu-14.04.4-server-amd64.iso --vnc \
--noautoconsole --os-type linux --os-variant ubuntutrusty
```

9. To connect to this, use Virtual Machine Manager, which can be launched searching for the Virtual Machine Manager in the Ubuntu dash.

10. Since this VM has two NICs, when you get to the installation screen prompting you to Configure the Network, select eth0: Ethernet as your Primary network interface.

11. Now create your compute node, with 2G of RAM and 1 NIC:

```
$ sudo virt-install --connect qemu:///system -n compute --vcpus=2 -r 2048 \
--network=bridge:virbr0 -f /var/lib/libvirt/images/compute.qcow2 \
-c /var/lib/libvirt/images/ubuntu-14.04.4-server-amd64.iso --vnc \
--noautoconsole --os-type linux --os-variant ubuntutrusty
```

With both servers up and running, you can log into them via ssh or interact through Virtual Machine Manager (see Figure A.1) to set up the systems as defined in Chapter 5, "Foundations for Deployments," and beyond.

Recommendations

Instead of interacting through Virtual Machine Manager for all your commands, you may want to install the openssh-server package on all systems. This will allow you to use SSH to connect to the machines and will make pasting commands into them easier.

Additionally, the Firefox web browser comes with the Ubuntu desktop you have installed. You can use this to interact with Horizon, the OpenStack Dashboard, without installing any additional software.

Figure A.1   Virtual Machine Manager. You can access the KVM
instances you created by using Virtual Machine Manager.

B

Other Deployment Mechanisms

In this book we explored using Puppet to do various deployments of OpenStack. However, Puppet is just one of your options in the vast OpenStack ecosystem. By having a variety of deployment mechanisms, OpenStack can be deployed in your organization without a switch in tooling or by having it run on different tooling than the rest of your environment.

All deployment mechanisms that are part of the OpenStack community itself can be found by browsing through the OpenStack code repository at https://git.openstack.org/cgit/openstack/.

The tools covered here are the most popular and mature, but this list of tools is always changing, and it's always worth doing a search for your favorite tool not listed here to see if there are OpenStack deployment instructions available or in development.

Chef

Chef cookbooks are available for OpenStack under the OpenStack project in the project git repository. They all begin with the prefix cookbook-openstack- and end with the specific project they are deploying. For instance, you will find the compute (Nova) project Chef cookbooks via this address: https://git.openstack.org/cgit/openstack/cookbook-openstack-compute/tree/.

The README.rst file in each repository provides a reference for each project. Each of them have some basic instructions about usage of the cookbooks and many link to an additional repository that describes how to use it in the context of a full OpenStack deployment.

Ansible

A series of Ansible playbooks are also available in the OpenStack project git repository, directly accessible for browsing from here https://git.openstack.org/cgit/openstack/openstack-ansible/tree.

Unlike Chef and Puppet, Ansible has provided a single deployment playbook that pulls in other components. Instructions for basic setup are included in the README.rst file, which includes a tour of some of the scripts available, depending on what kind of deployment you're looking to do, from boot-strapping to running playbooks individually and more.

SaltStack and Others

Other open source configuration management tools, such as SaltStack, also now have published OpenStack tooling in their official repositories. These are maintained outside of the direct OpenStack community, and instructions for download and usage can be found by searching the code repositories and documentation for these projects.

Vendor-Specific

Community-driven efforts with technologies such as Puppet, Chef and Ansible have come up to speed for production use in the recent past, but OpenStack had historically been complicated to deploy. As discussed in Chapter 14, "Vendors and Hybrid Clouds," vendors offer a vast array of vendor-specific deployment mechanisms. Some of these mechanisms are tightly integrated with what the vendor calls their own OpenStack distribution, which packages a lot of other tools in with their OpenStack offering. Red Hat and HPE are among companies with offerings. Other companies focus on using their deployment tools to focus on deployment, such as Juju by Canonical for the Ubuntu ecosystem.

The OpenStack Marketplace, hosted by the OpenStack Foundation, provides a comprehensive list of vendors who offer their own OpenStack distributions and appliances at http://www.openstack.org/marketplace/distros/.

C
Long-Lived Puppet

For each deployment example in this book we ran a setup script and then `puppet apply` to apply the manifests. This works well for working through each scenario to get a feel for how OpenStack works in various deployments, but it is not a maintainable way to run OpenStack. In order to take the Puppet deployments module and Hiera from this book and turn it into a real Puppet OpenStack deployment, there are some things that you will need to consider and changes that will need to be made.

Puppet Master or Masterless?

From the Puppet side, the first main thing you'll need to change is that you might not want to run Puppet using `puppet apply` like we have here. Although some OpenStack deployments use masterless Puppet, it has some disadvantages. First, all Puppet code and Hiera data needs to be copied to every node and kept up-to-date. You also cannot use things like exported resources (https://docs.puppet.com/puppet/latest/reference/lang_exported.html) with masterless Puppet. Compared to masterless, running Puppet with a Puppet master has a few advantages as well. First, it provides a single place to make a change and have it automatically deployed out to every node. By default, all the clients will request a catalog and do a Puppet run every 30 minutes. This means that within 30 minutes, updates will be applied and hand-made changes will be auto-reverted (as long as the resource that is changed is managed by Puppet). Although masterless Puppet also has some advantages too, such as no catalog compile bottleneck, you need to at least affirm that you want to be running masterless and weigh the pros and cons before you productize the solution provided in this book.

Hiera

In this book we use a key/value tool called Hiera from Puppet to store preferences for each deployment example. For simplicity reasons, the Hiera used in this book barely meets the definition of what Hiera is supposed to be. Hiera is supposed to allow overlapping values that are exposed based on a hierarchy. In this book we have a simple flat file. In any real deployment you will want to have a real hierarchy that exposes layers like region, node type, and whether the node is dev, staging, or prod. Think of a case where you might want your dev compute box to have a different version of a package than a production node. This is what Hiera is for. It can even be used to separate nodes geographically. A node in Europe will have different NTP and DNS servers than a node in the Americas. Read more about the power of Hiera at https://docs.puppet.com/hiera/1/.

Passwords in Hiera

Another issue you will need to solve is storing passwords in Hiera. Checking passwords into git unencrypted is not a good idea and is unsafe. Using the hiera-emyl back end is one solution to this problem. The passwords will be encrypted on disk and decrypted for catalog compiles (see: https://puppet.com/blog/encrypt-your-data-using-hiera-eyaml). This has the drawback that your Puppet master will need a decryption key but is a large improvement over plain text. There are other solutions to consider as well. Just keep in mind that managing passwords that hold the keys to your entire deployment should be a top consideration. Hiera includes passwords for the OpenStack admin user, RabbitMQ, and MySQL, any of which, if leaked, would be extremely dangerous.

Node Classification

As noted earlier, in this book you are choosing what type of node you have by manually running `puppet apply` on a given box. This method does not scale well and is error prone. What would happen to your OpenStack cluster if someone accidentally applied the foundations_public_cloud.pp catalog to a compute host? In order to run this in production you need to think about how you will do your Puppet node classification (https://docs.puppet.com/pe/latest/puppet_assign_configurations.html). This can be done using the Puppet console that ships with Puppet Enterprise (paid), but it can also be done with Hiera and the site.pp file. This is something you'll need to consider as you productize this code.

Module Management

One major consideration will be how you manage Puppet modules and stay in-sync with upstream. The versions of the modules are managed by the Puppetfile and then pulled by the Puppet deployment toolset r10k. For the most part, the Puppetfile shipped with this book puts you in good shape. Versions of non-OpenStack modules are locked to specific tags, which means that their code cannot "move" unless you move it. But new modules are tagged and released every day. In fact, many of the tags in that Puppetfile are probably already outdated. What system will you have for updating those tags and tracking new releases? How will you test the new modules? These are key considerations that you will need to make. I advise that falling behind and then trying to do a massive jump on all the modules at once is not a good plan. Plan on reviewing the module tags at least every few months to see if they can be upgraded. The following is an example of a module pinned to a tag:

```
mod 'stdlib',
  :git => 'https://github.com/puppetlabs/puppetlabs-stdlib.git',
  :ref => '4.6.0'
```

The OpenStack modules are not pinned to a tag. They're tied to a release branch, which may be represented like the stable/mitaka, or in the future this may be stable/newton. Based on the policy that the Puppet OpenStack team uses, this branch should be free of breaking changes and should only get better as fixes are backported. "Should" is the key word here. By not tying to a tag, we pick up fixes in these modules every time the stable/mitaka branch of Puppet OpenStack modules are updated, but we run the risk that something that breaks us is backported. In other words, every time r10k runs you probably will get something good, but you might get something bad. You will either need to live with this risk or pin these modules to a specific commit ID and update them on a cadence as is suggested with the other modules. Puppet OpenStack modules do not have tags on stable branches, so you will need to link to a commit-id if you want these locked. The following is an example of how you might have a module pinned to a branch:

```
mod 'neutron',
  :git => 'https://github.com/openstack/puppet-neutron.git',
  :ref => 'stable/mitaka'
```

A final note on modules—if you find issues, please file bugs and, if possible, please contribute a fix upstream. If the problem is with the Puppet modules you can ask in the #puppet-openstack channel on freenode (IRC) or file a bug against the module in Launchpad. See Appendix F, "Finding Help with OpenStack," for how to get help with or file bugs if your problem is more generally about OpenStack. If you would like to learn how to contribute, see Appendix D, "Contributing Code to OpenStack."

Software Life Cycle

With Puppet managing your OpenStack deployment, you will be living the "infrastructure as code" mantra that has become popular in modern IT. This means you will need to define a software life cycle for your Puppet code and Hiera data. This might include separate test environments, code reviews, a CI (continuous integration) process and determining how you will test, update, and deploy code. There's no right way to do this, but you need to consider it.

Roles and Profiles

The code in this book uses Puppet roles and profiles, which is an excellent design pattern for Puppet. It makes nodes easier to "remix" by moving features around and even creating new node types. However, the node types defined for this book may not meet your architecture requirements. You will need to consider your architecture and experiment with new node types or role modifications as you deploy your cloud. This appendix only scratches the surface of what can be done with roles and profiles. You'll want to consult the Puppet documentation to learn more.

Packages

In this book we are using the official Ubuntu packages for Puppet, but these are somewhat behind what Puppet is shipping. This code was tested against the 3.x series of Puppet and should work with the Ubuntu version or the latest 3.x package from Puppet. However, you may get better support in the Puppet community and with Puppet bugs if you are using the latest packages that Puppet ships. Although Puppet 4 has been released, it is quite new and not all modules support it yet. Whether you choose to use 3.x or 4.x, you should probably get the packages for Puppet, Hiera, and Facter from Puppet. For Ubuntu you can enable this repo by running the following:

```
$ sudo su -
$ apt-key adv --keyserver keyserver.ubuntu.com --recv-keys 0x1054B7A24BD6EC30
$ echo 'deb http://apt.puppetlabs.com/ trusty main dependencies' > \
/etc/apt/sources.list.d/puppetlabs.list
$ apt-get update
```

Revision Control

One of the strengths of using a configuration management system like Puppet is the capability to put everything into a revision control system. When using something like git you can track changes over time, revert to known working configurations and keep things like passwords and secret keys in a centralized place. If you're not using revision control today for your systems, we'd highly recommend it. This book uses a public GitHub git repository, but if you're storing critical information about your deployment, like IP addresses and passwords, you will probably want to set up a private git repo. One other note: you may be tempted to put all your Puppet modules into one repo and skip using r10k with separate repos. This might give you a quick initial boost in productivity, but it will cost you long-term. It quickly becomes unwieldy and is also difficult to sync with upstream module changes. Many others who tried this method for their deployments have switched to the method shown in this book that employs r10k to check out modules individually.

What Else Belongs in Your Composition Module?

At its heart, the deployments module is a composition module. The deployments module we created was written specifically for this book and basic OpenStack deployments. It glues together all the Puppet OpenStack modules along with supporting modules like MySQL and RabbitMQ and joins them to give you a running OpenStack cloud. What we've presented here is pretty minimal; there's a variety of other things that belong in an OpenStack composition module.

You will likely not want to use the composition module we have provided in a production deployment, instead creating your own that has the customizations that you require.

The following is not an exhaustive list but will hopefully help you prepare to take your cloud to production and build your own composition module:

- Setting up backups of critical elements of your deployment. An example would be MySQL.

- Managing apt repositories. The module, at present, only adds the Ubuntu Cloud Archive repo. You might need to add one for RabbitMQ or Puppet or other vendors.

- Working around packaging issues. Sometimes packages do not have proper dependencies on versions of packages. The composition layer can be used to enforce these dependencies for you.

- Adding additional OpenStack roles, users, and projects. If you have a standard set of roles or users that you want in your cloud, your composition layer can declare them.

- Working around upstream issues in Puppet OpenStack. While the Puppet OpenStack team tries hard not to release code with bugs, it does happen. If you have a bug or a corner case that your deployment has, you can sometimes work around it in the composition layer. Please still report bugs upstream!

- Setting up clustering and HA. Your composition module might also help you configure and deploy clustering or HA solutions such as HAProxy or Galera Cluster for MySQL.

- Tuning. Finally, the composition layer can help manage tuning in your OpenStack cluster. Tuning might include database tuning, system tuning with sysctl and tuning RabbitMQ.

More Information

There are a couple of conference videos available that can explain more about the OpenStack Puppet modules and the relationship between them and a composition module like the deployments module. In some of these talks you may hear the modules referred to as the "Stackforge" Puppet modules. The modules covered here have since been moved and renamed to the OpenStack Puppet modules.

This first video is from the OpenStack Summit in Vancouver in the spring of 2015. It provides a good introduction to the OpenStack Puppet modules along with examples of two different company's solutions for deploying them. "Building Clouds with OpenStack Puppet Modules" can be found at https://www.youtube.com/watch?v=j58VnW2LMM0.

The second video is from PuppetConf 2015 in Portland in the fall of 2015. It provides a similar overview of the OpenStack Puppet modules and a tour through the common components in OpenStack with these modules. "Deploying OpenStack with Puppet Faster than Light" can be found at https://www.youtube.com/watch?v=HjkEsPJ4p-s.

D

Contributing Code to OpenStack

The OpenStack project can loosely be described as a vast ecosystem of individual projects that come together to build the end result that we call OpenStack. Each of these projects is governed at a high level by the OpenStack Technical Committee (TC) but on a per-project basis has an elected Project Team Lead (PTL) and core code reviewers who are specific to just that project. The OpenStack ecosystem also supports projects the scope of which covers all of the project, including the Documentation, Internationalization (i18n) and OpenStack project Infrastructure teams.

Contributing to OpenStack can be daunting at first because of this large ecosystem, but by narrowing in on specific segments that this appendix discusses, you can be a successful contributor.

Contribution Overview

There are some key concepts that range across all of the OpenStack projects, including the use of Python as the core development language, the feature specification process, code review, release cycle and the testing infrastructure that all code must pass.

Contributors in the OpenStack project come from a vast array of companies, organizations and individual contributors. Many of the contributors are directly paid by an employer, but there are always some volunteer contributors who contribute for a variety of reasons. As OpenStack developers continue to be in high demand, familiarity with the OpenStack ecosystem can be a boon to your career in OpenStack.

Release Cycle

When you are new to contributing to OpenStack, the release cycle may not be of much interest. However, you may want to eventually understand it so that your changes are incorporated into the version of OpenStack you're targeting.

With the exception of a few projects that are not tightly coupled with the rest of OpenStack (for example: Infrastructure, Ironic, Swift), non-client projects in OpenStack are released on a 6-month cycle. This 6-month cycle is kicked off with an OpenStack Design Summit and Conference where users in the OpenStack community get together to learn more about OpenStack in a presentation and panel-driven conference setting.

Developers get together for Design Summit sessions where in-person meetings are held to work through key components of focus for each project during the next 6 months and beyond. Some teams also schedule an in-person mid-cycle event about halfway through the release in order to get together in person and discuss any outstanding challenges with completing work planned for that cycle.

Throughout the release cycle, there are milestones and release candidates that shift and change per release as the OpenStack project grows and evolves. Members of a project typically work together to meet certain deadlines throughout the release cycle so that focus toward the end can be on release candidates and only bugs that will impact the release.

Communication

OpenStack contributors come from various companies and live all over the world. When teams aren't working together in person at a Design Summit or at a mid-cycle, collaboration occurs online through various communication channels.

The OpenStack community is committed to transparent decisions that all contributors have access to. This means that communities are encouraged to use open source software platforms when communicating with the project and to make sure Internet Relay Chat (IRC) logs or recordings of these meetings are kept for community review.

Mailing Lists

The OpenStack project runs a series of mailing lists, a full listing of which can be found at http://lists.openstack.org/.

Development discussions across all projects occur on the openstack-dev mailing list and can be filtered based on topics in the subject. For instance, all discussions about Nova will have an email subject that includes [Nova]. This is a very high traffic list.

As an operator, you may be interested in the openstack-user and openstack-operators mailing lists. The Operators mailing list has a similar tagging system to that of the dev mailing list.

The other mailing lists cover a variety of topics, including the work going into Documentation, Internationalization (i18n), Infrastructure, Community and various local OpenStack groups communicating in their native language.

The archive, or record of all emails, for a mailing list can be found by going to its respective http://lists.openstack.org/ page and looking for the Archives link.

Internet Relay Chat (IRC)

Internet Relay Chat (IRC) is a popular, cross platform chat technology that has been around for decades and is popular for open source projects. Most projects have their own IRC channel, or chat room, where discussion on that project is held. OpenStack channels reside on the freenode IRC network and can be accessed via clients across all popular platforms (Mac, Windows, Linux, Android, iOS).

Day-to-day discussions about development of each component occur on IRC, with bigger discussions and decisions typically happening on the mailing lists. There are also bots on IRC that alert contributors when new changes are submitted for review in the code review system or merged into the repository.

Meetings are held in a series of meeting channels. The meeting schedule and links to logs for these meetings and general channel logs can be found at: http://eavesdrop.openstack.org/

> **Reminder**
>
> We're an international community. All meetings are scheduled in UTC time so it's clear to all contributors when the meeting is. If you can, use a time zone converter or add meetings to your calendar in the UTC time zone so you don't miss a meeting.

Support

While not strictly related to code submissions, a discussion of communication would be incomplete without mentioning support outlets that keep the OpenStack community running.

There is a high-traffic OpenStack mailing list where support questions should be sent (rather than to the OpenStack Development list, mentioned earlier): http://lists.openstack .org/cgi-bin/mailman/listinfo/openstack.

Operators who are seeking to collaborate, and share best practices around running OpenStack at scale can join the OpenStack Operators mailing list: http://lists.openstack.org/ cgi-bin/mailman/listinfo/openstack-operators.

Learn more about user-level support in Appendix F, "Finding Help with OpenStack."

Specifications

Whether you're seeking to propose a new feature or looking for work to do, familiarizing yourself with the specification process in the OpenStack community is important to making a difference.

Specifications outline the work that is planned for a project for a given time period, typically a release cycle. These start out as a peer-reviewed document that outlines various components of a proposed new feature or change to the project. Typically, these describe the change in detail, including rationale for the feature, discuss some of the alternatives that the submitter has explored and explain things like security, API and broader project impact.

All specifications can be found at http://specs.openstack.org/.

If you seek to add a feature, you will need to write a specification and submit it to the community for review. This will typically take several weeks as you work with the project members to get people to look at your specification and you respond to comments about it through the review tool. Once accepted, you can get to work writing the code and supporting material (documentation, unit tests) required for your new feature.

Specifications can also be valuable to a new contributor who is looking for something to work on. Each project has sorted specifications so you can determine what is currently being worked on, and, with the detailed description of it, can enable you to get up to speed with required components and start working with the team that is currently assigned.

In the short term, the specifications process enables anyone to see what is happening within a project during a given cycle and gives newcomers an opportunity to find something to work on. In the long term, specifications give detailed historical rationale for why specific decisions were made and document other strategies considered.

> **Tip**
>
> If you're interested in working on a specification, coordinate your work with the rest of the team. There are often already people working on specifications and you don't want to duplicate work.

Note that if you're just working to fix a bug or make a simple change that has been discussed with the project team, either in IRC or on the OpenStack Development mailing list, you do not need to go through the specification process.

Bug and Feature Tracking

The OpenStack project uses the open source project platform Launchpad at https://launchpad.net/ for bug and feature tracking. While the project continues to explore other options, one of the key things that Launchpad has offered the OpenStack project is the ability to mark bugs as impacting multiple projects. For a project that is made up of many pieces that build the larger project we call OpenStack, the ability to mark multiple projects is essential.

Git and Code Review

OpenStack uses Git for code revision control. All code for the OpenStack project goes through peer-review, through a code review system called Gerrit hosted at https://review.openstack.org/.

After passing a series of automated tests (see "Testing Infrastructure" later in this appendix), project members then do a thorough review of the code. Code review may consist of making sure the code is safe and well-written and generally adheres to project standards. Reviewers may also test the code and offer feedback about how it can be run more efficiently or leverage other components of the project more effectively. Code testing is also deeply ingrained in the culture of OpenStack, so it's common for reviewers to insist upon tests when the code touches certain components of the project, such as the API.

Review of your code can take days or weeks, depending on the code submitted and when in the release cycle it has been submitted. Best practices for getting your code included are as follows:

- Submit early in the release cycle—later in the cycle code contributions become more restricted.
- Submit small changes rather than large ones—small changes are easier to review so more likely to get reviews.
- Be diligent about quickly following up with any comments to your code.

For code to ultimately be included, it needs peer review from other community members and approval in the form of a +2 vote from at least two core reviewers in a project. Once code has two +2 votes, a core reviewer can then Approve the change for final testing.

> **Tip**
>
> Having trouble finding someone to review your change? Anyone can review and add a +1/-1 vote to a review, so build up goodwill in the community by reviewing changes submitted by other people. Increasing your review numbers through thoughtful, thorough reviews is also a way to start building a reputation so that you, too, someday could become one of the core reviewers.
>
> If all else fails, you can join the project IRC channel and ask for some feedback on your review. Do not send review requests to the development mailing list.

Full documentation for getting set up with Git and the code review system, including the process for getting an account, is in the Developer's Guide portion of the OpenStack Infrastructure User Manual http://docs.openstack.org/infra/manual/developers.html.

Testing Infrastructure

All code submitted to the OpenStack project goes through a series of automated tests completed by the OpenStack Continuous Integration (CI) test infrastructure. The test infrastructure runs a series of tests, including unit tests defined in the project itself, code consistency tests for Python code that include lint and pep8 tests and full integration tests where an instance of OpenStack (in this case, DevStack) is launched to confirm that code being tested for one project does not have adverse impact on any other projects in OpenStack.

As described in Figure D.1, all code goes through a series of servers on the journey to be tested. First, code is uploaded to the code review system from the developer's system. The code review system then notifies a tool called Zuul that queues jobs up for testing, noting dependencies and order to make sure all changes are properly tested against each other. Zuul hands off the change to a Gearman worker, which then decides where to pass it to for actual testing on the test slaves, which are managed in a fleet by Nodepool.

Many projects today also have third-party CI systems also voting on changes. These come from various companies and organizations to test both open source and proprietary solutions against the latest commits to the OpenStack project repositories. Typically, you want to have your code passing these tests as well, but there are a variety of reasons why you may see your code get approved while some of the third-party tests are failing (outages, misconfiguration, etc.).

This process is largely invisible to the developer. All they know is that they have submitted code for review and can track the status of their tests by visiting the Zuul status page at http://status.openstack.org/zuul/ and searching for the change number. Once tests have completed, a bot comments in the code review interface with test results and verifies whether they have passed or not by leaving a verification vote. From there, peers and core reviewers review the code and then approve it, as described earlier in the "Git and Code Review" section of this appendix. Once the code is approved, it then goes through final testing called The Gate, which makes sure no conflicts or changes have arisen since the first testing that now cause the code to fail to merge or work properly. Once the code passes these tests, it is accepted into the project.

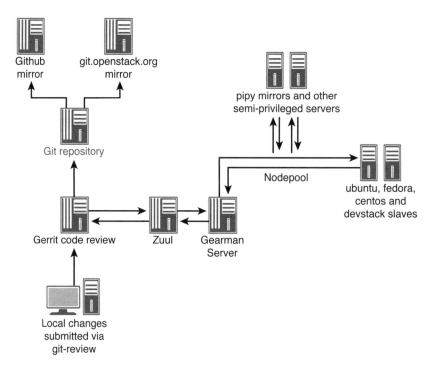

Figure D.1   OpenStack CI overview

> **Note**
>
> Want to learn more about the Continuous Integration system used by OpenStack? Visit the Infrastructure Team system documentation at http://docs.openstack.org/infra/system-config/ and see some of our slides decks at http://docs.openstack.org/infra/publications/.

Other Contributions

This appendix only provided a glimpse into the code-focused development efforts of the OpenStack project. No software project would be complete without the efforts of teams working on Documentation, Internationalization, Project Infrastructure, Release Management, Quality Assurance and more. All of these projects have distinct ways of getting involved which you can learn about by visiting the Project Teams lists maintained by the OpenStack Technical Committee at http://governance.openstack.org/reference/projects/.

OpenStack Client (OSC)

When you are exploring documentation and how-to guides in the OpenStack ecosystem, you will inevitably come across documents that describe per-service clients in order to run commands. Since these were all managed by individual teams, inconsistencies grew up between commands and overlap in functionality. For instance, some clients would have you use a hyphen between elements and you were able to do image calls from the compute client, as well as from the image client.

In 2015, projects began to deprecate these individual commands maintained by each project in favor of a consolidated client that includes support for all projects in a predicable manner: OpenStack Client (OSC). This book uses OSC for all services that support it at the time of writing. Neutron and Ceilometer currently do not have OSC support so we used their service-specific client as needed.

Basics

The bare minimum you need to know about using OSC is how to get it authenticated and the basic command structure so you can effectively use given commands and construct your own.

Authentication

In order to use any client, you need to pass it credentials. OSC mostly follows the credentials that the old clients used, and this is most easily done through an rc file. The rc files used in this book in /etc/openrc.admin and /etc/openrc.test were created by our Puppet manifests. These export a series of variables that are needed, some of them privileged (like the password).

For instance, looking at the openrc.test file you will see something like:

```
$ cat /etc/openrc.test
export OS_TENANT_NAME='test_project'
export OS_USERNAME='test'
export OS_PASSWORD='test'
export OS_AUTH_URL='http://192.168.122.38:5000/v3'
export OS_AUTH_STRATEGY='keystone'
export OS_REGION_NAME='RegionOne'
export OS_USER_DOMAIN_ID='default'
export OS_PROJECT_DOMAIN_ID='default'
export OS_IDENTITY_API_VERSION=3
```

By sourcing this file, your environment ends up with all the credentials you need to run OSC commands that your user has access to. You also have the option of passing all of these in-line at the command line when you run each command. For instance, you can use the following instead to run the image list command:

```
$ openstack --os-auth-url=http://192.168.122.38:5000/v3 --os-project-name=test_project \
--os-username=test --os-password=test --os-project-domain-id=default \
--os-region-name=RegionOne --os-identity-api-version=3 image list
```

This is quite unwieldy as a command to run, so using an rc file is recommended and preferred by most operators.

Commands

OSC has a predictable framework for calling commands as follows:

```
$ openstack <object> <action>
```

For example:

```
$ openstack compute service list
$ openstack image list
```

In the first command compute service is a two-word object and the action we're performing against it is a list of the compute services deployed. In the second command image is the object and we're also doing a list against that.

Just like the project-specific clients, some OSC commands require admin privileges to run, for example, openstack token issue and openstack endpoint create. You will get a detailed "You are not authorized to perform the requested action" error if you try to use a command as a user that you don't have access to.

Projects are always being added and functionality increased for existing services, so you can learn about the latest commands supported at http://docs.openstack.org/developer/python-openstackclient/.

Interactive Mode

OSC also has an interactive mode, which is a bit like a shell that enables you to use "openstack" on your system shell prompt alone, and then issue commands. For example, look at the following:

```
$ openstack
(openstack) image list
+--------------------------------------+-------------+
| ID                                   | Name        |
+--------------------------------------+-------------+
| 51f6c806-799a-4c01-b383-1d890b539828 | Cirros 0.3.4 |
+--------------------------------------+-------------+
```

Just as with running commands individually, you will have needed to pass credentials, either by sourcing an rc file before launching the client interactive mode or by passing values in-line. Note that if you do choose to pass them in-line, the credentials only need to be passed once, as the client then caches them as long as you have interactive mode running. Learn more about interactive mode at http://docs.openstack.org/developer/python-openstackclient/interactive.html.

Quick Reference

The following commands are a series of frequently used commands by operators who deploy OpenStack clouds.

List all of your running instances across your OpenStack cloud, as admin:

```
$ openstack server list --all-tenants
```

List all the instance images available to you:

```
$ openstack image list
```

List all the compute flavors available to you:

```
$ openstack flavor list
```

Show API endpoints available for use:

```
$ openstack endpoint list
```

List keypairs that have been uploaded:

```
$ openstack keypair list
```

Get a token:

```
$ openstack token issue
```

Retrieve the keystone catalog:

```
$ openstack catalog list
```

List OpenStack users, as admin:

```
$ openstack user list
```

Get a list of volumes:

```
$ openstack volume list
```

Show all your object storage containers:

```
openstack container list
```

Finding Help with OpenStack

OpenStack is a complicated infrastructure project that grows, changes and matures with every release. This book has given you a gradual introduction to various types of deployments by running your own scenarios on some local machines, but as you move into production you will inevitably have questions that are beyond the scope of what we've been able to cover here.

The OpenStack community is made up of developers, users and experienced operators from a variety of companies around the world. This community forms the basis of an online community that shares resources with each other and can help newcomers with problems they encounter as they begin to use and then grow their deployment of OpenStack. The following are various mechanisms for finding help in the OpenStack community.

Documentation

Official OpenStack Project documentation can be found at http://docs.openstack.org/.

There you will find step-by-step installation guides for various Linux distributions, guides for APIs and various operations and administrative guides. The following guides are recommended by the author:

- Benefit from the expertise of experienced operators with the OpenStack Operations Guide: http://docs.openstack.org/ops/.
- Find out more about managing and troubleshooting a production OpenStack cloud with the OpenStack Cloud Administrator Guide: http://docs.openstack.org/admin-guide-cloud/.
- Always find the latest step-by-step installation instructions for Ubuntu 14.04 with the manual OpenStack Installation Guide for Ubuntu: http://docs.openstack.org/mitaka/install-guide-ubuntu/
- Learn more about the history and philosophy around OpenStack with the Project Team Guide: http://docs.openstack.org/project-team-guide/.

This documentation portal is also where you will find contributor guides if you wish to learn more about the development of and contribute back to an OpenStack project. You can also learn more about contributing code in Appendix D, "Contributing Code to OpenStack."

Mailing Lists

OpenStack has dozens of mailing lists collectively found at http://lists.openstack.org/. Of particular interest to users are the following:

- OpenStack General mailing list, a user list where newcomer questions are welcome: http://lists.openstack.org/cgi-bin/mailman/listinfo/openstack.
- OpenStack Operators mailing list, a list where more experienced operators of OpenStack clouds share experience and make plans for working with developers to prioritize needs of the community: http://lists.openstack.org/cgi-bin/mailman/listinfo/openstack-operators.
- OpenStack Community mailing list, which includes the weekly news from the OpenStack community as well as updates to resources from the OpenStack Foundation (not for technical questions): http://lists.openstack.org/cgi-bin/mailman/listinfo/community.

If you are unfamiliar with using an open source community mailing list, you may also want to browse the Etiquette guidelines before posting a message: https://wiki.openstack.org/wiki/MailingListEtiquette.

Web-Based

The OpenStack project runs a service called AskBot to power the web-based https://ask.openstack.org/ forum service. A question-and-answer service with voter ranking of answers, this site serves the needs of OpenStack users who are more comfortable with a web-based resource.

If you're new to this style of question and answer based service, it's recommended that you begin by reading the Frequently Asked Questions (FAQ) first: https://ask.openstack.org/en/faq/.

Chat

The vast majority of collaboration between OpenStack developers happens over text-based chat called Internet Relay Chat (IRC) on the freenode network. This makes it a valuable place to also get support for OpenStack in channels like #openstack and #openstack-101. Note that most people in these channels are doing support on a volunteer basis rather than as part of their jobs, so if you ask a question there, be prepared to stay connected and wait for some time for an answer.

If you're familiar with IRC, you can connect to chat.freenode.net to access these resources. If not, visit this wiki page to learn more about IRC and where to find a client to connect with: https://wiki.openstack.org/wiki/IRC.

Conferences and User Groups

Conferences and user groups are a major part of learning for most people who work with OpenStack. Users, operators and vendors get together for a variety of types of events each year. A high-level overview of OpenStack events can be found at http://www.openstack.org/community/events/.

OpenStack Summits

Every six months, members of the OpenStack community gather in a single city for an OpenStack Summit. These summits are held all over the world in order to make it easier for a broad swath of OpenStack users, operators and developers to attend. These summits have keynotes from major companies who are building products and services on OpenStack as well as hundreds of talks, panels and other events throughout the week that touch upon various aspects of using, deploying, scaling and developing OpenStack. Learn the latest about the next summit by visiting https://www.openstack.org/summit/.

Videos from these summits are made freely available by the OpenStack Foundation and can be accessed by going to the pages for past events. Even if you're unable to attend the summit, these videos are a treasure trove of information for people across the OpenStack community, from newcomers to seasoned operators who are looking to improve their work in production with the latest improvements from developers and tips from other operators.

OpenStack Ops Meetup

Originally focused on developers, many teams also get together between summits to collaborate, and Operators are no exception. At Ops Meetups, experienced operators gather together to share best practices, plan for approaching developers with collective needs and generally get to know other operators. Typically, a few Project Technical Leads of OpenStack projects also attend these Meetups to get to know operators.

Learn about upcoming Meetups by visiting the wiki page for their events at https://wiki.openstack.org/wiki/Operations/Meetups, and keep up with latest plans by reading the OpenStack Operators mailing list (see the section "Mailing Lists" earlier in this appendix).

OpenStack User Groups

All over the world OpenStack community members are getting together for OpenStack User Group meetings. These meetups range from casual gatherings of other people who find OpenStack interesting or are just getting started, to full-fledged monthly events with high profile presenters and hundreds of attendees. Find one near you by visiting https://groups.openstack.org/.

Vendors

Finally, beyond the fleet of volunteers in the OpenStack community, there are several avenues of paid support. By exploring the OpenStack Marketplace at http://www.openstack.org/marketplace/ you will find links to training programs and integration and consulting vendors around the world. The integration and consulting vendors offer a vast array of support, from doing all the work of bringing OpenStack into your organization with their custom solution to being a resource you can contact when you need support. The Marketplace will also give you the ability to explore offerings for public and private clouds, appliances built with OpenStack components and a driver database for hardware that works with OpenStack.

Index